KENNEDY BABYLON

A Century of Scandal and Depravity

Volume 1

HOWIE CARR

TABLE OF CONTENTS

ACKNOWLEDGMENTS

THIS IS A WORK in progress. When I began, I anticipated that this subject could be adequately covered in one volume. Obviously, despite observing the Kennedy family closely for my entire life, I underestimated the extent of their corruption.

The book that you hold in your hands could have never been produced without the assistance of so many others, starting with my lovely wife Kathy, who has again flawlessly handled all the business arrangements.

I would also like to express my gratitude to everyone at the *Boston Herald*, where I have worked off and on (mostly on) for almost 40 years. Many of the outstanding photographs in this book were taken by the *Herald's* photographers. Thanks to *Herald* publisher Pat Purcell, editor-in-chief Joe Sciacca, editors John Strahinich and Joe Dwinell and photo editor Jim Mahoney for allowing the use of these memorable photos.

I would also like to thank former *Herald* photographer Kevin Cole, freelance photographer Paul Adao and former *Herald* librarian Martha Reagan for their invaluable help. Thanks also to the staff of my radio show—Jared Goodell, Steve Robinson and Grace Curley. My gratitude extends to Allison Barrows, who did the fine cover art.

Some of the photos were sent anonymously by my readers and/or listeners—thanks as well to them, and to Al Rounds of South Carolina, who allowed me access to photos that I plan to use in Volume 2. Jennifer Welsch at Bookmasters did another great job in putting the book together quickly and professionally.

Thanks also to Bob Maynes of Mathews Brothers, one of our earliest radio sponsors and a great friend of the show. In addition to all of his great moral support, Bob provided the gray Mathews Bros. notebooks I used for all of my research notes. Bob, your notebooks are now dog-eared, and they fill a large storage box in my basement.

After the book's publication, my radio affiliates supported my "Kennedy Babylon" speaking tour all through the spring and summer, which turned out to be great fun. Among the stations that assisted me in finding the right venues and then promoting the events were WRKO, WCRN, WBSM and WHYN in Massachusetts, WGAN and WVOM in Maine, WFEA and WKBK in New Hampshire and WVMT in Vermont.

Market Basket also came through for me in a big way, allowing me to hold weekend book signings in so many of their great supermarkets across New England. Thanks to everyone at Market Basket, especially Arthur T. Demoulas and Jay Rainville. Market Basket is a great company and the best supermarket chain anywhere. Also, best wishes to Bill Marden on his retirement. It is well-deserved.

Finally, I would like to express my appreciation to all my listeners and readers who have supported me over the years. I can't begin to tell you how grateful I am for your loyalty. I hope you will enjoy this latest book.

Howie Carr

CHAPTER ONE

INTRODUCTION: "TRADITIONAL EASTER WEEKEND"

S EN. EDWARD MOORE KENNEDY, liquor on his breath, needing a haircut, wearing a suit he'd bought when he was perhaps 50 pounds lighter, stepped out into an open-air foyer on the campus of the Massachusetts Institute of Technology in Cambridge.

Cambridge, May 1991: "I WAS NOT TOLD!"

It was a warm spring afternoon in May 1991, six weeks after the Kennedys' "traditional Easter weekend" in Palm Beach, when his nephew William Kennedy Smith had been accused of raping a 29-year-old single mother. The sordid tale had quickly become the symbol of the Kennedys' ruined greatness, of the family's descent into decadence and depravity, as one witness after another stepped forward, "telling tales," as in an old Kinks song, "of drunkenness and cruelty."

A day earlier, the victim's sworn affidavit describing her terrifying ordeal had been released by state prosecutors in Florida, detailing the late-night attack by Smith on the beach in front of the Kennedy mansion on Easter Saturday, at the end of March.

The alleged rape had occurred at the end of a day of epic drinking. Ted Kennedy had been imbibing steadily for more than 12 hours when he awakened his nephew Smith, and his son, Patrick, a soon-to-be 24-year-old senior at Providence College who was also a Rhode Island state representative and recovering cocaine addict.

The senior senator had convinced his younger kinsmen to join him as he headed down to Au Bar, a new island hotspot off Coconut Row. He'd made his first visit to Au Bar two nights earlier, almost as soon as he'd landed in West Palm, and confirmed for himself the stories he'd been hearing about the bar in DC. The rumors were true; he and his son had picked up two young women there that night.

As Good Friday turned into Holy Saturday, the Kennedy men were again on the prowl, much the worse for wear. After picking up two more young women, they had returned to La Querida, the family's 11-bedroom, 15,347-square-foot mansion at 1095 North Ocean Boulevard. Willie had convinced his date, a woman from nearby Jupiter, to stroll with him down onto the dark beach. Once there, without a word he began to remove his pants—a family tradition, as it would turn out. Suddenly fearful, the woman decided to return to the mansion. But according to the police report, Smith had grabbed her by the leg. She broke free and started running through the sand. But Smith tackled her and then raped her.

"The victim said that she remembers hearing herself screaming," the police report would say, "and wondering why no one in the house would come out and help, especially since she knew that Sen. Kennedy was in the house."

She said that when she told Willie to stop, he replied, "Stop it bitch!"

Afterward, as he rolled off her, she escaped his grasp and ran into the house, where she hysterically telephoned friends. As Smith barged back into the house and began yelling her name, she tried to flee back outside.

"I didn't know what he was going to do to me then," she said in the police report. "I was petrified that he was going to start hitting me, or that he was going to rape me again, or that he was going to kill me."

Smith dragged her into another room and flung her onto a couch. He then flopped down into an easy chair and, according to the woman, "crossed his legs and appeared very composed and sure of himself."

"You raped me," she said.

"I did not," she quoted him as saying, "and no one will believe you anyway."

She was not the first woman to quote a Kennedy as saying that, nor would she be the last. It had just never made the front pages before. But it was 1991 now, and Ted Kennedy's Senate spokesman had already been forced to issue a denial, saying the senator had "heard absolutely no screams that night."

That night.

William Kennedy Smith mugshot, Palm Beach County Sheriff's department, 1991.

* * *

It was exactly six weeks later as Teddy was facing the press, in Cambridge. Outside the MIT building, on Memorial Drive, a moving truck from a company called Camelot Rental had pulled up. The bemused TV cameramen had shot videotape of it—another brief shining moment was apparently about to be hauled away.

Teddy's hands were shaking as he approached the microphones and began his halting, disjointed denial that he had deliberately fled Palm Beach ahead of schedule in order to avoid giving local cops a statement on the alleged rape. He again denied hearing any screams "that night."

Teddy said he had only learned of the sexual assault on Easter Sunday, from "Mr. Barry," a retired FBI agent, who had been with Sen. Robert Kennedy at the Ambassador Hotel in Los Angeles when he was assassinated in 1968. William Barry had also flown down for the weekend, and he had been tasked with meeting with the Palm Beach police when they arrived on North Ocean Boulevard during Easter dinner. Teddy began quoting what he said Barry had told him:

"There's some additional something going on here, vaguely, and it's going to involve some kind of, uh, sexual harassment on Willie on that because I was not told—"

At this point he began shouting—"I WAS NOT TOLD EVER, EVER WAS TOLD—"

He paused to glance at the Boston reporters and cameramen, some of whom looked puzzled at the unmistakable panic in a Kennedy's voice. This was not something they were accustomed to. Somehow Teddy regained enough composure to lower his voice.

"—that the Palm Beach Police wanted to speak to me about an alleged incident of Willie Smith raping some girl."

Some girl. This was the same senator who on the Senate floor a few years earlier, thundering against the nomination of Robert Bork to the Supreme Court in righteous anger, demanding to know if the Senate was nothing more than "an old boys' club."

"I was never told that!" Teddy repeated about the charges against his nephew. "And the record when you see it and when it comes out will never, will not suggest that I was, and since from the time that, uh, I found out that was the allegation, I have been available, uh, to the police and responded to all those questions and I certainly would have if I knew that the charge had been rape, would have done it."

As he spoke, he would thrust his right hand out. The hand would start shaking. He'd stick his hand back into his pocket. Then he'd whip it out again to make a point, but would again be unable to stop the shaking, after which he'd once more thrust the hand back inside the pocket of his too-small suit jacket.

"But that was never," he bellowed, "that was never, I was never told that. If I had been told that—if I had been told that I certainly would have. But I was never told that and you're gonna have to look at the records of who told what to who."

Whom, he should have said. His mother Rose would have corrected him, but she was 100 years old, and everyone else was either dead, like Kenny O'Donnell, or had deserted after one or another of the earlier scandals, like Ted Sorensen after Chappaquiddick.

Still, Teddy Kennedy was incredulous at the turn his traditional Easter weekend had taken. How could this happen to him in Palm Beach? Everything bad that happened to a Kennedy got straightened out in Palm Beach, even his brother Jack's impulsive marriage to a twice-divorced Protestant in front of a justice of the peace in 1947.

Their father—the Ambassador, as his children always called him—had solved the problem quickly by giving one of Jack's friends a bag of cash. He'd gone over to the clerk's office and purchased the only documentation of the marriage that existed, thus saving JFK's political career from destruction almost before it began.

Palm Beach—this was the Kennedys' real hometown, a "restricted" island where as late as the 1960s black people had been prohibited from buying property. Palm Beach was the ultimate "sunny place for shady people," in Somerset Maugham's turn of phrase.

The Kennedys' next-door neighbor was the former ambassador to Cuba and future town mayor, Earl Smith, whose late wife, the former Florence Pritchett, had been another of the president's long-term girlfriends.

One day in the early sixties, the Secret Service detail at the mansion realized the president had vanished. Frantic, they began calling the local FBI office and the Palm Beach police. The chief, an old family friend named Homer Large, chuckled and told them to go next door. There the Secret Service had found the president and Mrs. Smith cavorting in the ambassador's pool.

"And they weren't doing the Australian crawl," Chief Large later said. In Palm Beach, as the old saying went, money didn't talk, it screamed.

The Kennedys had always been protected in Palm Beach. A female visitor had died of a drug overdose at the mansion in 1967; nothing had come of it. When Bobby's wayward son David Kennedy, age 29, died of a drug overdose in a downtown hotel during the traditional Easter weekend of 1984, the drugs in his room, some of which had apparently been stolen from Rose Kennedy, were mysteriously flushed down the toilet before the body was officially discovered.

The two Kennedy cousins seen at the hotel that morning were allowed to give pro forma statements denying that they had destroyed evidence. The only two people indicted for David Kennedy's death were a couple of bellhops at the hotel.

Palm Beach was where the Ambassador first had Gloria Swanson at the old Royal Poinciana Hotel in 1927, while her husband was conveniently deep-sea fishing with the old man's most loyal aide, Edward Moore, after whom Joe would name his youngest son a few years later.

In her memoirs, Swanson recalled how the patriarch, after months of unrequited lust, had finally gotten her alone in her hotel suite. Breathlessly, he began pulling at her kimono.

"He kept insisting in a drawn-out moan, 'No longer, no longer. Now.' He was like a roped horse, rough, arduous, racing to be free. After a hasty climax he lay beside me, stroking my hair. Apart from his guilty, passionate muttering, he had still said nothing cogent."

In other words, Kennedy men didn't take "no" for an answer—especially in Palm Beach.

What had happened on the beach that night wasn't the first time a woman had been raped at the ramshackle mansion by a Kennedy. In 1946, the future Pamela Harriman, the former daughter-in-law of Winston Churchill, had been visiting Florida as a guest of her wartime friend Kathleen "Kick" Kennedy Cavendish. Jack Kennedy often advised young women visitors to lock the doors to their guest rooms because, as he put it, "the Ambassador has a tendency to wander at night."

But Pamela apparently didn't get the heads-up from Kick. In his final novella, *Answered Prayers,* Truman Capote recounted in fictional form what Harriman had told him.

"The old bugger slipped into my bedroom," he quoted Harriman as saying. "The sheer ballsy gall of it—right there in his own house with the whole family sleeping all around us. But all those Kennedy men are the same; they're like dogs. They have to pee on every fire hydrant."

Afterward, she said, in the morning, Joe Kennedy was nonchalant about the assault, much like his grandson would be 45 years later.

"Can you imagine?" Capote quoted Harriman as saying. "He pretended nothing had happened, there was never a wink or nod . . . There should have been some sentimental acknowledgment, a bauble, a cigarette box . . ."

By 1991, though, even the Palm Beach police couldn't broom a rape. The world had changed, and the Kennedys hadn't.

* * *

"Never, NEVER used the word rape," Teddy was yelling again. "I thought this was something that Willie-yum Smith, uh, uh, that I had no knowledge of, no awareness of, Willie-yum Smith had left, uh, uh, according to schedule and ha-ha-ha-ha-he never mentioned it to me."

He had run away, in other words, not unlike Uncle Ted himself at the Dike Bridge on Chappaquiddick. Flight from a crime—another family tradition. In 1969, Teddy had waited nine hours to mention the drowning of "some girl" to anyone—any cops, that is.

He had telephoned a number of people after freeing himself from the submerged Oldsmobile, starting with his Palm Beach mistress. He'd called her because he knew she had the phone number for the family fixer, his brother-in-law, Stephen Smith, the father of Willie-yum Smith, now indicted for rape.

For six weeks now, the media had been in full attack mode, especially publisher Rupert Murdoch's two gritty urban tabloids, the *New York Post* and the *Boston Herald*, both of which Teddy had tried to shut down two years earlier, in a rider anonymously attached to a Senate spending bill. He had been angry that a *Herald* columnist called him "Fat Boy."

The *Post* and the *Herald* had survived the attack, and now it was payback time. The *Herald* had renamed the mansion, La Querida, after the old Pink Floyd song, "Comfortably Numb by the Sea." Both papers were gleefully printing the depositions of the witnesses (and the victim) as they were publicly released. They read like anthropological monographs on the lifestyles of the rich and depraved. Now the world knew that the younger Kennedys had long since figured out that the quickest way to get laid in Palm Beach was to buy a woman a few drinks and then offer her a tour of what had once been known as "the winter White House."

Ted Kennedy resented being called "Fat Boy" by the Boston Herald.

Like the family itself, the old mansion had seen better days. It was owned by one of the family's trust funds, and family matriarch Rose refused to approve spending any money for upkeep on any property that didn't have her name on the deed. But still, even among women too young to remember Camelot, the words "winter White House" carried a certain cachet. They certainly did for a 24-year-old woman named Michele Cassone, whom Patrick Kennedy had picked up at Au Bar.

In the weeks after the rape, she would be variously described, in true Palm Beach style, as both a "waitress" and an "heiress." She would recall that like Willie and his date, she and Patrick—known in New England as "Patches"—had walked hand in hand down the beach. What Cassone was about to see was like nothing she had ever read about the New Frontier in her high-school history textbooks.

"I noticed a woman walking naked into the ocean," she said, in one of her many television interviews, "and I made a comment, 'There goes a naked woman.' . . . I saw a girl walk into the ocean and I never saw her again. I don't think it fazed them."

But what Cassone recalled most clearly about that early morning was the terrifying image of a drunken Ted stumbling about the first floor of the mansion at 3 a.m. after his 15-hour Good Friday drinking binge, a tumbler of Chivas Regal, perhaps his 20th of the day, in his right hand.

"(He) was kinda wobbling, and he came into the room, and he's just like staring at us, and he had his shirt, just his long Oxford shirt on. And I don't know what he had on under that, but he didn't have his slacks on any longer."

She elaborated to the *Boston Herald*: "Ted had a really weird look on his face. I saw his bare knees and freaked out. I said, 'I gotta go. This is getting weird . . .' He did not say a word. He was just there without pants."

As Patrick walked the 24-year-old Cassone back to her car, she watched the senator, "swaying slightly," reeling across the lawn toward the beach, drink still in hand, without his pants.

Ted Kennedy, tribune of the underclass—the American *sans culotte*, as it were—was now ridiculed as *sans culotte* himself, without trousers, comfortably numb by the sea.

The *New York Post* headline: TEDDY'S SEXY ROMP.

It was as though Rupert Murdoch and his cutthroat crew of ink-stained wretches were toying with him. What had become of all those credulous, fawning "journalists" of yesteryear—Arthur Krock, Ben Bradlee, Roone Arledge, everyone at the *Boston Globe*?

Wasn't anything off the record anymore?

Just 30 years earlier, the Kennedys had been on top of the world. In 1961, before his stroke, the Ambassador had summarily decreed that Teddy, not even 30 yet, would run for JFK's old seat in the U.S. Senate– "I paid for that seat and it belongs to our family!"

One of Teddy's sisters had anonymously defended the decision to install Teddy in the Senate by telling one of the family's house journalists, "Teddy had to do something!"

As terrible as the murders of his two brothers had been, their deaths had immunized Teddy and everyone else in the family from any criticism, let alone prosecution. Teddy—the Senator—could in fact get away with anything, and had, at Chappaquiddick. But now the Senator's Teflon had turned to Velcro. Everything stuck to him.

Not so long ago, he could keep the Boston press at bay simply by inviting them down to the compound in Hyannis Port for a late-summer clambake. Now, at MIT, half the reporters had those damnable cockney or Australian accents that marked them as Murdoch hands. All they cared about were their circulations and their TV ratings. The Kennedys were good copy, the best, because in the decades when they enjoyed carte blanche to do anything, they had grown even more careless and sloppy than they had been at the height of their power . . . and now they had next to no one to back them up.

Soon, Teddy instinctively knew, he would have to give a deposition. His lifestyle would be under a microscope. And he would be under oath.

"Do you," a prosecutor would ask him, "consider yourself a sound or light sleeper?"

"Sometimes sounder than others."

* * *

That weekend Willie Smith had been bunking with Patches. In a generation in which almost all of the Kennedys had become "filmmakers" or "community activists" or lawyers, or had at least passed the bar exam, sometimes even on the first try, William Kennedy Smith appeared to be an exception. He seemed to be making something of himself. He had been an outstanding student through prep school, Duke University and then Georgetown University Medical School.

But now this had happened, and like all the earlier scandals, it had to be made to go away. The only problem was that the family fixer, Steve Smith, Willie's father, was gone, dead of lung cancer at age 62 the previous summer. He'd handled not just Chappaquiddick, but later, all the drug arrests, the OUIs, the overturned Jeeps and, yes, the failed bar exams.

On his passing, Teddy had issued a statement that could be interpreted in more ways than one, depending on how you felt about the Kennedys:

"There wouldn't have been a Camelot without Steve Smith."

In Cambridge, the senator was still prattling on about Mr. Barry, the FBI agent who had been assigned to clean up this latest ugly mess. After the rape, the victim had decided to take something from the mansion, to protect herself against the not unreasonable assumption that the Palm Beach cops wouldn't believe her story about one of the Kennedys. As a local, she understood that even in 1991, she might be up against it in a courtroom in West Palm Beach.

"Mr. Barry indicated that the police wanted information about the alleged stolen property which I knew nothing about and which I didn't even recognize but was identified by, uh, Nellie McGrail who has worked for the family over a long period of time."

"What was taken?" a reporter asked.

Willie and his mother Jean Smith in Georgetown, 1991.

"My mother's yearn."

A yearn. Not an urn, or even a urinal. Rose's yearn.

"I had no knowledge that my mother's property had been stolen and I was enormously relieved that my mother's property was recovered."

On and on it went, the Senator denying everything.

"Never . . . ever . . . never, ever, ever . . . never . . . slept through the night . . . no knowledge, no knowledge . . . Never told."

In front of the MIT building in Cambridge, the truck from Camelot Rental was pulling away. And watching Ted Kennedy at age 57, it was easy to forget that there was a spot, for one brief shining moment, that was known as Camelot.

JFK Library, 1994: Willie enjoys a chat with another accused rapist, President Bill Clinton.

CHAPTER TWO

THE MORE THINGS CHANGE . . .

ENERATION AFTER GENERATION, CERTAIN patterns recur in every family. Karl Marx said that history repeats itself first as tragedy, then as farce. With the Kennedys, as well as with their various kinsmen like the Fitzgeralds and the Skakels, history is often farce the initial time as well.

Some of the behavioral traits are passed down from father to son. For instance, Jack Kennedy once told Clare Booth Luce that, "Dad told all the boys to get laid as often as possible."

As president, JFK was once photographed shirtless on a beach. When he saw the pictures, he grimaced at his flabby chest, especially at what he described to his friend Ben Bradlee as "the Fitzgerald breasts."

That wasn't the only thing passed down in the family's maternal genes. Two of Rose's maternal uncles died of what was known in the Hannon family as "the curse of the Irish." Three of Honey Fitz's brothers were alcoholics. And in the later generations, the curse of the Irish seemed to grow even more pernicious.

Christopher Lawford once said that among his generation, it was easier to put together an Alcoholics Anonymous meeting than a touch football game. In 1998, RFK Jr. said that at least nine members of his generation were AA members. People close to the Kennedys also tended to become alcoholics. Kenny O'Donnell, JFK's top aide, died of cirrhosis of the liver in 1977. The mother of the babysitter Michael Kennedy raped in the 1990s likewise died of alcoholism. When Teddy began to be blamed in the 1970s for Joan's problems, he angrily told his aide

Rick Burke that Joan's alcoholism was genetic—through her mother, another drunk.

Like so many rich Bostonians, the Kennedys preferred to dry out close to home—at McLean Hospital in Belmont. Joan Kennedy made at least four visits over the years. The three "Lost Boys" who became heroin addicts— Bobby Jr., David Kennedy and Chris Lawford—all eventually made their way to McLean. At least three Kennedys have been arrested for possession of marijuana: Bobby Jr., Teddy Jr. and

Teddy shows off what JFK called "the Fitzgerald breasts."

Bobby Shriver. By the 1970s, drug use had become so prevalent among the family's "Lost Boys" that Steve Smith, the family spokesman, came up with a euphemism that, while used specifically for David Kennedy, could have been used for any number of family members.

David, his aunt's husband told reporters, was suffering from "an ailment similar to drug addiction."

That's not the only euphemism they've employed over the years.

When David's brother Joe burned his 16-year-old son Matthew with illegal fireworks in Massachusetts, a press release from the congressman's office described the mishap as being caused by a "sparks-emitting device."

Their sex lives were and are messy, to say the least. For the most part they were lousy lovers. As one of the help in Palm Beach said after William Kennedy Smith was charged with rape in 1991, "Willie and the Senator don't like to take no for an answer."

Nor did the family patriarch, Joe. And it wasn't just with Pamela Harriman either. Another time in Palm Beach, he got inside a young woman's bedroom early one morning. As she groggily realized she wasn't alone, he dropped his pajama bottoms and told her, "This is going to be something you'll always remember."

Even young Patrick, sometimes described as the runt of the litter's runt of the litter, had his own pattern of abominable behavior with women. In the late 1980s, a hysterical young woman on a yacht he had rented called the Coast Guard asking to be rescued.

"She seemed concerned for her safety," a Coast Guard spokesman said later. "She did not feel safe on the boat, and she wanted to be removed."

They passed around their women too. There was a sort of competition among them all. More than one of their girlfriends described the whole family as "incestuous." Shortly before his assassination, JFK had one of his usual quickies with Marlene Dietrich, who had also known his father on the French Riviera before World War II. Afterward, he asked her if she'd slept with his father, now paralyzed by his 1961 stroke. Dietrich lied, and said no.

Patrick Kennedy: cocaine addict, alcoholic, terror on the high seas.

"I knew it!" said the president. "I knew it!"

Judith Campbell, whom JFK shared with Frank Sinatra and Chicago Mafia boss Momo Giancana, told JFK that Teddy had made a pass at her the night she met the brothers in Las Vegas. In her book, *My Story*, she recalled that one night, lying in bed with the then-senator, he told her, "Boy, if Teddy only knew, he'd be eating his heart out!"

In the late 1940s, dining in New York with gossip columnist Cholly Knickerbocker, Joe was introduced to a beautiful Swedish model named Hjordis Tersmeden. He made a crude pass at her, but she rebuffed him. Later she married British actor David Niven, and on JFK's 46th and final birthday in 1963, he got Mrs. Niven below deck on the presidential yacht for a quickie, as Sen. George Smathers kept Jackie occupied. Hjordis later reported that it was a memorable lay; JFK gave her a dose of the clap—chlamydia.

David Niven and his wife Hjordis, to whom JFK gave a venereal disease in May 1963.

The competition extended to the in-laws. When RFK began his affair with Marilyn Monroe, he was so proud that he wanted his brother-in-law, George Skakel, to know about it.

"George would keel over if he knew who I was screwing," RFK bragged to a mutual friend. "Just tell George I've had Marilyn's pussy."

By some accounts, JFK had sex with his sister-in-law, Lee Radziwill. After her husband's death, Jackie became Bobby's lover, and maybe Teddy's as well. (His diaries will not be unsealed until 2032.) Marilyn Monroe was passed down from JFK to RFK. During his New York hospital stay in 1954, Sen. Kennedy was visited in his private room (and according to some accounts fellated) by actress Grace Kelly.

Decades later, long after the death of both JFK and Princess Grace, her daughter, Princess Stephanie of Monaco, was romantically linked both to JFK Jr. and to Teddy Jr.

Another recurring pattern with the Kennedys: they liked hookers.

When Patricia Kennedy told her father Joe that she was engaged to actor Peter Lawford, he had a background check done on the English thespian. After Joe got the reports back, he called in Lawford.

"If there's anything I like less than an English actor, it's an English actor who wears red socks," he said.

But Lawford had a couple of saving graces. A contract player at MGM, he had a healthy bank account. And more significantly, the report showed, he liked hookers. Obviously, in Joe's eyes, he was Good People.

Ted Kennedy too enjoyed the company of prostitutes. During his brother's 1960 campaign, Teddy was—at least nominally—the manager of JFK's efforts in the western states, including the nation's 50th state, Hawaii.

George Jacobs, Frank Sinatra's longtime valet, picks up the story from there in his book *Mr. S*:

"(Teddy) showed up at a campaign appearance in Honolulu with three of the cheesiest-looking bimbos. You couldn't find junkie hookers this low in the worst part of Times Square, but somehow Teddy had dug deeper and hit paydirt. Even if they weren't hookers, they *looked* like hookers."

A year later, the family was grooming Teddy to run for Jack's seat in the U.S. Senate. Taking a break from his $1-a-year job as an assistant district attorney in Boston, Teddy went on a grand tour of South America. He sought out various Castro wannabes and conducted himself in the usual Kennedy manner—an FBI report quoted a State Department official in Lima, Peru, who described him as "pompous and a spoiled brat."

That FBI report also noted that "while Kennedy was in that city, he made arrangements to 'rent' a brothel for an entire night. Kennedy allegedly invited one of the Embassy chauffeurs in for the night's activities."

In the 1950s, Bobby visited the Soviet Union with Supreme Court Justice William O. Douglas. One of RFK's first requests to his official Soviet guide: that "a woman of loose morals" be sent up to his hotel room. Until near the very end of JFK's presidency, the Kennedys never worried about the sex scandals that brought down lesser mortals.

C05584132

SECRET

M. A. Jones to DeLoach
RE: EDWARD M. "TEDDY" KENNEDY (D)
SENATOR-ELECT--MASSACHUSETTS

(b) (6), (b) (7) (C) -1 per

9-2-60. The purpose of this call was not known; however, it is noted that ▢ was FBI sentenced by a North Carolina court on 11-3-60 to a two to three year sentence for conspiracy and four to six year sentence for felonious larceny. ·

On 1-24-61 the Boston SAC advised that (b)(6), (b)(7)(C) -3 per FBI
(b)(6), (b)(7)(C)-3 per FBI Boston, Massachusetts, had confidentially advised that Joseph P. Kennedy had expressed an interest in placing "Teddy" as the Assistant District Attorney of Suffolk County. [(b)(6), (b)(7)(C) -3 per FBI] advised he had heard statements attributed to the President that he was not satisfied with political conditions in the Democratic Party in Massachusetts and surmised that the President was using this way to get "Teddy" into politics. It is noted that "Teddy" was sworn in as an Assistant District Attorney on 2-7-61. Kennedy indicated he would accept a fee of $1 and waive the remainder of his $5,000 salary.

In July, 1961, Edward Kennedy made a familiarization and orientation tour of Central and South American countries. During this tour, the Mexico City Legal Attache reported that Kennedy had expressed an interest in meeting with "Leftists" to talk with them and determine why they think as they do. Kennedy met with a number of individuals known to have communist sympathies. While in Mexico City, Kennedy asked the Ambassador to invite left-wingers to the Embassy where he could interview them; however, the Ambassador refused to do so and stated that if any such interviews were to be conducted, all arrangements would have to be made by Kennedy himself. Subsequently, a State Department official in Lima, Peru, confidentially advised that Kennedy had made a similar request in Peru, and this official described Kennedy as "pompous and a spoiled brat."

(S)

(b)(1), (b)(3) per CIA [(b)(1), (b)(3) per CIA] while Kennedy was in that city, he made arrangements to "rent" a brothel for an entire night. Kennedy allegedly invited one of the Embassy chauffeurs in for the night's activities.

In August, 1961, a confidential source advised that Edward Kennedy had recently dined with Dr. Lauchlin Bernard Currie, former White House Aide to President Roosevelt. Currie's name had been mentioned in Washington investigations of Soviet spy rings. It was also noted that Dr. Currie had recently been invited to the U. S. Embassy at Bogata, Columbia, where Currie presently resides.

In October, 1961, a confidential source on Portuguese matters advised that Edward Kennedy was planning to enter politics and had retained one [(b)(6), (b)(7)(C)-1 per FBI] an attorney in Boston, to be his advisor on how to obtain Portuguese votes in Massachusetts. This source described [(b)(6), (b)(7)(C) -1 per FBI] as being a rightest and an extremist on behalf of the Portuguese Government. Inasmuch as there was a question as to whether [(b)(6), (b)(7)(C) -1 per FBI] should be registered as a foreign agent with the Department of Justice, Attorney General Kennedy was advised, and he spoke to "Teddy" about this. [(b)(6), (b)(7)(C)-1 per FBI] subsequently registered as a foreign agent on 12-29-61.

- 2 -

SECRET

FBI-MSJ-4 ·

1961 FBI Report: Teddy rented out an entire brothel in Lima, Peru.

JFK's cavalier attitude was that no one would dare print anything about his philandering while he was alive, "and after I'm dead, who cares?" Threesomes ran in the family too. According to multiple sources, JFK enjoyed them with hookers, Hollywood starlets, at least one in-law, his Harvard classmates, etc. One of Teddy's teenage Senate interns told his aide Rick Burke that she didn't mind sleeping with him until he tried to bring a second woman into the bedroom. RFK Jr. has likewise been accused of trying to get his second wife, who later committed suicide, into a *menage a trois*.

With the Kennedys, it's not birds, but in-laws of a feather that flock together. Michael Skakel, Ethel's nephew, served time in prison in Connecticut after being convicted of murdering his 16-year-old neighbor. Maria Shriver's husband, California Gov. Arnold Schwarzenegger, impregnated one of the family's maids.

Of course, like many Kennedy women, Maria Shriver also had a wild side, although before her marriage to the Terminator, she liked to portray

July 1990: Future California Gov. Arnold Schwarzenegger with wife Maria, left, mother-in-law Eunice, right, holding his legitimate daughter Katherine Eunice, age 10 months.

herself as a good Catholic girl. But in Palm Beach, she was well-known among the help for smuggling her boyfriends into La Querida.

As family maid Nellie McGrail used to say with a chuckle, "She'll never die wonderin'."

Frank Gifford, the former New York Giants running back and later *Monday Night Football* anchor, was the father-in-law of Bobby's third son, the late Michael Kennedy. Gifford cheated on all three of his wives and was set up by a supermarket tabloid in a hotel-room sex sting, recorded on videotape, in which he begged an airline stewardess for anal sex.

That scandal happened the same year Gifford's son-in-law, Michael Kennedy, was accused of statutory rape of the family's 14-year-old baby-sitter. As for the flight attendant who stung Gifford, she is now a real estate agent . . . in Palm Beach.

The former Jacqueline Bouvier's family has likewise been roiled by scandal. Her father, Black Jack, was a Yale College classmate of Noel Coward, and often joined him on his lifelong quests for "working-class males," as the young boys they sought were sometimes described. In 1953 Black Jack was so drunk at his daughter's wedding that he could not walk her down the aisle. Jackie's much younger half-brother, James Auchincloss, was convicted in 2010 of possession of child pornography.

Teddy Kennedy's second wife, the former Victoria Reggie, likewise came from a family with a criminal past, involving millions of dollars in multiple frauds. In 1992, Teddy flew to Louisiana to ask her father, Judge Edmund Reggie, for Vikki's hand in marriage. A few months later, the judge was indicted on federal charges, which involved the looting of the bank he had founded in 1959.

Reggie eventually pleaded guilty to a single count of misapplication of bank funds, a felony. The U.S. attorney asked for $5.1 million in restitution; the judge let off Sen. Kennedy's father-in-law with a $30,000 fine and 120 days of home detention.

Then there was Teddy's brother-in-law, Raymond Reggie. On the occasion of his second federal indictment, the U.S. attorney in Baton Rouge described him as a "flim-flam con artist" and a "serial fraudster."

By then Teddy was dead, so his brother-in-law could expect no Kennedy-style brooming of his crimes.

"It was a non-traditional pay agreement," Teddy's brother-in-law told the court in his plea for mercy. "I am 100 percent not guilty."

After his statement, the judge sentenced the Kennedy in-law to prison. He was released in June 2016.

Another family tradition: flunking the bar exam. It's understandable that heroin addicts might have a problem with the test, as indeed Bobby Jr. and Chris Lawford did. More embarrassing were the two failures in New York of John F. Kennedy Jr., whose futility in the law resulted in a famous tabloid headline, "The Hunk Flunks."

Teddy was never arrested for drunk driving, but his wife Joan was, three times.

Before his fatal overdose in Palm Beach, David was bagged once for OUI. Anthony Shriver was once stopped in Palm Beach for "erratic"

May 1991: Joan Kennedy surrenders her driver's license in Quincy after yet another DUI conviction.

driving, but not arrested—like many other family members pulled over down through the decades. Kerry Kennedy Cuomo was arrested in Westchester County in 2012 for driving while impaired.

On the morning she was arrested, the *New York Daily News* reported that she "ate carrots, cappuccino and Ambien."

When her case went to the jury, her mother Ethel appeared at the Westchester Courthouse in a wheelchair. Once the not-guilty verdict was announced, Ethel leapt up and quickly made her way downstairs to the bank of microphones, without any assistance.

In the early years, the Kennedys had been eager to show off their indomitable toughness, their imperviousness to pain. Only one or two photos exist of JFK wearing his back brace (one in Palm Beach with his neighbor Ambassador Earl Smith, whom he cuckolded). But less than a decade later, Teddy would wear a neck brace to the funeral of Mary Jo Kopechne. And later, his son Patrick likewise would be photographed wearing his own neck brace in Boston.

The country was changing, growing softer, and so were the Kennedys.

Kerry was not the only family member with a taste for Ambien. It was one of her cousin Patrick's go-to drugs as well. In 2006, when he slammed into barricades near the Capitol and had to be driven home, he claimed he thought he was on his way to a roll-call vote—at 3 a.m. He told police that the last thing he remembered was gobbling a few Ambien and heading out for a roll call, or was it last call?

Cocaine has been another popular Kennedy drug down through the generations, starting with JFK. Frank Sinatra's valet saw him snorting lines with his brother-in-law Peter Lawford in Palm Springs as early as 1960.

"It's for my back," Kennedy lied.

"Don't tell Frank!" a panicked Lawford said.

Later, Lawford would snort with his own children. For Christopher's 21st birthday, he gave him a few grams of cocaine. Teddy likewise did drugs with his children. Even after Patrick had gone into rehabilitation for cocaine addiction as a high-school senior in 1985, he and his father often drank together.

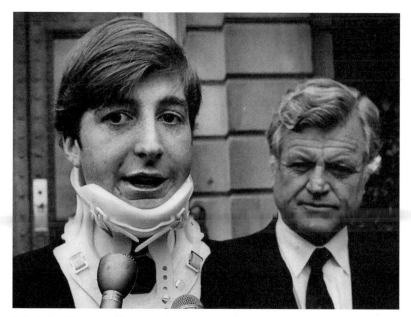

Like father like son: Teddy in a neck brace in Hyannis, 1969, son Patrick in a neck brace in Boston, 1988.

From JFK on, the Kennedys liked convertibles. JFK used to drive one around Palm Beach, eluding his Secret Service protections on the way to one assignation or another. As attorney general, Bobby was easy to spot in his convertible, driving around Washington with his black Newfoundland dog Brummus beside him.

Jimmy Hoffa was recorded by the FBI musing how easy it would be to take RFK out with a high-powered rifle as he drove in Washington. Indeed, a year later, JFK was killed in Dallas while riding in a convertible. He had personally rejected the Secret Service's recommendation of a bubble.

In 1962, when Bobby was regularly flying out to the West Coast to meet Marilyn Monroe, he insisted on borrowing a car from the special agent in charge of the FBI's Los Angeles office. It was a white Cadillac convertible.

In the 1980s, when Teddy bought a convertible for himself, he started a fad among his fellow Democratic senators. John Kerry soon had one, as did Howard Metzenbaum of Ohio.

Teddy's final auto accident came in the convertible. After a torrential rainfall, a tree fell on top of the car as Teddy was driving. This time, no one was killed. On Good Friday 1991, Teddy was too wasted to drive from the mansion to Palm Beach to Au Bar, so he handed his son Patrick the keys—to a white Cadillac convertible.

Teddy's nephew Michael also drove a convertible when he lived on the South Shore before his fatal skiing accident in 1997. Locals in Hingham remembered it well, because when he brought it into the local gas stations for service, they would notice the pornographic videos, magazines and books scattered haphazardly on the backseat.

Just like their brothers, the Kennedy women cheat. During the Kennedy administration, at least three female relatives of the president reportedly came on to Secret Service agents. One was codenamed "Rancid Ass."

Like the Kennedy men, the Kennedy women have never been renowned for their prowess in the bedroom. Peter Lawford said that before having sex, his wife Pat insisted on saying a prayer, after making the sign of the cross.

"It was like fucking the Pope," he told one of his later wives.

The same people keep reoccurring in the Kennedy family history. Alan Jay Lerner was in JFK's class, first at the Choate School and then at Harvard College. He was the composer of the Broadway musical *Camelot,* which Jackie Kennedy cited as the basis of the myth she created about her late husband's administration. Like JFK and Jackie, Lerner was also a patient of Dr. Max Jacobson, "Dr. Feelgood"—the quack doctor who provided illicit narcotics to a clientele of bold-faced celebrities in the 1960s.

After JFK's assassination, Lerner began an affair with Jean Kennedy Smith. Finally, the lovers agreed that they would rendezvous in Paris and begin their new lives together. Jean arrived in Paris and waited . . . and waited. Alan Jay Lerner never appeared.

Another of JFK's and Lerner's classmates at Harvard was Frederick Ayer Jr. After graduation, he became an FBI agent. One of his first bugging assignments was of a suspected Nazi spy named Inga Arvad and her Navy boyfriend, whom the FBI somehow could not positively identify. Ayer dutifully recorded their lovemaking in a hotel in Charleston, South Carolina. As they began a post-coital conversation, Ayer recognized a familiar voice—his Harvard classmate, JFK.

Twenty-two years later, JFK attended Harvard's graduation ceremonies as the grand marshal. So did Ayer, according to author Seymour Hersh the president was in the formal procession, wearing a top hat and tails, walking regally toward the stage, when suddenly Ayer shouted out:

"How's Inga, Jack?"

"You son of a bitch!" JFK hissed back, according to Seymour Hersh.

Inga worked at the *Washington Times-Herald,* which also employed, at various times, Kathleen "Kick" Kennedy and, after World War II, Jacqueline Bouvier. Patterson's brother was the founder of the *New York Daily News.*

The *Daily News* was where Caroline Kennedy would work as an intern. In 1977, after the death of Elvis Presley, she would travel to Memphis as an assistant for columnist Pete Hamill, who at the time was the boyfriend of her mother Jackie.

But the Kennedys had deeper ties to the Hearst organization. During the Depression, Joe helped William Randolph Hearst, "the Chief," restructure his finances. Walter Winchell, the gossip columnist for Hearst's *New York Mirror*, was a conduit for stories Joe Kennedy wanted to get out. When Jack took up with Inga Arvad, Winchell printed a blind item as a warning to Jack—"Pa No Happy."

Kerry Kennedy Cuomo's marriage to future New York Gov. Andrew Cuomo broke up in 2003 after she pursued and bedded a polo-playing heir to a McDonald's fortune. After her divorce, she wrote a book entitled *Being Catholic Now*. The polo player's name was Bruce Colley, and his wife was named Ann. The *New York Post* would later report that Kerry's brother, RFK Jr., had bedded Ann Colley. She would deny it.

Over and over again the same names reappear in connection with family embarrassments. Consider Momo Giancana, with whom JFK shared Judith Campbell. When Giancana was working with the CIA on plots to eliminate Fidel Castro, Momo became suspicious of another one of his girlfriends, singer Phyllis McGuire of the McGuire Sisters.

Momo thought she was spending altogether too much time in the company of nightclub comic Dan Rowan, who a few years later co-hosted what was briefly the most popular comedy-variety series on television, *Rowan & Martin's Laugh-In.*

In 1960, Momo asked his CIA handler if he could put a bug in Rowan's hotel room. The CIA operative tried to oblige, but the associate he'd assigned to handle the black-bag job ended up arrested, and had to be bailed out of the Clark County Jail by Momo's Outfit associate, Johnny Roselli (who had grown up, like Joe Kennedy, in East Boston).

When Momo heard about the botched CIA wiretap on Rowan's phone, he reportedly laughed so hard that he almost swallowed his cigar. Meanwhile, Dan Rowan's role in the ongoing Kennedy family saga would rate another farcical footnote a decade later.

After divorcing his wife Pat, Peter Lawford would take Rowan's daughter Mary as the second of his four wives. Lawford was 30 years older than Mary Rowan; Dan was not nearly as amused as Momo had been in 1961.

For the Kennedys, it's a very small world. For example, Carter Burden was a New York socialite who went to Portsmouth Priory a decade and a half after Bobby Kennedy was expelled from the school in 1942 for cheating (another recurring family tradition; Teddy would be expelled from Harvard in 1951 for having another student take a Spanish exam for him).

Burden was later elected to the New York City Council from Manhattan. His wife was Amanda Burden—a descendant of John Jay, the first chief justice of the U.S. Supreme Court, who was also an ancestor of one of JFK's girlfriends, the former Helen Husted. After her divorce from Carter Burden, Amanda would become another of Teddy Kennedy's many girlfriends.

Rose Fitzgerald Kennedy was very religious. But the rest of her family hasn't exactly distinguished itself in its devotion to Roman Catholic doctrine. Kennedy weddings were usually presided over by cardinals, princes of the church, but Joe Kennedy dismissed priests as "little men in black dresses." Off the record, JFK told Ben Bradlee that he had no particular problems with abortion.

The concept of an afterlife is a comforting thought to many, but not the Kennedys.

After JFK's assassination, the wife of columnist Joe Alsop said she attempted to comfort Jackie "so I mumbled something like, 'At least Jack is resting peacefully with God.'"

To which Jackie responded, "That's the silliest thing I've ever heard."

Likewise, RFK was skeptical of Church doctrine about an afterlife.

Following JFK's death, Bobby and his political allies would often gather to discuss national issues. Inevitably the question would turn to what should be done next. And sometimes Ethel Kennedy would chime in, saying, "Well, Jack will take care of that. He's up in heaven, and he's looking down on us, and he'll show us what to do."

Finally, after one such statement, Bobby piped up and said, "The voice you just heard belongs to the wife of the attorney general of the United States. Let's hear no more out of her."

Thirty years later, Bobby's son, Cong. Joseph P. Kennedy II, was getting a divorce from his Protestant wife, Sheila Rauch. He was trying to get her to agree to an annulment, so that he could marry his new younger girlfriend in the church. When his first wife demurred, he brushed aside her objections, saying the annulment was just a bunch of "Catholic gobbledygook."

"Nobody actually believes it," he scoffed.

Sheila didn't know her marriage had been annulled until Joe Kennedy got married in a Catholic church. Ditto, Joan Kennedy when Teddy married Victoria Reggie in 1992.

Another family tradition is butchering names. Like the "alcohol gene," as Max Kennedy once described it, and the "Fitzgerald breasts," as JFK described them, this trait seems to come from the Fitzgerald side of the family.

During his grand tour of Europe in 1912 as mayor, Honey Fitz saluted his audience in the great city of "Dusselberg," and said he and his party were looking forward next to visiting "the great German cities" of Vienna and Budapest.

Remembering other people's names has always been a problem for the Kennedys.

The final event of the 1960 campaign was a huge rally at the old Boston Garden, memorably described by Theodore H. White in *The Making of the President 1960.* JFK appeared, hatless, in a sea of old-line politicians wearing homburgs and soft hats like those favored by his late grandfather Honey Fitz.

JFK introduced the statewide Democratic ticket to the adoring audience. When he got to the candidate for secretary of state, Kevin White, he called him "Calvin White."

Former Boston mayor John "Honey Fitz" Fitzgerald with his granddaughter Rosemary before her father had her lobotomized.

Four years later, RFK was running for the Senate in New York. He made the obligatory trip to Coney Island to campaign at Nathan's Hot Dogs and introduced the founder, Nathan Handwerker, as "Nathan Hamburger."

But Ted was the worst. When he first entered the race for president in 1979, Teddy agreed to have a network camera crew film him as he went about his daily Senate business. At one point in the piece, the phone in his office rings. His aide, Rick Burke, who would later write a tell-all memoir, *The Senator*, tells him it's the newly elected congressman from Malden, Ed Markey.

As Teddy takes the receiver, a look of panic crosses his face.

"Ricky, what's his name? What's his name?" He cups the receiver. "Markey."

"No, no, no. What's his first name?"

"Ed." Kennedy nods and takes his hand off the receiver. A smarmy smile crosses his face: "Oh Ed, how are you?"

In 1989, when he was trying to force Rupert Murdoch to sell the *Boston Herald* and the *New York Post*, he was interviewed on a radio talk show as he was being driven to the Cape. As the interview wore on he began slurring his words.

Finally, Teddy began referring to the Australian press baron as "Rudolph Murdoch," and finally told the host he didn't have to put up with any more of his "dribble."

In 1992, a young State House hand named Marty Meehan ousted the incumbent congressman from the Merrimack Valley district in the Democrat primary. A few days later, Teddy came to Lowell to address a fundraiser for Meehan at the Speare House. He spoke upstairs, in a room completely festooned with blue signs saying "Marty Meehan US Congress." Despite the signs, Teddy stood up and began bellowing about his good friend "Andy Meehan." Over and over he shouted about how much he liked "Andy Meehan."

Even though he endorsed Barack Obama, Teddy had trouble with his name as well. Once, in 2008, attempting to slough off reporters' questions, he quipped, "Well, why don't we just ask Osama bin, Osama Obama, er, Barack Obama."

Sports figures didn't escape having their names mangled. Once he saluted the great home-run kings "Sammy Sooser and Mike McGuire."

After his death in 2009, Ted's son Patrick returned to Massachusetts to campaign for the Democratic Senate candidate, Martha Coakley. Patrick called her "Marsha" Coakley.

Teddy Kennedy, and to a lesser degree, his nephew Joe II, were famous for incoherent statements. Asked on CBS by family friend Roger Mudd in 1979 why he was running for president, Ted replied:

"Well, it's a a-on-on what-on-you know, you have to come to grips with the—the different issues that we're—we're facing."

Thirty years later, it was Caroline Kennedy's turn to continue the family tradition. She was campaigning to be appointed to the U.S. Senate seat being vacated by Hillary Clinton. Despite her lack of experience of any kind, she expected to be coronated. She was, after all, a Kennedy. So she agreed to be interviewed by various media in New York.

They were all disasters. Her verbal tic was "You know." In her interview with the *New York Times,* she repeated the words "you know" 200 times. She was asked how being a senator might affect her husband and children.

"I think they understand that it will make—you know, bring change for them. But you know, again, I think this is, you know, I think he's someone who's committed to, you know, education, science education, you know, he makes children's museums, you know, this is, he—"

And what about your uncle Ted, the *Times* asked.

"He loves the Senate, it's been, you know, the most, you know, rewarding life for him, you know I'm sure he would feel like somebody that he cared about had that same kind of opportunity, and I think he really—and so do I, think the impact he's had on, you know, working people, you know?"

A few days later, you know, she issued a statement asking to be withdrawn from consideration, you know.

Jack Kennedy sold his house in McLean, Virginia to his brother Bobby in 1957. Joe Kennedy II sold his house in Hingham, Massachusetts, to his brother Michael in 1986. In the 1920s, Joe had no relatives who could afford his home in Brookline. So he sold it to his closest aide, Edward Moore, his trusted aide and procurer, after whom he would name his youngest son.

Another family tradition: shipping out troublesome children. Edward Moore had charge of Rosemary Kennedy for a number of years before her lobotomy in 1940. After RFK's assassination in 1968, Ethel Skakel Kennedy sent at least a couple of her sons to live with . . . well, whoever would take them. One of those who was sent away was Robert F. Kennedy Jr. He is now continuing the family tradition—in the fall of 2016 he dispatched his troubled daughter Kyra off to boarding school in Italy.

Often when a Kennedy is called out for bad behavior, say, for jumping a line, or spitting ice cream in the face of a cop, they will cry out: "Do you know who I am?!"

At a nightclub in 2015, Kyra gave the family's eternal question a 21st century spin:

"Do you know who I am? I'm a Kennedy. Google me!"

Kyra's brother Conor is continuing another family tradition—bad behavior in Aspen, Colorado.

In 1980, Chris Lawford was arrested there for impersonating a physician—he was trying to score drugs.

At Christmas 1997, his cousin Michael Kennedy, having just dodged a statutory-rape rap in Massachusetts, skied into a tree in Aspen and killed himself.

During Christmas week 2016, the Kennedys were back in Aspen, and Conor Kennedy, age 22, was arrested after a brawl outside the Bootsy Bellows nightclub at 1:40 a.m.

Conor Kennedy, of course, has been continuing yet another tradition—dating show-biz celebrities. When he was 18, in prep school, he briefly hooked up with Taylor Swift.

Conor Kennedy mugshot, Aspen, Colorado, December 2016.

Small airplanes have figured prominently in a number of family tragedies. JFK Jr. was not the first member of the family to die needlessly. In 1944, Joe Jr., a Navy lieutenant, was killed in what amounted to a suicide mission to bomb a Nazi rocket base that had already been abandoned. He had already completed 50 missions; he volunteered for the last fatal one.

Navy Lt. Joseph P. Kennedy Jr., died in a plane crash in 1944.

(In the plane behind Joe Kennedy was Elliott Roosevelt, FDR's son; the Kennedys and the Roosevelts crossed paths again and again, right up until 1986, when Joe Kennedy II defeated James Roosevelt for the congressional seat once held by Jack Kennedy.)

Kathleen "Kick" Kennedy Cavendish, right, died in a plane crash in 1948.

John F. Kennedy Jr., died in a plane crash in 1999.

Four years after Joe's death, his sister Kick died in a plane crash in France with her married English boyfriend.

In 1955, Ethel Skakel's parents were killed in a private plane crash in Oklahoma. In 1966, her brother George died in Idaho when the small plane he was on overshot a rural runway.

In 1999, John F. Kennedy Jr., his wife and his sister-in-law were killed in yet another private plane crash, off Martha's Vineyard.

The only Kennedy to ever survive a plane crash was Ted Kennedy. In 1964, he was severely injured, and one of his aides killed, when their small plane crashed in western Massachusetts.

No one likes to pay taxes, but few people run for political office demanding higher taxes . . . on other people, while aggressively minimizing their own obligations. Oliver Wendell Holmes Jr. once said that, "Taxes are the price we pay for a civilized society." The Kennedys have always believed taxes are the price other people pay for their civilized society.

In 1941, Joe Kennedy transferred his legal domicile from Bronxville to Palm Beach. Then, as now, Florida had no income tax, or inheritance tax. He began investing in oil. The depletion allowances provided an unbeatable tax shelter.

In 1957, New York City needed Kennedy's parcel at 70 Columbus Avenue for the Lincoln Center project. He held out for $2.5 million. The city ending up paying Kennedy $62.88 per square foot, while the adjacent buildings had been snapped up for an average of $9.58 per square foot.

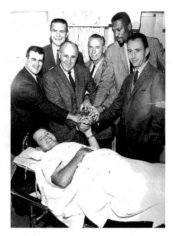

Recuperating from his 1964 plane crash, Sen. Ted Kennedy is visited by Boston sports figures, including Celtics Tom Heinsohn, Red Auerbach, Bill Russell and Bob Cousy. Center: Bruins' great Milt Schmidt.

Even more exasperating to taxpayers, only a year earlier Kennedy's lawyers had contested the building's valuation of $1.75 million as too high. The real value, they said in filings, was $1.1 million—less than one-half of what the city paid a year later.

The city tried to claw back the money, but a judge quickly ruled that although Kennedy had in essence swindled the city, the court "cannot constitutionally deprive the owner of just compensation because the latter was greedy enough to try to pay less than its fair share of taxes."

In January 1995, Rose Kennedy died in Hyannis Port. She hadn't set foot in Florida in at least 12 years. Yet the Commonwealth of Massachusetts allowed the family to probate her will in Palm Beach County. They saved millions in inheritance taxes, which her son Ted Kennedy voted to raise whenever he had the opportunity in the Senate.

The Kennedys treat almost everyone around them terribly, and always have.

When JFK was running for president, a fellow Democratic senator told a reporter for the *Wall Street Journal*: "The thing that bothers me most about Jack is this attitude that everybody is on earth for the sole purpose of helping him."

When Ted's son Patrick was learning to play tennis, his coach at one point told him to retrieve the balls from his side of the court. Patrick refused to budge. At age 10, Patrick understood what he took to be his exalted status.

"We Kennedys hire people to pick up our balls."

During Prohibition, the Bugs & Meyer gang once hijacked a load of the old man's bootlegged liquor. In a gun battle, several of Kennedy's men were killed. As a later biographer of Meyer Lansky noted of Joe, "For months afterward he was beset by pleas for financial help from the widow and relatives of the killed guards."

Kennedy didn't want to pay out any death benefits.

Forty years later, in exile in Israel, Lansky told his biographers that Kennedy "held his grudge," and that after Bobby became attorney general, "they were out to get us."

In 1961, during the Bay of Pigs fiasco, four pilots of the Alabama Air National Guard had defied orders to stand down and had instead flown their B-26s to Cuba to provide air cover for the Cuban freedom fighters. Before finally being shot down, the U.S. warplanes wreaked havoc on the Communist forces.

The fates of the four Alabamans were still unknown the next day when the top CIA officer, Richard Bissell, appeared at the White House. RFK was in a panic, afraid that one or more of the pilots would be paraded before the cameras in Havana, as the Soviets had done with captured U-2 pilot Francis Gary Powers a year earlier.

"He was short," Bissell recalled of Bobby's height. "But (he) got right in my face as best he could. The first words out of his mouth were, "Those American pilots had better goddamned well be dead.'"

As it turned out, they were. But Bissell was shocked at Kennedy's callousness, his unconcern about anything other than the embarrassment that the administration might face. He later told his wife, according to Seymour Hersh, "I don't like to tell you this. Bobby wanted them dead."

Then Bobby tried to halt the payment of any pensions or death benefits to the families of the dead Guardsmen, in order to put over a cover story about their deaths. A major campaign contributor from Texas finally had to threaten to go to the newspapers before the pensions were approved.

The Kennedys were just as high-handed with their own help. Barbara Gibson was Rose Kennedy's assistant in the last years of her life.

"The Kennedy women were volatile, cheap and domineering when it came to household help," she recalled. "They held their staffs in disdain, rewarded loyalty with low pay, and made unrealistic demands."

Jackie later told Paul Newman that Rose insisted that even as the family were served steaks and other prime cuts of beef, the help were expected to eat hamburgers. Until 1964, it was a "mortal sin" for Catholics to eat meat on Fridays. While the Kennedys would dine on lobster, the staff would be served canned tuna fish.

During the Cuban missile crisis, meetings were going on around the clock at the White House. One aide recalled that one evening, as the president, the attorney general and five or six of their top aides huddled, a White House waiter arrived with a tray with two cups of lobster stew.

He carefully placed the bowls in front of the Kennedy brothers, along with spoons and napkins. They ate in front of "the help," never offering them anything.

After Joe's stroke, he required round-the-clock nurses wherever he was, either in Hyannis Port or Palm Beach. According to Rita Dallas, the head nurse, Rose never allowed any of "the help" to share her table, even the top medical specialists flown in from New York to treat the Ambassador. Rose was also so concerned about the coffee the nurses drank on their shifts that she spoke to Dallas about what she considered the intolerable expenses.

"Would you post a note on the bulletin board," Rose asked Dallas, "to the effect that I would appreciate it if the nurses would please confine themselves to, say, one cup of coffee a shift? Or perhaps it might be a good idea if they would fix themselves a little thermos at home."

During trips to Palm Beach, the Kennedy women would often shop in the fashionable stores on Worth Avenue. They would buy dresses, wear them once and then return them, or more precisely, have Gibson return them. Sometimes when they arrived from Washington or New York, they would have several expensive outfits with them, often with stains or other signs of wear and tear, that she would be expected to return to the shops for a full refund. Some stores eventually stopped selling to the Kennedys.

The Kennedy women have never changed their ways. In 2016, Caroline Kennedy was the U.S. ambassador to Japan. A report by the State Department's inspector general (IG) described her management of the embassy in Tokyo as a disaster. There was "confusion among staff," the IG said, and said her management had caused "major . . . challenges."

As one 2016 Internet headline put it: "Boss from Hell? Caroline Kennedy's Work as Ambassador Slammed in Government Probe."

Getting paid by the Kennedys has always been difficult for "the help." In Aspen, one caterer had to eventually sue Ethel to get the money he was owed. On Cape Cod, they shoplifted, knowing that the police would never be called, or, on the rare occasions that they were, no charges would be filed.

Another family tradition was never carrying cash. JFK was often borrowing $10 or $20 from his much less well-heeled friends, who would have to dun him for months before he would finally repay them. Some got into the habit of just sending invoices to the Park Agency, which administered the financial affairs of the children.

Once Bobby Kennedy went to Mass with one of his aides, Peter Maas. When it was time for the collection, Bobby looked over at Maas and held out his hand. Maas handed him a one-dollar bill.

Bobby shook his head and said to Maas, "Don't you think I'd be more generous than that?"

But perhaps the most enduring pattern in Kennedy family behavior is that, no matter how appalling, or criminal, their behavior, in the end they always skate.

Consider the case of Michaela Kennedy Cuomo, daughter of Kerry Kennedy Cuomo and her former husband, New York Gov. Andrew Cuomo. Michaela is a chip off the old block in more ways than one—in 2015, EMTs were called to her mother's house in New York when she was reported to be "unconscious."

As a teenager, Michaela decided to begin lobbying at least one state senator in Albany on behalf of a farmworkers' bill. Her unlicensed lobbying came to the attention of Adam Skelos, the son of the Republican majority leader of the state Senate. Both father and son were about to be indicted on a variety of federal corruption charges. Adam was angry that he was looking at a lengthy prison sentence for his machinations in Albany, while Michaela was being lionized for her unlicensed lobbying.

"I mean, how is that—how can she get away with that?" Adam Skelos asked his father. It was, obviously, a rhetorical question.

"All right," he finally said. "I can't stand this family. I really can't stand this family."

A year earlier, the younger Skelos had sent his father a link to a story about Michaela's unlicensed lobbying.

"So," he wrote his father, "because she's a Kennedy she's allowed to lobby?"

His older, wiser father replied: "Always double standard when it comes to the Kennedys."

Adam and Dean Skelos were both convicted at trial in 2016. They are free pending appeals. Adam has been sentenced to 6½ years in prison.

Michaela Kennedy Cuomo is an undergraduate at Brown University.

CHAPTER THREE

1946: CONGRESS AND . . . CONGRESS

For John F. Kennedy, the year 1946 would prove to be particularly memorable—not only was he elected to Congress, but he also may have impregnated at least two women, and in January 1947 he married for the first time, more than six years before his "storybook wedding" to Jacqueline Bouvier.

Even as JFK was serving in the Pacific on PT-109, his father was laying the groundwork for the political careers of his two oldest sons. After his disastrous stint as ambassador to the Court of St. James, Joe realized his political ambitions were permanently dashed. So he transferred his dreams to his sons, specifically Joe, his first-born and namesake.

Joe Kane was Joe's first cousin, an irascible but canny Boston political operative. He had tangled with Joe back in 1918, when Kennedy put up his father-in-law Honey Fitz to run against incumbent Cong. Peter Tague, who had refused to go along with Kennedy's schemes at the Fore River Shipyard. Kane was Tague's campaign manager.

After a scandalous election marked by massive voter fraud (another family tradition in the making), Honey Fitz won a narrow victory. Tague, however, appealed the results to the U.S. House of Representatives, producing a mountain of evidence of fraud, while Honey Fitz's only defense was that he was "framed."

In October 1919, Honey Fitz was expelled from Congress and Tague was immediately sworn in to replace him.

(Like so many other family embarrassments, this episode has largely been expunged from the Kennedys' hagiographic chronicles. Doris Kearns Goodwin dismissed it in a few words, writing that Honey Fitz returned to Boston not in humiliation but "as exuberant as ever . . . the local newspapers still considered him the leading citizen of Boston.")

Years later, the two cousins, Kane and Kennedy, reconciled. Pragmatists, they realized they needed one another. Kane went on Joe's payroll, laying the groundwork for his younger cousins' postwar political careers. Kane's first move came in 1942, as GOP Sen. Henry Cabot Lodge was seeking a second six-year term. His opponent would be an attractive young Democratic congressman from Clinton named Joseph E. Casey.

Kane and Kennedy were concerned that if Casey were elected to the Senate at age 44, he might block the Kennedys' upward mobility indefinitely into the future. So they decided to take him out.

Kane asked Joe, "Is your father-in-law doing anything this year?"

And so Honey Fitz, at the age of 79, began his final campaign, as a straw candidate to drain votes and weaken Casey for the general election. To accomplish his mission, Kane simultaneously began a whispering campaign against Casey—spreading the lie that his future wife had been pregnant when she married Casey in 1939. It was both scurrilous and ironic, given the Kennedys' own track record.

In Boston, Kane hired a priest to spread the rumors. Even JFK got into the act, writing back from the Pacific to friends in Boston that Casey had gotten married because he had "one in the oven."

Among those shocked by the false charges was Cong. John McCormack of South Boston. He and his wife were the godparents of the Caseys' child.

In a 1967 interview for the JFK library, Casey recalled the whispering campaign against him. Among other things, he said, the Kennedys claimed that "I was living with a lot of loose women up on the Fenway . . . It was a complete fiction, sure, but that never bothered these people."

In the Democratic primary, Honey Fitz got 40 percent of the vote. Another straw, Dan Coakley, a disbarred Governor's Councilor who had once represented Honey Fitz's old girlfriend Elizabeth "Toodles" Ryan in an alienation of affection suit, drained off still more support from Casey. In November Lodge easily defeated Casey, ending his political career.

Mission accomplished.

In January 1944, Jack returned from the Pacific. The next day, the *Boston Globe* ran a story and a photo of Jack on the front page. The headline was "Tells Story of PT Epic: Kennedy Lauds Men, Disdains Hero Stuff."

The West Coast stringer who wrote the story was Inga Arvad, his old girlfriend from Washington. It may have been the first time a Kennedy was in bed with the *Globe*, but it wouldn't be the last.

On August 12, 1944, everything would forever change for the Kennedy family. U.S. Navy Lt. Joseph P. Kennedy Jr. was killed in a top-secret mission to bomb a Nazi rocket factory that, as it turned out, had already been abandoned. His bomber, a B-24 Liberator loaded with 10 tons of bombs, exploded in midair before it even reached the English Channel. No body parts were ever recovered.

The next day two priests delivered the news to the family in Hyannis Port. Joe Kennedy would never really recover, but his ambitions for the family didn't end, they were just transferred to his second son. Recuperating from his combat wounds, JFK knew his fate.

"The burden falls to me," he told his Navy friend Red Fay. "I can feel Pappy's eyes on the back of my neck."

The question was which political office JFK would now seek.

Joe Kane had picked up rumors of a promising development. After a 30-year hiatus, James Michael Curley was back in Congress, having defeated a Yankee Democrat named Thomas Eliot in a new district. Curley didn't live in the district, but he had made use of a potent campaign issue. He accused his opponent of being a Unitarian.

Curley won going away, but he had other problems. He owed $42,000 after a civil fraud judgment, and a federal criminal indictment loomed. At the age of 71, Curley wanted to run for mayor one more time, and the timing seemed fortuitous. His arch foe, Mayor Maurice Tobin, a fellow Irishman from Roxbury, had given up the mayoralty after being elected governor in 1944. Curley figured his chances of prevailing over a placeholder at City Hall were much greater than a rematch against the Tobin machine that had crushed him in 1939.

It was just the kind of parochial Boston political infighting that Joe Kennedy so disdained, but this time it meant opportunity. One of Joe's henchmen, Joe Timilty, delivered $12,000 cash to Curley as a down payment on his mayoral campaign.

It was, of course, a bribe, but both Curley and Kennedy trusted Timilty. He was an old Kennedy family pal who had traveled to Rome with the

Police Commissioner Joe Timilty was accused of taking hundreds of thousands of dollars in payoffs to protect gambling czar Harry "Doc Jasper" Sagansky.

family in the late 1930s to meet the Pope. Timilty, a devout Catholic layman, had been Curley's police commissioner, and had continued serving until earlier in the year, when he was indicted after the Republican attorney general discovered $300,000 cash in his safe-deposit boxes. (The indictments were later dismissed.)

Now "the Comish" was working as Joe's bagman. His first delivery was to his old boss, Curley.

"The ambassador paid him to get out of the congressional seat," Joe Kane recalled, "and Curley figured he might need the money."

That Christmas, 1944, JFK wrote to his pal Lem Billings that he might go to law school at Harvard but that "if something good turns up while I am there I will run for it. I have my eye on something pretty good now if it comes through."

JFK spent 1945 recuperating, first at a spa in Arizona, then in Hollywood. Among his conquests was Sonja Henie, a former champion Norwegian ice skater who included among her prewar European fans Adolph Hitler, to whom she publicly gave the Nazi salute in 1936.

She'd parlayed her ice skating fame into a mediocre career in the movies, but never overcame the Nazi taint.

Joe strongly advised his son to get rid of her—"the Nazi thing," he explained.

Tagging along with his friend, actor Robert Stack, JFK next talked his way into the home of Olivia de Havilland, younger sister of Joan Fontaine, whom his father was pursuing, unsuccessfully. JFK thought he had handled himself quite suavely until it was time to leave for the evening. Looking for the front door, he opened a closet door and a cascade of the A-lister's high heels tumbled down on his head. The woman who'd played Maid Marion opposite Errol Flynn subsequently declined a dinner invitation.

"Do you think it was my walking into the closet?" he asked his friend Chuck Spalding. "Do you think that's what really did it?"

By July JFK was back in Boston. Curley was running away with the mayor's race. The caretaker mayor, John E. Kerrigan, a bachelor from South Boston, had fallen for a Scollay Square showgirl. When she decamped for New Orleans, he followed her, like a puppy. He had been gone for weeks, his whereabouts unknown. So much for the advantages of incumbency.

Joseph P. Kennedy Jr. might be dead, but his memory still had its uses. As his younger brother introduced himself to the voters, the Navy commissioned the destroyer U.S.S. *Joseph P. Kennedy Jr.,* built at the Fore River Shipyard his father had once run. Young Joe received the Navy Cross posthumously. A new VFW post named after him was incorporated, with Jack Kennedy as the president. The family started a foundation in his name, and at a well-attended media event, JFK presented a check for $600,000 to the Archdiocese, with Archbishop Richard Cushing accepting.

But the question remained, which office would Jack run for? Curley had been true to his word. Once elected mayor, he announced that he would not seek reelection to Congress, and waived his salary for 1946.

But another office was open—lieutenant governor. The incumbent Democrat governor, Maurice Tobin, wanted JFK as his running mate and Joe was tempted. The U.S. senator up for reelection was David I. Walsh, a closeted homosexual who in 1942 had been linked to a Nazi-run male brothel on the Brooklyn waterfront. The Boston papers had hushed it up, and J. Edgar Hoover had cleared him, but the facts were common knowledge in Massachusetts.

(Prior to his scandal, Walsh had served as chairman of the Senate Naval Affairs Committee. In 1942, when JFK was a young ensign whose girlfriend was suspected of being a Nazi spy, Honey Fitz arranged an interview for his grandson with Walsh. Walsh was quite taken with the rail-thin officer, writing back to Honey Fitz: "Frankly, I have not met a young man of his age in a long time who has impressed me more favorably." To JFK he wrote, "I am looking forward to keeping in contact with you.")

Walsh was 73 and in failing health. Joe Kennedy fantasized about Walsh being reelected, then dying in office. Gov. Tobin would appoint himself senator, and Jack would become governor. It was a nice dream, but

Gay Sen. David I. Walsh loved sailors, especially Ensign Kennedy.

Joe Kane reminded him that Henry Cabot Lodge, who had resigned his Senate seat in 1943 to join the military, would be running against Walsh.

In March 1946 Kane wrote a memo to Joe: "Has it ever occurred to you Tobin might be licked and Jack win?"

In those days, the governor and lieutenant governor of Massachusetts were elected separately, every other year. If a Republican took the governorship while JFK was elected lieutenant governor, the state GOP would never acquiesce to Jack becoming governor, even if Walsh died in office. Anyway, as Kane pointed out, in the last 32 years, only one lieutenant governor had ever attained the governorship of Massachusetts.

The alternative was a fallback to the original plan, Curley's 11th Congressional district. The bird in the hand . . .

JFK moved into a two-bedroom apartment in the Bellevue Hotel atop Beacon Hill, across from the State House. His grandfather, Honey Fitz, lived down the hall. Early in the campaign, Honey Fitz used to wander uninvited into JFK's strategy conferences.

One day, Kane was lecturing the troops when he looked up and saw his ancient nemesis. He pointed a finger at Honey Fitz as he looked at Jack.

"Get that son of a bitch out of here!" Kane yelled. Jack was stunned.

"Who? Grandpa?"

The campaign almost ended before it began. First of all, Jack, as a resident of Florida, had to register as a Democrat 30 days before the filing deadline. By the time he did, it was only 27 days to the deadline. For the right price, the documents were backdated. Then his campaign neglected to file his nomination papers with the Secretary of State before that deadline. A few hours after the office closed, it was reopened to accept JFK's certified signatures.

Eunice Kennedy asked her father, "Daddy, do you really think Jack can be a congressman?"

"You must remember," he famously answered, "it's not what you are that counts, but what people think you are."

The Kennedys sold JFK "like soap flakes," as Joe bragged later. Joe operated out of the Ritz, with Eddie Moore and Joe Timilty his top lieutenants. Joe Kane came up with the slogan, "The New Generation

Offers a Leader." At the age of 67, Kane taught his young cousin the nuts and bolts of politics.

He told Jack that he would have no friends in politics, only co-conspirators. It was, Kane said, like a jewelry store smash-and-grab.

"You conspire to grab the diamonds," he said, "and everybody runs, see?"

Another of Kane's sayings was, "Politics is like war. It takes three things to win. The first thing is money, the second thing is money, the third thing is money."

He had plenty of all three. The other candidates couldn't compete. Former Cambridge Mayor Mike Neville was his most prominent challenger. Neville took out a $25,000 mortgage on his home, but it wasn't nearly enough. One day he walked into the State House press gallery with a $10 bill hanging out of his breast coat pocket.

"It's a Kennedy campaign button," he bitterly explained to the reporters.

The Kennedys took it right to Neville in his hometown. Bobby Kennedy, 20 years old, fresh out of the Navy, was given East Cambridge to run. More importantly, the family organized "teas," inviting Democrat voters to formal introductions of the candidate. In Cambridge, the tea took place at the Commander Hotel outside Harvard Square. Hours before it began, women, in their finest clothes, with matching hats and gloves, began queuing up in the lobby, down the steps and out onto the sidewalk.

Joe Russo was a Boston city councilor in the fight. Soon another Joe Russo was on the ballot. He was a janitor from the West End.

The young street guys, just back from World War II, were looking for the main chance. That was Jack Kennedy, it quickly became clear. Soon JFK's fellow veterans began peeling away from the candidates from their own neighborhoods that they'd known their entire lives.

Dave Powers had been with the Charlestown state rep who was in the fight, but he defected, and Jack had the guy who would become for him what Eddie Moore had been for his father, a jack of all trades, one of which was pimp.

For the campaign, Joe hired a public-relations man named John Dowd. Dowd brought along some of his staff to provide back-office support, including a young secretary. One of the volunteers later explained to Nigel Hamilton, author of *JFK: Reckless Youth*, what JFK did next:

"The first thing he did was to get one of Dowd's staff pregnant. I went in one day—I was taking a law degree after leaving the Navy—and I found him humping this girl on one of the desks in his office. I said, 'Sorry,' and left! Later the girl told my wife she had missed her period, then learned she was expecting."

The volunteer told JFK the bad news.

"Oh shit!" he responded.

The volunteer told Hamilton: "He didn't care a damn about the girl—it was just the inconvenience that bothered him. In that sense, he was a pretty selfish guy."

As the campaign progressed, a new phenomenon began to occur. Women, especially younger women, were reacting to JFK the way Sen. Walsh had—head over heels. At East Boston High School, it was reported, before he delivered a speech the young female students rushed him, shouting "Sinatra!"

Fanueil Hall 1946: Candidate JFK is joined on stage by, left to right, Rose Kennedy, Mary and Honey Fitz Fitzgerald, Mayor James Michael Curley and (in uniform) George Curley.

It was the same at other girls' schools—"like Frank Sinatra in the old days," Red Fay recalled. "They would scream and holler and touch him—absolutely, in 1946. I mean, these girls were just crazy about him."

The day before the primary in June, Jack marched in Charlestown's Bunker Hill Day parade. It was hot, and he wore no hat. At the end of the route he buckled and collapsed, and was carried to a nearby doctor's house. It never made the papers.

The next day, in the primary that was tantamount to election, JFK cruised to victory. At his nephew's victory party, Honey Fitz sang "Sweet Adeline." Mike Neville asked rhetorically, "How do you beat a million dollars?"

Jack had 22,183 votes to Neville's 11,341. The nine other candidates trailed even further behind.

For the record, Joe Russo got 5,661 votes. Joe Russo got 779 votes.

Once the campaign was over, JFK went on a victory tour of sorts. The "extra's delight," as he signed his letters when he was in Hollywood, was back in business. In New York, he squired actress Gene Tierney and his old newspaper flame from the *Journal-American*, Flo Pritchett. And he reconnected with his first true love, Inga Arvad. She'd been going out with two older men—John Gunther, the successful author of the Inside series of nonfiction books, who was 12 years her senior. And she was also dating Tim McCoy, an old cowboy movie star. McCoy was 55, 23 years older than Inga.

One of the best books on Jack's early life is *The Search for JFK,* written by Joan and Clay Blair Jr. and published in 1976. By the time they began their research, Inga had died, at the age of 63. The Blairs interviewed her son, Ronald McCoy, who told them that she saw JFK for the last time in mid-November 1946, about the time she became pregnant.

When Ronald was in college, he told the Blairs, he came home one weekend and Inga pulled him aside and said she wanted to talk to him about something she'd never mentioned before. Then she told him never to discuss what she was about to tell him with his brother or father.

As Ronald recalled the conversation for the Blairs, his mother said to him: "I was pregnant when I married your father . . . I didn't know who your father was for sure. I really don't know if it was Jack or Tim."

The Blairs went back and checked the records. Inga married Tim McCoy in upstate New York on February 14, 1947. Ronald was born six months later, on August 12.

As always, Jack headed to Palm Beach for Christmas. Soon he had latched onto Durie Malcolm, a beautiful blonde socialite originally from Chicago. Like Inga, she was older than Jack, but only by five months. She had already been married twice, and she was an Episcopalian.

In January 1947, the *New York World-Telegram* even carried

Durie Malcolm, JFK's first wife.

an item about their whirlwind courtship, describing them as "inseparable at all social functions." At some point in January 1947, Jack married her, after a drunken party, in a civil ceremony. One story is that Durie refused to sleep with him before marriage, another is that she was pregnant. Whatever the truth, the marriage was known to everyone in both families.

Over a late-night bottle of Scotch in Bolivia in 1958, Seymour Hersh reported, Richard Cardinal Cushing told a group of young missionaries about the marriage. Morton Downey Jr. told Hersh that his father, Morton Downey Sr., a close friend of Joe Kennedy's, often cited the story when warning his son not to do anything as foolish as JFK had done.

According to Hersh in *The Dark Side of Camelot*, Joe had a "shitfit" when he heard about the marriage. He immediately dispatched JFK's friend Chuck Spalding and a lawyer to either Palm Beach Town Hall or the county courthouse in West Palm to get the records and destroy them—cost be damned. They were apparently successful; no such records exist today. Malcolm died in Palm Beach at age 91 in 2007. To the end of her life, she denied ever having been married to JFK.

"I didn't care for those Irish micks," she told a London newspaper in 1996, "and old Joe was a terrible man."

Six months later, she married for the third or fourth time, to another Palm Beach socialite named Thomas Shevlin. It was his second marriage; his first wife, Lorraine later married John Sherman Cooper, a Republican senator from Kentucky. Despite their party differences, JFK and Cooper were close friends. Hersh reported that sometimes when the Kennedys and the Coopers were at parties together, JFK or Lorraine Cooper would tell the other guests, "We're related by marriage." Lorraine and JFK would then start laughing, greatly amused that no one else got their little inside joke.

Durie Malcolm: JFK was her third husband.

After JFK's assassination, LBJ and RFK wanted to stack the Warren Commission with both Republicans and Democrats who could be counted upon not to rock the boat. Almost immediately, Sen. John Sherman Cooper was selected as one of the Republican members of the Commission.

He knew where the bodies were buried.

CHAPTER FOUR

COPS AND ROBBERS

JOE KENNEDY DIDN'T BELIEVE in making enemies needlessly—especially if they were cops or gangsters. There was just no upside to it, or at least not enough to justify the risks.

Joe was, at bottom, a street guy from East Boston. And he tried to shield his sons from the family "business." It may have been Joe's worst mistake as a father. Ultimately, Jack and Bobby were totally unprepared to deal with either cops or gangsters, especially once their father was incapacitated by a stroke in December 1961.

Joe understood what his sons were—and weren't. As he told Tip O'Neill in 1952 after his election to Congress:

"Never expect any appreciation from my boys. These kids have had so much done for them by other people that they assume it's coming to them."

And they assumed it more than ever after JFK's election as president in 1960, when he named his younger brother as his attorney general.

But there were two ruthless, powerful men who likewise assumed that they did have something coming to them from the Kennedys. They expected to be taken care of, or at least treated with kid gloves, by the new administration.

One was a cop, FBI director J. Edgar Hoover.

The other was a gangster from Chicago, Sam "Momo" Giancana.

Even if his sons didn't, Joe Kennedy understood what the Kennedys owed Hoover and Giancana.

Joe had always taken good care of Hoover because he knew how much blackmail material the director had on his oldest surviving son. Hoover had two sets of audio tapes of JFK engaging in scandalous extramarital sex—one from 1941, with suspected Nazi spy Inga Arvad in Room 132 of the Fort Sumter Hotel in Charleston, and the other with his 23-year-old Jackie-lookalike Senate aide, Pamela Turnure, in 1958.

Jack had been complaining about the Arvad tapes since the early 1940s. He wrote to one of his friends from Stanford, Henry Adams, about how much he loved Inga:

"She's warm, she's affectionate, she's wonderful in bed. But you know, goddammit Henry, I found out that son of a bitch Hoover had put a microphone under the mattress."

As soon as he was elected to Congress in 1946, JFK began talking about getting the tapes from Hoover.

"That bastard," he told his friend Langdon Melvin Jr., "I'm going to force Hoover to give me those files."

Of course, when someone has that kind of leverage over you, it's wise not to threaten him. Joe Kennedy understood this. He had the same philosophy as the Godfather: Keep your friends close and your enemies closer.

Joe Kennedy flattered Hoover. He treated Hoover the same way as he handled his pet journalists, lavishing gifts on them. Every Christmas, Joe would send J. Edgar a case of his favorite liquor, Jack Daniel's Black Label. Hoover's top assistant, Clyde Tolson, who was also his homosexual lover, got a case of his preferred Scotch, Haig & Haig.

When Joe was in Washington, he and Hoover would go out to lunch

FBI Director J. Edgar Hoover with his gay "partner," Clyde Tolson, Boston, 1957.

together and swap gossip. Knowing what Hoover had on his son, Joe once confided that he should have had Jack "gelded."

Soon, the FBI opened a small satellite office in Hyannis, a favor of sorts to Joe. In 1953, the local agent attended Jack's wedding to Jackie in Newport, and JFK made sure to seek him out and thank him for his courageous service to the nation.

Two years later, in 1955, Joe wrote a letter to Hoover basically urging him to run for president, and offering to raise whatever money he needed to win the White House, whether he ran as a Democrat or a Republican.

Hoover was so proud of the letter that he had it framed. It hung in a prominent place in his office for the rest of his life.

Flattery would get the Kennedys somewhere, but the more important goal for Hoover was keeping his job. His 70th birthday—and mandatory retirement under federal regulations—would come on January 1, 1965, after JFK's presumed reelection in 1964.

Hoover wanted a waiver, but he knew the younger Kennedys didn't like him. On the other hand, he had those tapes, and hundreds of pages of reports detailing JFK's obsessive need for "poontang," as he called it.

In March 1960, for example, an FBI report from New Orleans quoted an informant as saying "Senator Kennedy had been compromised with a woman in Las Vegas . . . He stated that when Senator Kennedy was in Miami, Fla., an airless hostess named (redacted) was sent to visit Kennedy."

One of Hoover's top assistants, Cartha DeLoach, reported that "on the top of Kennedy's desk a photo (is) openly displayed. This photo included Senator Kennedy and other men, as well as several girls in the nude. It was taken aboard a yacht or some type of pleasure cruiser."

Much of this material was likely turned over by Hoover to Lyndon Johnson before JFK suddenly decided to make LBJ his running mate in August 1960, although a definitive account of those hours in Los Angeles has never emerged.

As JFK told his press secretary Pierre Salinger: "The whole story will never be known. And it's just as well it won't be."

ALL INFORMATION CONTAINED
HEREIN IS UNCLASSIFIED
DATE ___ BY ___

April 19, 1960

Mr. Toison	
Mr. Mohr	
Mr. Parsons	
Mr. Belmont	
Mr. Callahan	
Mr. DeLoach	
Mr. Malone	
Mr. McGuire	
Mr. Rosen	
Mr. Tamm	
Mr. Trotter	
Mr. W. C. Sullivan	
Tele. Room	
Mr. Ingram	
Miss Gandy	

MR. MOHR:

Re: SENATOR JACK KENNEDY

Mr. James Dowd, Departmental Attorney who has been handling the Hoffa case in Florida, dropped by yesterday and spoke with Leinbaugh in my office. Mr. Dowd met the Director recently in his office. Dowd passed along the following information concerning Senator Kennedy on a strictly confidential basis:

Dowd said that in July 1959, just prior to leaving his practice in West Orange, New Jersey, he had met ⎰ ⎱ and their conversation turned to politics. ⎰ expressed great concern over Senator Kennedy's presidential aspirations. He said he felt Kennedy was extremely vulnerable and had shown "damn poor judgment."

⎰ said he was checking offices in the Senate Building one night and noted on the top of Kennedy's desk a photograph openly displayed. This photo included Senator Kennedy and other men, as well as several girls in the nude. It was taken aboard a yacht or some type of pleasure cruiser. ⎰ ⎱ Dowd that the thing that disturbed him most was that the Senator would show such poor judgment in leaving this photo openly displayed and said that other members of the guard and cleaning forces were aware of the photograph and that Kennedy's "extracurricular activities" were a standard joke around the Senate Office Building.

⎰ he felt he was a man of high principles who is reliable; that he would have no reason to question the story.

The above is for information.

RESPECTFULLY,

C. D. DeLoach

HPL'emb:geg
(2)

1960 FBI report re: JFK's Senate desk photo of "several girls in the nude."

RFK agreed: "The only people who were involved in the discussions were Jack and myself. We both promised each other that we'd never tell what happened."

At any rate, there was a standoff of sorts between Hoover and the Kennedys. The day after his narrow victory over Richard M. Nixon in

1960, the president-elect went out on the lawn in Hyannis Port and announced, among other things, that Hoover would be staying on.

"You don't fire God," JFK said, but only privately, not on the lawn at the compound.

Hoover had a reprieve, but he understood his continuing vulnerability.

The problem for Hoover wasn't so much Jack as his brother, Bobby, who as attorney general would now be the Director's boss, at least nominally.

"You have to get along with the old man," JFK told Bobby.

Part of the problem between the two was the age difference. Hoover instructed the tour guides at the Justice Department building to inform tourist groups that he had been director since before RFK was born. They were also told to mention that RFK had applied to become a G-man, only to be rejected as "too cocky."

RFK was equally scornful of the Director.

In his biography, *J. Edgar Hoover: The Man and the Secrets,* Curt Gentry reported that Bobby used to pass the John Dillinger exhibit case outside Hoover's office and quip, "What have they done lately?"

Even Ethel Kennedy took a swipe at the insecure old man. One day she saw the FBI "suggestion box." She scribbled out a note: "Chief (William) Parker in Los Angeles for director."

But the larger problem between Hoover and RFK may have been the Director's homosexuality. RFK had a lifelong aversion to gay men. In his final years, he managed to somewhat temper his rabid anti-Semitism, but he never changed his low opinion of gays.

In 1968, shortly before his assassination, he was complaining about having to work with a gay editor in New York on his latest book.

Roy Cohn, Bobby's sworn enemy since their feud in the early 1950s while working as aides for Sen. Joe McCarthy, was flamboyantly gay, and he was close to Hoover. According to one perhaps apocryphal account, in the 1950s, Hoover was spotted in full drag in a New York hotel room—either at the Plaza or the Waldorf-Astoria, depending on who's telling the story.

The room—or apartment, again depending on the story—was supposedly rented by Cohn.

As early as 1933, *Collier's* magazine noted that Hoover walked with "a mincing step." *Time* magazine reported that he is "seldom seen without a male companion, most frequently solemn-faced Clyde Tolson."

Tolson had caught the Director's eye early. It took Tolson just three years to go from rookie agent to assistant director of the Bureau. Truman Capote joked that he wanted to do a magazine piece, "Johnny and Clyde."

As time went on, mobsters would be picked up on bugs or wiretaps discussing Hoover. In Philadelphia, one gangster accurately told boss Angelo Bruno why RFK was trying to get rid of the Director:

"He wants Edgar Hoover out of the FBI because he is a fairy. I heard this before . . . Listen to this: Edgar Hoover is not married and neither is his assistant. Read back in his history."

According to Anthony Summers in his biography *Official and Confidential: The Secret Life of J. Edgar Hoover,* the director was arrested in the 1920s on a morals charge in New Orleans.

The pinch was straightened out by a well-connected FBI agent who would later be set up on a $75,000 bribery sting in Washington during World War II. After the ex-agent complained directly to Hoover, the sting was aborted and the agent was allowed to keep the $75,000—a huge sum in those days.

Pete Hamill, a New York newspaperman and later a boyfriend of Jackie Onassis, reported that he was told by a Mob associate in Las Vegas that the underworld had photos of Hoover *in flagrante delicto* with Tolson.

Gangster Meyer Lansky had supposedly obtained the pictures. Another version of the story is that James Jesus Angleton, a top CIA officer, had what Summers described as "a picture of him (Hoover) giving Clyde Tolson a blow job . . . (including) a close shot of Hoover's head. He was totally recognizable."

During World War II, Angleton had served in the Office of Strategic Services (OSS), which worked closely with Lansky and other New York gangsters on the Brooklyn waterfront to prevent Nazi sabotage.

Hoover was always obsessively protective of his turf, and after the war he tried to prevent the OSS from morphing into what would become the CIA. It would have been only natural for Angleton et al. to seek their own insurance policy against a crafty bureaucratic infighter like Hoover, and to share their blackmail material with their former gangland allies.

Or vice versa.

Hoover was also said to worry about the potential for his agents to be bribed or otherwise compromised if they started going up against powerful gangsters with large bankrolls and other enticements. And indeed, that would be a problem for the Bureau in cities like New York and Boston later in the 20th century.

Whatever the reasons, Hoover had next to no interest in going after organized crime until the Apalachin Mafia conference in 1957. That was a gathering of dozens of Mafia leaders from around the country in upstate New York.

Local and state police raided the house where they were meeting and arrested 56 high-ranking mobsters, while others escaped into the woods.

After the resulting national headlines, Hoover was reluctantly forced to pay more attention to a criminal organization he had previously claimed did not exist. Thus began the Top Hoodlum program.

Bobby had always detested the Mafia. In the 1950s, when he had told Joe about his plans as a Senate investigator to take on both corrupt unions and the Mob, his father was apoplectic. He knew JFK would need union support when he ran for president in 1960. Joe also understood that any investigations of corrupt union leaders would inevitably lead back to the Mob.

Bobby didn't care. First he subpoenaed gangsters to testify in Washington, then he humiliated them at the hearings. RFK was particularly disdainful of the boss of the Chicago Outfit, Sam "Momo" Giancana.

RFK: Would you tell us anything about your operations or will you just giggle every time I ask you a question?

Giancana: I decline to answer.

RFK: I thought only little girls giggled, Mr. Giancana.

Still, in 1960, at the behest of his good friend Frank Sinatra, Giancana made his peace with the Kennedys. He delivered Chicago to the Democrats, and JFK carried Illinois.

Judith Campbell, the girlfriend of Giancana, Sinatra and JFK, later claimed the Mafia leader told her, "Listen, honey, if it wasn't for me, your boyfriend wouldn't even be in the White House."

In return, Giancana expected a good leaving alone from the Kennedys.

When JFK became president in 1961, both Hoover and Giancana were determined to get along with him. About 10 days after the inauguration, Hoover presented Bobby with information that an Italian magazine had printed a story about a woman, Alicia Purdom Durr, who

Alicia Purdom Durr: another of JFK's girlfriends, whom his father Joe called "a goddamn Polish Jew."

claimed to have been engaged to JFK in the early 1950s. Later, the FBI reported, "it was further alleged that the woman became pregnant."

Bobby knew the story well. According to some accounts, he had been detached from his brother's campaign the previous year to deliver the woman a hush money payment of $500,000.

Hoover was most likely using the Durr story to remind Bobby of just how much dirt he had on his brother. Giancana, on the other hand, actually came through in a big way for JFK in the early days of his administration.

A young heir to a swank Los Angeles restaurant fortune had foolishly married a promiscuous Hollywood starlet named Judi Meredith. The kid's relatives wanted to extricate him from the woman's clutches, so they hired Fred Otash, the former LAPD detective turned private eye, to dig up dirt on the woman.

In short order, Otash discovered a long list of her paramours including, among others, most of the Rat Pack, as well as Jerry Lewis and the new president of the United States.

When word got out that the husband's lawyer was planning to name them all, including JFK, as co-respondents, Otash got a phone call from Giancana's man in Hollywood, Johnny Roselli. The gangster wanted a sit-down with the ex-cop at the Brown Derby in Hollywood.

In his biography *Peter Lawford: The Man Who Kept the Secrets,* James Spada recounted what Otash told him about his conversation with the Chicago hoodlum:

"He said to me, 'I'm representing the Kennedys.' I said, 'Are you kidding me?' I couldn't believe my ears—here's Roselli, a guy who's a fucking mobster, intervening on behalf of the White House."

The case was quickly settled out of court. Meredith got a modest check and a set of furniture and was sent on her way.

Despite the Mob's assistance in such matters, as well as in the anti-Castro plots the Kennedys had inherited from the Eisenhower administration, RFK was still determined to bring the underworld to heel. He directed Hoover to turn the FBI loose on the Mafia.

On March 14, 1961, Hoover sent a memo to his field offices, instructing them to "infiltrate organized crime groups to the same degree that we have been able to penetrate the Communist party and other subversive organizations."

The first to feel the heat was Carlos Marcello, the boss of New Orleans. The Kennedys had tried to recruit him to the JFK campaign in 1960. But instead he'd donated hundreds of thousands in cash to Nixon, perhaps because Bobby had humiliated him by forcing him to take the Fifth Amendment at another of Bobby's show-trial Senate hearings in the late 1950s.

Along with Giancana and Teamsters boss Jimmy Hoffa, Marcello was close to the top of RFK's personal Hit Parade.

New Orleans Mafia boss Carlos Marcello in New York, 1966.

He'd been born in Tunisia in 1910, but had lately taken to claiming he was born in Guatemala.

On April 4, 1961, Marcello showed up at the federal office building in New Orleans for what he thought would be a routine immigration hearing. Instead, he was grabbed by federal agents, hustled to the airport, and flown to Guatemala—deported.

It took Marcello weeks to make his way back to the States, an arduous journey that involved hacking his way through dangerous jungles, accompanied only by his lawyer, who had flown to Guatemala to join his client.

When he finally returned to Louisiana, Marcello was indicted for fraud, perjury (for saying he was born in Guatemala) and illegal reentry.

Santo Trafficante, the boss of Tampa, was equally angry at the Kennedys. In the 1950s, when he and Meyer Lansky were

Second generation Tampa Mafia boss Santo Trafficante, who supplied whores for JFK in Havana.

running the casinos in Havana, JFK and Sen. George Smathers had often vacationed there.

The mobsters had provided the senators with their best Cuban hookers, and had even watched them cavorting with their "dates" through two-way mirrors. According to T. J. English in *Havana Nocturne: How the Mob Owned Cuba and Then Lost It to the Revolution,* Lansky and Trafficante later rued the fact that they didn't film the future president's escapades.

Trafficante, who had been arrested at the Apalachin conference in 1957, was briefly jailed again in Cuba when Fidel Castro took power in January 1959. (So was Lansky's brother Jake.) Trafficante subsequently worked on various CIA plots to take out the Communist dictator, and he was also close to Jimmy Hoffa, the president of the Teamsters Union and another of RFK's targets.

By mid-1961, Trafficante was complaining to whoever would listen about the "honesty" of the Kennedys.

Mobbed-up Teamsters boss Jimmy Hoffa, center. Left: William McCarthy of Boston Local 25, ex-con who later became the national Teamsters president.

But the angriest mobster of all may have been Giancana. He had done more for the Kennedys than anyone else in the underworld, and now he was under close FBI surveillance wherever he went.

On July 12, 1961, he flew back to Chicago from Phoenix with his girlfriend, the singer Phyllis McGuire. Local FBI agents grabbed them at O'Hare Airport.

William J. Roemer Jr., a high-ranking Chicago G-man, separated them and then got Giancana in a room by himself. What happened next has been recounted many times.

According to Roemer in his first book, *Roemer: Man Against the Mob*, Giancana began screaming about Hoover and RFK and then said to the agent, "Fuck your super, super boss!"

Roemer, bemused, asked Giancana who his "super, super boss" was.

JFK, the enraged mobster replied. Roemer said he doubted the president cared about Momo Giancana.

"Fuck John Kennedy!" Giancana shouted. "Listen, Roemer, I know all about the Kennedys, and Phyllis knows more about the Kennedys, and one of these days we're going to tell all."

At the time, Roemer wrote more than 20 years later, he had no idea what Momo was talking about.

"Fuck you!" Giancana continued. "One of these days it'll come out. You wait, you smart asshole, you'll see."

According to Roemer, Giancana then said something else the FBI agents didn't understand at the time.

"The fucking United States government is not as smart as it thinks it is, is it? You made a deal with Castro to overthrow Batista if he would kick us out of Cuba, and now that deal has backfired on you, hasn't it?"

Back in Washington, RFK was going out of his way to get under Hoover's skin. Bobby wandered the halls of the Justice Department building in shirtsleeves, which offended the fastidious Hoover.

RFK brought his large un-housebroken dog into the building, and when Brummus pissed on the floor, Hoover angrily called a meeting of his top staff to discuss what could be done about this affront to the dignity of his office.

Bobby and his aides repeated all the old jokes about Hoover and Tolson. One was that when an ambitious FBI agent's wife gave birth to a boy, it would be named Edgar. If it were a girl, the child would be named Clyde.

They called the Director "J. Edna," and later, "Gay Edgar Hoover."

One day it was brought up at a Justice meeting that Tolson was having minor surgery.

"For what," Bobby asked, "a hysterectomy?"

Hoover, always the consummate bureaucrat, suffered in silence. But now he had a new weapon. The bugging and wiretaps, which Hoover had resisted for so long, were in fact proving to be a boon, both for Mob prosecutions and for his own personal files that his devoted secretary, Helen Gandy, kept under tight lock and key.

Not only was he turning up ever more dirt on JFK, but Hoover was also learning about RFK's secret life. Bobby, as Peter Lawford used to say, had contracted the "adultery virus" from his older brother.

In early September 1961, through his liaison to the Justice Department, Hoover sent over files to RFK detailing how an informant was reporting that the attorney general had been seen in the desert near Las Vegas on a blanket with two young women.

A photographer in the employ of organized crime, the informant continued, had used a telephoto lens to obtain compromising pictures of the attorney general.

Bobby listened to the liaison, an FBI agent, in icy silence. He then calmly asked the agent if he had any special plans for the Labor Day weekend.

A quarter century later, the liaison told a Hoover biographer that the exchange "probably did happen as described."

From his Chicago wiretaps, Hoover would soon know that Judith Campbell was calling private lines at the White House on a regular basis, from Giancana's home.

And from his bugs on Giancana's headquarters at the Armory Lounge in suburban Oak Park, he would also discover how angry Giancana and his associates were that Frank Sinatra seemed unable to deliver on the promises he had made to them a year earlier, during the campaign.

Sinatra, in fact, was still trying to call in the Mob's chits, using Joe Kennedy as his go-between to the brothers. But after advancing his sons enough cash to build a swimming pool at the White House (which JFK was soon enjoying with his female staffers), Joe began to get the brush off from his offspring.

At age 73, Joe's blood pressure had risen to dangerously high levels, and his physicians began prescribing various medications, which Joe resisted taking.

On December 11, 1961, Hoover sent Bobby a transcript of another bugged conversation between Giancana and Roselli at the Armory Lounge in Forest Park.

They were discussing what they had expected when Sinatra had brought them the offer of a hands-off administration if they came through for JFK in the 1960 campaign.

Roselli: Sinatra's got it in his head that they (the Kennedys) are going to be faithful to him. (By which he meant organized crime.)

Giancana: In other words, the donation that was made . . .

Roselli: That's what I was talking about.

Giancana: In other words, if I ever get a speeding ticket, none of these fuckers would know me?

Roselli: You told that right, buddy.

But the Kennedys had reneged on their pledge. Hoover must have been ecstatic when he read the transcript. The smoking-gun word was "donation." The Mafia had "donated" to JFK's campaign.

With the transcript, Hoover included for Bobby his own taunting description of what he now had Giancana saying on tape:

"He made a donation to the campaign of President Kennedy but was not getting his money's worth."

It will never be known what the Kennedy brothers did next, but a week later, on December 18, their father suffered a massive stroke while playing golf in Palm Beach.

Joe survived, but he was totally incapacitated. He would never speak again.

If the brothers were devastated by Joe's stroke, so was Frank Sinatra. Bobby hated him, and so did Jackie. When the boys leaned on Sinatra, he could always call Joe. Joe hadn't been able to get his sons to lay off the Mob, but before the stroke, there had always been a chance that eventually he could convince his sons to fulfill their end of the bargain.

Now no one would be able to talk sense to the two spoiled rich kids.

In his book *Mr. S: My Life with Frank Sinatra*, Sinatra's valet George Jacobs described his boss's post-stroke panic:

"Only that master strategist Old Joe could tell Frank how to sort this thing out, but by now Old Joe wasn't talking. What a can of worms!"

Within three months, Sinatra himself would be totally cast out of Camelot, after Hoover told JFK what he knew about his girlfriend Judith Campbell and her ties to Sinatra and Giancana.

Giancana's associates were as livid about the Kennedys' double cross as their boss. Johnny Formosa was one of the Outfit's front men in Las Vegas. He knew what should be done to Sinatra.

"Let's hit him!" he told Giancana.

Then, Formosa continued, he would personally exterminate the Rat Pack.

"Let's show 'em. Let's show those fuckin' Hollywood fruitcakes they can't get away with it as if nothing happened . . . I could whack out a couple of those guys. Lawford, that Martin prick, and I could take the nigger and put his other eye out."

Giancana was able to calm Formosa down, but the overlords of organized crime were coming to a consensus. Yes, Bobby was a problem, but ultimately the source of his power was the president of the United States.

In August 1962, Meyer Lansky was recorded on an FBI bug telling his wife about another of RFK's affairs.

Lansky's wife, Teddy, blamed it all on Sinatra, describing him as "nothing but a procurer of women for those guys. Sinatra is the guy that gets them all together."

Lansky disagreed.

"It starts with the president," he said, "and goes right down the line."

Ditto with the harassment by the FBI. Within a month, the rumblings of retaliation by the underworld against both brothers were becoming even more ominous. Jimmy Hoffa, whom RFK had been trying to get the goods on for years, was talking with one of his Teamsters local presidents about the best way to assassinate the AG.

Hoffa mentioned RFK's convertible, and how he could be taken out by a sniper in a tall building as he drove by. It would be best, Hoffa said, to kill Bobby in the South, so that segregationists would be blamed.

But, Hoffa said, he preferred to blow up RFK. He asked the president of the Teamsters local if he could obtain plastic explosives. Soon thereafter, the union president became an FBI informant, and told agents of his conversation.

This time, Hoover passed on the information to the Kennedys. They were shocked enough to ask Hoover to give his informant a lie-detector test. The union president passed.

That same month, September 1962, Carlos Marcello was drinking with two of his underworld associates at his swampy 6,400-acre plantation outside New Orleans.

One of the hoodlums commiserated with the Mafia boss about the problems Bobby was giving him. That set off Marcello, and he began yelling in his native Sicilian dialect:

"*Livarsi na petra di la scarpa!?*" (Translation: "Take the stone out of my shoe.")

Then he switched back to English for the benefit of his Anglo associate:

"Don't worry about that little Bobby son of a bitch. He's going to be taken care of."

None of his men would be directly involved, Marcello continued. The job would be done by "a nut." But, he added, it wasn't Bobby who was going to be hit. It would be his brother, the president of the United States.

"The dog will keep biting you if you only cut off its tail," Marcello said.

In other words, if Bobby were murdered, JFK would come after them all. But if the president were dead, RFK would be out of power as well.

That same month, in Tampa, Santo Trafficante met with one of his old Havana associates, Jose Aleman, now an exile from Cuba, much like Trafficante himself. Trafficante told his old friend how angry he was about Bobby's crusade against his friend and business associate Hoffa.

"Have you seen how his brother is hitting Hoffa, a man who is a worker, who is not a millionaire, a friend of the blue collars? He doesn't know that kind of encounter is very delicate."

Very delicate. Joe Kennedy would have known what Trafficante was getting at. But Joe Kennedy was no longer in the picture.

Then Trafficante made an even more direct threat. Aleman would later say that he twice passed on what Trafficante said to a pair of FBI agents that he knew.

Years later, the two now-retired agents refused to confirm or deny that Aleman had informed them of Trafficante's threats.

"I wouldn't want to do anything to embarrass the FBI," one of them told a reporter from the *Washington Post.*

At any rate, there is no evidence that Hoover ever informed the Kennedys what Trafficante next said to Aleman.

"Mark my words," Trafficante told the Cuban, "this man Kennedy is in trouble, and he will get what is coming to him."

Aleman agreed that JFK probably wouldn't get reelected. Trafficante shook his head.

"No Jose," he said, "he is going to be hit."

There was no way this was going to end well.

CHAPTER FIVE

JFK: "TWO-MINUTE MAN"

FILL IN YOUR OWN cliché about the prodigious womanizing of the Kennedy men—they got more ass than a toilet seat. They touched everything but the third rail. They would have fucked the crack of dawn. Any rude description applies.

But one other fact seems indisputable—the Kennedy men have always been lousy lovers. In a letter to his best friend Lem Billings, young Jack Kennedy described himself as a "slam-bam-thank-you-ma'am" kind of lover.

He was, all agreed, an attractive guy.

"He does not wear a hat and has blonde curly hair which is always tousled," an FBI agent reported about him in 1941, when he was dating suspected Nazi spy Inga Arvad.

The report on JFK continued: "Known only as Jack."

He always liked to visit Hollywood. As he later told Frank Sinatra's valet, "I want to fuck every woman in Hollywood."

But was he really "the extra's delight," as he signed those letters from Hollywood? Most of the reviews of his amorous techniques were far from positive.

Here are a few notices about JFK's performances, culled from various sources:

In February 1942, the FBI was bugging the room at the Francis Marion Hotel in Charleston, South Carolina, where he was having sex every night with Inga Arvad. The report noted that Arvad accused JFK of "taking every pleasure of youth but not the responsibility."

Inga-Binga, as JFK affectionately called her, was worried that she might be pregnant with his child. She wondered what she would do.

"She spoke of the possibility of getting her marriage annulled. It was noted that Kennedy had very little comment to make on the subject."

Truman Capote quoted JFK's first wife, Durie Malcolm, as saying that JFK "was a pig about hogging all the fun for himself."

Fred Otash was a legendary Hollywood private detective who planted any number of show-biz and political wiretaps. He claimed his targets included the last home of Marilyn Monroe in Brentwood, and Peter Lawford's beachfront Santa Monica home where JFK had occasional assignations with Monroe.

Years later, Otash described JFK as a "two-minute man," who was "hung like a cashew."

Angie Dickinson has never publicly acknowledged that she was JFK's lover, but the quote attributed to her of their lovemaking is that it was "the best 20 seconds of my life."

Marlene Dietrich, believed to have had sex with Joe, Joe Jr. and JFK, described Jack's techniques as "weak lemonade," and said that their final coupling in the White House in 1963 was "three to six minutes of ecstasy."

Bettie Page, the famous pinup girl of the 1950s, had sex with JFK at Frank Sinatra's mansion in Palm Springs.

"It was nothing out of the ordinary," she said. "He wanted me on top."

Jayne Mansfield, the poor man's Marilyn Monroe of the 1950s: "I had to teach him some tricks . . . Jack seemed to just want to get his jollies and the women didn't seem to matter."

(As for JFK, he had his own take on Mansfield: "I'd rather have Marilyn Monroe or Lana Turner, but if they're not available, I'd happily switch from the A-list to the C-cup.")

Henry Kissinger said power is the ultimate aphrodisiac, and for Marilyn Monroe, it certainly was. She told a Hollywood gossip columnist: "Jack won't indulge in foreplay because he's on the run all the time."

Judith Campbell Exner, one of JFK's more famous paramours, said in her first memoir, *My Story*:

"He refused to wear a condom, claiming it deadened the sensation for him."

At the beginning of their affair, when he was running for president in 1960, "He couldn't have been more loving, more concerned about my feelings, more considerate, more gentle. Later, because of his bad back and an arrogance that overtook him in the White House, he developed a cavalier attitude in bed, as if he were there to be serviced."

Tempest Storm, the stripper, in her book, *Tempest Storm: The Lady Is a Vamp*: "He told me that he was not happily married, that Jackie was cold toward him . . . In my memory Jack Kennedy's sex drive lives up to the legend that has developed around it since his death. The man just never wore out."

Gunilla von Post, a Swedish beauty from the 1950s, in her book, *Love, Jack*: "His back trouble was always a critical factor."

Mimi Alford, JFK's 19-year-old White House intern, in her book *Once Upon a Secret*: "I don't remember the President *ever* kissing me—not hello, not goodbye, even during sex."

CHAPTER SIX

"BEAUTIES IN THE WHITE HOUSE"

O N THE MORNING OF June 11, 1961, more than a million Americans picked up the Sunday editions of their favorite Hearst newspapers, all of which carried the Hearst Sunday supplement, *The American Weekly.*

In New York, Los Angeles, San Francisco, Boston, Baltimore and a number of other cities, a few million readers saw the *Weekly's* lead story—"Beauties in the White House."

The story began in italics:

"Led by the prettiest First Lady in our history, the White House female contingent makes up a beauty contest with brains."

It was only slightly more gushing than the purple prose being printed about the new president almost everywhere else, even after the recent disaster at the Bay of Pigs. But probably no one who picked up a *Chicago American* or *San Francisco Examiner* had any idea exactly how well Jack Kennedy knew the beauties.

The first staffer profiled was Pamela Turnure, age 23, described as "closest to the Kennedys." What

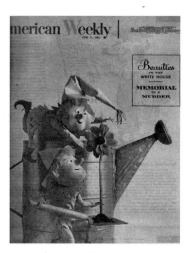

Three of JFK's girlfriends—"Beauties in the White House"—were profiled in the Hearst newspapers' Sunday supplement of June 11, 1961.

wasn't mentioned, but was obvious to any reader, was that she was a Jackie lookalike—brunette bouffant hair. As Kitty Kelley later noted, Pam even dressed like Jackie—sleeveless dresses, chokers and pumps with low heels.

She was Jackie's press secretary, but before that she had worked in JFK's Senate office. She had lived in an upstairs apartment owned by a devout Catholic couple named Kater. One night in 1958, they were awakened by the sound of pebbles hitting the upstairs window outside Turnure's room.

Florence Mary Kater looked out and was amazed to see her tenant's boss, the very married Sen. Jack Kennedy, looking up at the window. It didn't take her long to figure out what was going on, and on an almost nightly basis, as she was soon to realize.

Pamela Turnure, Jackie lookalike.

An obsessive sort, Mrs. Kater wired Turnure's bedroom and soon had salacious audios. One night, as the junior senator left her house, she managed to get a photograph, although the future president had the wherewithal to cover his face.

Soon she was shopping the photo and the tapes to newspapers, calling JFK a "'debaucher' of a girl young enough to be his daughter," as an FBI report dated October 27, 1961, noted. But only the *Washington Star* would print as much as a blind item.

JFK fleeing Turnure's apartment, 1958.

Next she did what any good American would have done in 1958. She sent copies of the JFK sex tapes to the nation's most incorruptible cop, J. Edgar Hoover. Little did she know what Hoover would do with the tapes. As his longtime deputy, William Sullivan, once said, the Director was a "master blackmailer."

Senate Majority Leader Lyndon Johnson had always taken a prurient interest in "ole Jack" and his sex life. In DC, LBJ was a neighbor of Hoover's, and according to LBJ aide Bobby Baker, the Director was soon playing the Turnure sex tapes for LBJ's amusement and edification.

Turnure was definitely JFK's type: upper class, a Northeastern debutante. Once she moved into the White House, Jackie apparently developed a friendship with her. Later, after the assassination, when Jackie moved to New York, Turnure followed her and continued working for Jackie until she got married.

On the facing page of *American Weekly* were the two secretaries known as Fiddle and Faddle. They had gone to work for JFK during the campaign out of Goucher College. Priscilla Wear, "Fiddle," was still

Jill "Faddle" Cowan and Priscilla "Fiddle" Wear.

only 20. She worked as an assistant to JFK's secretary, Evelyn Lincoln. The supplement noted her green eyes and the fact that "she sees the President a dozen times a day." Like Jackie, she was a graduate of Miss Porter's School in Farmington, Connecticut.

Fiddle's roommate in Georgetown was Jill Cowan, a 23-year-old Jewish relative of the family that owned the Bloomingdale's department stores. Her nickname was Faddle. In 1965, as part of the JFK library's oral history project about the administration, Faddle was asked what her duties were at the White House.

"It varied," she said.

Sometimes Fiddle and Faddle would be seen in the Oval Office, massaging the president's hair with gel. They often accompanied him on trips—but only if Jackie was not along, which she wasn't most of the time. Their secretarial duties were minimal. Their services were seldom required before noon, when they would be summoned to the White House pool. As they arrived, the president would already be waiting for them. After all, as his aides Kenny O'Donnell and Dave Powers later noted in their sycophantic joint memoir, *Johnny, We Hardly Knew Ye,* "The president disliked swimming alone in the White House pool . . . If Dave was not available to join him, he would bring another friend to the pool."

Or two.

When JFK was in the pool with Fiddle and Faddle, it was off-limits, even to the Secret Service. Jackie had no illusions about their "varied" duties. One day, she was escorting a reporter from the French magazine *Paris-Match* on a tour of the White House. They reached the Oval Office and Jackie said hello to Evelyn Lincoln, noticed Fiddle and then turned to the reporter, speaking to him in French.

Caroline Kennedy in the White House with her father's 21-year-old gal pal.

"This is the girl who supposedly is sleeping with my husband."

Jackie apparently didn't know— or perhaps didn't care—that her fellow Miss Porter's alumna also spoke French.

According to Ron Kessler in *The First Family Detail*, one afternoon Jackie was out, and JFK was frolicking in the pool with Fiddle and Faddle, who were clad as usual only in wet T-shirts, the better to highlight their nipples. Suddenly, Jackie unexpectedly returned to the White House. Only in such an emergency was the Secret Service authorized to enter the pool area, and agent Anthony Sherman bolted inside to warn the president and his guests.

Janet Des Rosiers, Leicester High School yearbook photo, 1941.

As all three clambered out of the pool, JFK handed his Bloody Mary to Sherman.

"Enjoy it," he said. "It's quite good."

Another "White House beauty" not included in the story was Janet des Rosiers. She was 37, somewhat older than the other beauties, and her claim to fame in the White House was that she had been the longtime girlfriend of the president's father.

From Leicester, Massachusetts, Des Rosiers had hooked up with Joe in 1947, when she was 24 and he was 60. She'd been his "assistant" for years, accepted even by Rose.

Des Rosiers, seated, was often photographed with Joe—and Rose.

Growing tired of her dead-end job as an old man's mistress, when the 1960 presidential campaign began des Rosiers became the stewardess on JFK's plane, the *Caroline*. Of course, JFK put the moves on her—"Don't you think it's about time you found me attractive?" was his come-on line, she wrote in the memoir she self-published in 2015 at the age of 92.

She never succumbed to his blandishments, but Janet did use her time on the plane wisely. Speaking to crowd after crowd around the clock, JFK often struggled with laryngitis. His doctors told him that to preserve his voice, he should communicate whenever possible with written notes. Des Rosiers began collecting his discarded notes, and later sold them at auction. Perhaps the most famous note, in JFK's unmistakable longhand: "I got into the blond."

But another one may be even more telling. Looking ahead to a possible victory, Sen. Kennedy sadly wrote:

"I suppose if I win—my poon days are over."

Actually, nothing changed when the new president moved into 1600 Pennsylvania Avenue. JFK used to say that he got migraine headaches if he didn't have sex at least once a day. There are no reports of him suffering any migraines during the 1,000 days of his administration.

Fiddle wasn't his only girlfriend from Miss Porter's School. He also carried on with the former Helen Husted, a first cousin of John Husted, whom Jackie had dumped to marry JFK. Helen had married a member of the Romanov family that had ruled Russia until the Bolshevik Revolution. When JFK met her in 1960 she was 26, with two children, divorced, and her name was Helen Chavchavadze. Through a newspaper pal, he had requested that she be invited to a dinner party in Georgetown he was attending by himself, and that night he followed her home in his own car and seduced her.

Helen had assumed that once he became president, their affair would be over. But a couple of weeks after his inauguration, in the winter of 1961, JFK had appeared at her front door, on a weekday morning, accompanied not by his Secret Service escort, but by Sen. George Smathers, his fellow philanderer down through the years. The message to JFK's gal pal couldn't have been any clearer—the president would continue to live his life the way he always had.

Another White House staffer on JFK's string was Diane deVegh, one more in his long line of Social Register WASPs. DeVegh was descended from John Jay, one of the authors of the Federalist Papers. JFK had met her in 1958 when she was an undergraduate at Radcliffe and he was running for reelection to the Senate from Massachusetts. Soon Dave Powers, JFK's most trusted aide, was picking her up at her dorm in Cambridge.

McGeorge Bundy, then the dean of the Harvard faculty, was shocked. For one thing, JFK was serving on the Harvard Board of Overseers. Making their May-to-December affair even more scandalous, deVegh's father was on a couple of visiting Harvard committees.

"You have to stop it!" Bundy told Kennedy.

Bundy was a respected academic, with the bluest of Brahmin blood-lines, a nominal Republican whose brother Bill would also work in the New Frontier. The Bundys may have been loyal liegemen to the arriviste young Irishman, but JFK couldn't resist giving the needle to the old-line Yankee establishment, the way his father did when he named his post-Prohibition liquor importing company after the ultra-exclusive WASP social club on Park Street, the Somerset.

After appointing McGeorge Bundy to head the National Security Council, JFK decided to send him a young aide—the now 22-year-old Diane deVegh. It was a reminder to Bundy who was now calling the shots. Bundy endured the indignity in silence. When Jackie was away, deVegh would often dine alone at the White House with JFK and his two closest Boston Irish aides, Kenny O'Donnell and Dave Powers.

DeVegh soon realized that being the president's mistress was not a good long-term career move. She left Washington and eventually became an actress on the soap opera *All My Children*, 20 years before JFK's nephew Chris Lawford would join the cast.

Washington was a very small town in those days. Everyone knew—and often had sex with—one another. For instance, during her affair with Kennedy, deVegh was also sleeping with Cord Meyer, a CIA operative who himself was also going out with Jill Cowan, aka Faddle.

October 1978: Former JFK aides McGeorge Bundy and Dave Powers both knew a lot about Diane de Vegh.

Meyer had just split up with the former Mary Pinchot, another Brahmin whose sister was married to JFK's closest journalist friend, Ben Bradlee, the future *Washington Post* editor who was then working for *Newsweek* magazine. Like the Bundys, Bradlee was another Boston Brahmin who idolized Kennedy. Bradlee soon realized that if he wanted to retain his access, he would have to learn to look the other way, and not ask questions about, among other things, the increasing amount of time his sister-in-law was spending with the married president.

One of the Meyers' sons had been run over in 1956, and Mary's marriage to Cord had disintegrated in the aftermath of their child's death. She was available, and accessible.

JFK had known the beautiful Mary Pinchot since his youth at the Choate School back in the 1930s. As the '60s began, they had something else in common: drugs. Both had become "patients" of Dr. Max

Jacobson, a refugee from Nazi Germany who operated out of a squalid office on East 72nd Street in Manhattan.

JFK had been introduced to "Dr. Feelgood" by his old college roommate, Chuck Spalding, during the 1960 campaign. He got his first shot September 26, 1960, hours before his first televised debate against Richard Nixon. After the injection, Kennedy had sex with a prostitute. As O'Donnell and Powers later wrote, "We were annoyed by later reports that Kennedy had spent three days resting and studying the issues before the decisive first debate."

During that first televised presidential debate, JFK appeared relaxed and totally in control, while Nixon seemed nervous, perspiring. It was a huge win for the Democrats, and Dr. Feelgood became the president's regular connection to the drug demimonde. JFK called his New York office directly, identifying himself as "Mrs. Dunn."

Soon Jacobson was providing "vitamins" for both Jack and Jackie. They were just two more boldface names in Dr. Feelgood's clientele—a Who's Who of celebrities, gangsters and entertainers.

Author Truman Capote described the rush after an injection: "Instant euphoria. You feel like Superman. You're flying. Ideas come at the speed of light."

The crash was spectacular as well, which was why JFK eventually invited him to move into the White House. Dr. Feelgood wisely declined that opportunity, but he accompanied JFK on at least a couple of foreign trips, and became a familiar face in Hyannis Port and Palm Beach. The president even gave him a PT 109 tie clasp—the ultimate insider honor in JFK's White House.

According to Seymour Hersh, Jacobson's name appears on the White House visitors' logs more than 30 times. RFK, who had no tolerance for either illicit drug use or Jews, quickly became suspicious of Jacobson. So did JFK's physician of record, Dr. Janet Travell. As the president's connection, Jacobson was a much more important person in JFK's life than Travell, but he couldn't fire her—during the 1960 campaign, Travell had lied to the press about JFK's Addison's disease. She knew too much.

Bobby eventually obtained a vial of the "vitamins," and had them analyzed by the Bureau of Narcotics and Dangerous Drugs. The analysis, later obtained by the press through a Freedom of Information Act (FOIA) request, showed that Dr. Feelgood was injecting his famous clientele with, among other things, amphetamines, vitamins, painkillers, steroids and human placenta.

RFK showed a list of the ingredients to his brother, who shrugged. "I don't care if it's horse piss, it makes me feel good!"

According to Jacobson's 2013 biography by Richard A. Lertzman and William J. Birnes, the next time Jacobson flew to DC, he brought along one of his friends, Mike Samek.

When Bobby noticed Jacobson and Samek wandering the White House halls, Samek recalled in the book, RFK exploded in one of his typical anti-Semitic tirades.

"What are you fuckin' kikes doing in the White House? You Jews aren't welcome here. Go back to New York with the other Jews."

Jacobson promptly cut off the president. Frantic after going cold-turkey for a few days, JFK flew to New York and checked into the Carlyle. But this time he wasn't rendezvousing with Judy Campbell or Marilyn Monroe or anonymous "mulatto prostitutes," as one FBI report from 1961 had described some of the president-elect's visitors. JFK called Dr. Jacobson from the Carlyle and begged him to come downtown. The physician finally relented and arrived a short while later.

Like a junkie coming down, JFK begged for a potent injection. Dr. Feelgood administered a powerful dose to the president and then left. In a few minutes, it became clear that he'd overdosed Kennedy. JFK ripped off his clothes and began dancing around his hotel suite.

The Secret Service agents were amused until the leader of the Free World ran out into the hallway, naked, and took off running. They couldn't let him reach the lobby, where reporters and cameras crews were awaiting his departure. Finally, according to Jacobson's biographers, JFK was wrestled down and dragged back into the suite. A call was placed to another Manhattan physician, who came over and tranquilized the president with another massive injection, this time of phenobarbital.

Jacobson's biographers list Mary Pinchot Meyer as another of his patients. But by the time she began sleeping with JFK in 1962, she had her own sources of more common drugs like marijuana. By 1962 she was an occasional visitor to the White House—five times that summer. In 1976, a down-on-his-luck former *Washington Post* executive sold a story to the *National Enquirer* about how Meyer had introduced JFK to street drugs.

James Truitt had been an executive of the *Washington Post*, a member of Ben Bradlee's inner circle. But his alcoholism had cost him his job, and by the time Truitt approached the supermarket tabloid, he was destitute.

For $1,000, he told the *Enquirer* that Mary had turned JFK on to pot in July 1962. Within a few months she'd become fascinated with a newer, more exotic drug—LSD. Here Dr. Timothy Leary, the legendary Harvard-trained guru of LSD, picks up the story in his autobiography *Flashbacks.*

Phil Graham was the publisher of *The Washington Post* and married to Katherine, whose father had bought the paper out of bankruptcy during the Depression. Katherine would run the paper during its Watergate glory years. Her husband Graham was close to both JFK and LBJ; he had been a fraternity brother of Kennedy pal Sen. George Smathers at the University of Florida.

But Graham was going insane. In January 1963, he flew out to an Associated Press publishers' convention in Arizona with his mistress. He got drunk at a dinner, stumbled up to the podium and began an obscenity-filled rant about the corruption of the press, and how newspapers refused to print anything of substance. Like, for instance, the affair that the president was having with his friend Mary Meyer. He also mentioned the president's assignations at the Carlyle Hotel in New York, not then a widely known fact.

Graham was quickly hustled off the stage. Alarmed, JFK sent an Air Force plane to bring him back to Washington. When Graham was wheeled off the plane in DC on a stretcher, in a straitjacket, he yelled at an old lady, "It's all right ma'am, I'm only dying of cancer."

Afterward, Katherine Graham wrote an abject note of apology to JFK for her husband's behavior. Graham committed suicide a few months later with a shotgun.

Soon thereafter, Leary wrote in his 1983 book, Mary flew to Boston, checked into the Ritz-Carlton and called the guru of LSD. He drove into the city from his rented house in suburban Newton and was instantly impressed by her patrician beauty—"late thirties. Good looking. Flamboyant eyebrows, piercing green-blue eyes, fine-boned face. Amused, arrogant, aristocratic."

Leary suggested they go downstairs, to the hotel's famous café, but she nervously demurred, opting for room service. Meyer wanted to learn how to run an LSD "trip" session for her "very important" friend. Leary then offered to conduct one for her and her friend in Boston.

"Out of the question!" she snapped. She then told him the story of Graham's drunken public rant, without mentioning any names.

"I got exposed, publicly," Leary quoted her as saying.

"Your boyfriend's married, I gather?"

Chuckle. "To say the least."

Leary told her he hadn't read about any big scandals recently.

"No," she said. "Here's the scary part. Not a word was printed about it."

Nothing was resolved at that meeting, and by the time she called again, Leary had moved to Millbrook, New York. She flew to LaGuardia, Leary wrote, rented a car and drove to his new home. After asking if he could hide her out if necessary, she handed Leary a small bottle of pills.

"This is supposed to be the best LSD in the world. From the National Institute of Mental Health (sic). Isn't it funny that I end up giving it to you?"

As she drove off, Leary said he asked himself, "What trouble could she be in?"

All of these third-rate romances, low-rent rendezvouses were common knowledge among a still small but ever-growing number of connected people. In May 1963, The Thunderbolt, a racist monthly published in Georgia by the National States' Rights Party, ran a story based on Kater's tapes and photographs, under the headline, "JFK Accused of Adultery."

A New York publishing executive for whom Jackie later worked told author Sally Bedell Smith, author of *Grace and Power: The Private World of the Kennedy White House,* that he was sleeping with a girlfriend late one night when the phone beside her bed rang. It was JFK, inviting her to fly to Palm Beach the next day for the weekend. She accepted.

The daughter of Treasury Secretary Douglas Dillon told her father that JFK was sleeping with one of her friends, a "very decent" person.

The managing editor of *Time* magazine had an exclusive interview with JFK at the White House in April 1961. Forgetting his hat, he returned a few minutes later to the president's private quarters to retrieve it and saw on the sofa "a striking blonde, about 35 years old, wearing a short black dress . . . Jack handed me my hat, and I left."

Another *Timesman,* Hugh Sidey, worked at the White House covering the administration. JFK seemed to like him; one night in Palm Beach he was invited to the compound for a small dinner foursome—himself, JFK and Fiddle and Faddle. Late that night, Sidey got up to go back to his hotel downtown, and he asked the two "White House beauties" if they were leaving too.

There was a moment of uncomfortable silence, but finally they all went out to their rented cars. As Sidey waited for them in his car, they got out of their own vehicle and told the columnist they couldn't start it. The battery was dead. They told Sidey they'd have to wait for a jump start, and then they ran back inside. Sidey never filed anything about the incident.

Later, in March 1963, Sidey sent an eyes-only memo to his prurient bosses in New York, telling how the Kennedys had flown in black prostitutes from New York for a New Year's orgy in Palm Beach.

Somehow RFK got a copy of the memo, and summoned Sidey to his office.

"I thought you were a different kind of guy," RFK scolded him. Sidey asked how he'd gotten the memo.

"I have my ways," RFK told him.

But most of the time, the reporters never even put their observations on paper, let alone into print.

Some of JFK's women were recognizable—Marilyn Monroe in Los Angeles, Angie Dickinson in Palm Springs. Others were anonymous.

Faddle working out at the Georgetown apartment she shared with Fiddle.

Bob Pierpont of CBS News saw the president and a young woman coming out of a cottage in Palm Beach early one morning and dash to a waiting limousine. Like the others, Pierpont filed nothing.

Traphes Bryant was the longtime White House kennel keeper, and in 1975 he wrote his own memoirs *Dog Days at the White House.* It was one of the first books to effectively debunk the myth of Camelot.

The danger for White House staff, Bryant wrote, was taking the back elevator to the second floor. Nobody ever knew what they'd see, at least if Jackie was away. He recalled one staffer saying she had heard "lovey-dovey talk," and another as seeing "a naked woman walking from the kitchen."

Bryant himself quoted from his contemporaneous diary: "Just as the elevator door opened, a naked blonde office girl ran through the hall between the second-floor kitchen and the door leading to the West Hall. Her breasts were swinging as she ran by."

Bryant also passed on the story about an alleged $1 million pay-off from Joe Kennedy in the 1950s—"when a 15-year-old babysitter accused the senator of making her pregnant."

This was written 20 years before Michael Kennedy, JFK's nephew, was accused of raping his own 14-year-old teenage babysitter—yet another Kennedy family tradition, apparently.

Bryant was perhaps the first author to print JFK's famous quote: "I'm not through with a girl till I've had her three ways."

Another of JFK's well-known pensées on women was, "Blondes for fun, brunettes for marriage." Bryant said his penchant for blondes made it even more difficult for the White House staff to clean up after his romps. If any telltale strands of blond hair remained, Jackie would know—for sure.

Bryant also pointed the finger at Dave Powers as JFK's main pimp, at least in DC, just as his "brother-in-Lawford" was in charge of Hollywood procurements.

According to Fiddle and Faddle in their 1965 oral histories for the JFK Library, the president greatly appreciated their efforts.

Faddle on Powers: "I think Dave, probably, was his best friend."

Fiddle on Lawford: "He knew he could count on Peter any time to do anything."

One night in late 1961, during JFK's visit to Seattle, a local sheriff brought a pair of "high-class" hookers into the presidential suite at the Olympic hotel. The sheriff had wanted to personally present them as a gift to the president, but the Secret Service stopped him, according to an account by Seymour Hersh in *The Dark Side of Camelot*.

The sheriff settled for warning the call girls, "If any word of this gets out, I'll see that both of you go to Stillicoom and never get out."

Stillicoom was a local mental institution.

A couple of hours later, the Secret Service agent found several security posts assigned to the local police unmanned. He finally located the cops on a fire escape, passing around a pair of binoculars. They were watching Kenny O'Donnell having sex with two young female staffers.

Dave Powers had the task of smuggling the Hollywood women in the White House. A Secret Service agent told Hersh that once "I saw Dave Powers bring in two starlets who were easily recognizable. He had one put a scarf over her head."

There was no romance, the agent said—"it might be their career if they told their agent in Hollywood they didn't want to play." Afterward, on the way back to the airport, the women were warned by Powers that, "If any of this ever gets out in any way, your careers are through."

Bryant once recalled Powers asking his boss what he wanted for his birthday.

"He named a TV actress from California. His wish was granted."

When they arrived at the White House, the women had to sign into what are called the Usher's Logs, a detailed record of visitors, both official and unofficial, to the White House. The logs are public record, but one set is missing.

According to Hersh, despite Bobby Kennedy's grief for his murdered brother, one of his first calls after the assassination was to White House usher J. B. West, demanding the logs from January 20, 1961, to November 21, 1963. Early on Saturday morning, November 23, Bobby returned to the White House and picked up the logs from West. They would never be seen again.

It was less risky, of course, and more convenient, if the women were White House staffers. But JFK always needed new "strange," to use another slang term of the era. One of the president's youngest White House conquests was a 19-year-old intern then named Mimi Beardsley—still another graduate of Miss Porter's School, one more Northeastern Protestant debutante with a patrician background, another Brahmin notch on JFK's Irish-Catholic belt.

She was 19 and had just finished her freshman year at Wheaton College in Norton, Massachusetts, when she became a White House intern. She was a virgin. On her fourth day of work, according to her memoir *Once Upon a Secret*, she was invited to join the president and others at the swimming pool. Soon afterward, Jackie and the kids left for Glen Ora, their rented house in the Virginia horse country. Mimi was invited to a private dinner upstairs at the White House with JFK, Powers, O'Donnell and Fiddle and Faddle.

The men were 50, 45 and 36 years old, respectively. The women were 24, 21 and 19.

Soon the future Mrs. Mimi Alford was alone with the president, and after showing her the view from his second-floor balcony, he directed her into his bedroom and undressed her. Guiding her to the bed and mounting her, JFK thought to inquire, "Haven't you done this before?"

When she said no, he asked, "Are you okay?" She wrote that it was a question he repeated several times as he deflowered her. Afterward, as he put his trousers back on, JFK pointed to the corner of the room. "There's the bathroom if you need it," he said.

As she wrote, "I wouldn't describe what happened that night as making love. But I wouldn't call it nonconsensual either."

In her book, she remembered that although she was not practicing any form of birth control, JFK never wore a condom, "either because of his Catholicism or recklessness, I could never be sure."

Once, when she was back at college in Massachusetts and her period was two weeks late, Mimi got on the White House phone with JFK, who left messages at her dorm as "Michael Carter." He "took the news in stride." Soon Dave Powers was on the phone to her, with the name and phone number of a woman in New Jersey who could if necessary put her in touch with an abortionist. So the president had almost instantly put at least three buffers between himself and any potential abortion.

In that summer of 1962, Mimi became one of the president's favorites. She was working in press secretary Pierre Salinger's office, along with Faddle. It was more than suspected among reporters that she often slept over at the White House. But the press had no interest in revealing anything derogatory about their hero.

In his boudoir, the president had a state-of-the art stereo system installed under his bed by the Army Signal Corps, according to Bryant. He put another speaker mounted on the second-floor balcony. That was where he had first seduced Mimi, in what she called "the fading June light."

Despite his pioneering attitudes about "free love," the president did not embrace another hallmark of "his" decade—rock 'n' roll. The gossip columns may have reported that he learned the Twist, but in private, with Mimi and all the others, he much preferred the old standards.

"His taste tended toward anything by Tony Bennett or Frank Sinatra," she recalled. "It wasn't music I could relate to."

Quickly, the other White House secretaries learned to resent the poor little rich girl who could neither type nor take shorthand. She was soon making trips on Air Force One that the others could only dream of.

One night she and Fiddle were on a western swing, and JFK was spending the night at Bing Crosby's high-end ranch in Palm Springs. As she told the story in her book, the party was raucous, and suddenly a bowl of poppers—yellow amyl-nitrate capsules—was being passed around. JFK offered her one, and she declined, but suddenly he popped a capsule and held it under her nose.

(Peter Lawford told a variation of this story, in which he provided the then-exotic drug, but refused to give any to JFK because of the potential dangers it posed to the heart. In Lawford's recollection, as told by his third wife in her book, the drug was then given to "either Fiddle or Faddle," who had the same adverse reaction Mimi Alford wrote about in her 2012 book.)

When Alford inhaled, she recalled, her heart started racing and her hands began shaking. She panicked and ran from the room, weeping. Dave Powers ran after her, and "then sat with me for more than an hour until the effects of the drug wore off."

Of course, Powers may have felt a little guilty. In the summer of 1962, JFK and Mimi were swimming in the White House pool. Dave Powers was the only other person present, sitting on a towel, his feet in the shallow end of the pool but otherwise fully clothed.

JFK swam over to Mimi and said, "Mr. Powers looks a little tense. Would you take care of him?"

Alford wrote that she knew that her boyfriend wanted her to fellate his pal. He was, after all, JFK's best friend.

"I'm ashamed to say that I did. It was a pathetic, sordid scene . . . The president silently watched."

Afterward, as she got out of the pool, she heard Dave Powers addressing JFK "in as stern a tone as I ever heard him use with his boss."

May 1986: On what would have been JFK's 69th birthday, Dave Powers reminisces with Caroline about those wonderful days in the White House pool.

"You shouldn't have made her do that!" Powers said.

"I know," JFK said. "I know." Later, he would apologize to them both.

In October 1963, JFK visited Boston for what would be the final time, for the Columbia-Harvard football game and then later a black-tie fundraiser for the state Democratic party. O'Donnell and Powers as usual put a glossy, nostalgic sheen on the trip, having the president (minus the traveling press corps) visiting the grave of his infant son Patrick in Brookline, and then heading to the old Schrafft's ice cream parlor downtown on West Street for a butterscotch sundae, just like the ones he used to enjoy nightly after finishing his campaign appearances in his Congressional and Senate races. As he ate at the counter, they reported, "He said to Dave, 'Get me a chocolate frappe with vanilla ice cream to take out, so I can have it later at the hotel.'"

Mimi Alford, however, has a different recollection of the president's wishes that evening. By the time she arrived at the Sheraton Plaza, the president was in his tuxedo, as was his 31-year-old brother, the freshman senator Teddy.

"Mimi," the president said, "why don't you take care of my baby brother. He could stand a little relaxation."

Hearing the same words he'd spoken to her 14 months earlier in DC, this time she had a very different reaction. "For the first time," she said, she rebuked one of the president's requests.

"You've got to be kidding. Absolutely not, Mr. President."

In her book, Alford wrote that the president immediately dropped the subject.

The last time she saw JFK was November 15, 1963, the Friday before his murder, at the Carlyle Hotel in Manhattan. He handed her $300 cash for a shopping spree and told her he'd call her after he got back from Texas.

She'd already told him she was engaged and that she would be getting married in January.

"I know that," he said. "But I'll call you anyway."

October 1963: JFK with New England's four Democratic governors, an hour or so after he'd asked his 19-year-old girlfriend to fellate Teddy.

Pamela Turnure always attracted a lot of attention.

As time went on, the president's behavior seemed more and more out of control. Too many people knew. Finally, RFK tried to have Fiddle and Faddle fired. Faddle's boss, press secretary, Pierre Salinger flatly refused Bobby's order. Salinger knew his boss.

Since his first experience with the three-dollar white whore in Harlem in 1934, JFK had enjoyed the company of prostitutes, and they too were plentiful in the White House. Again, Powers was in charge of procurement. The president liked to memorialize, as it were, his escapades.

At the White House, he had someone, most likely an official White House photographer, take pictures of himself with various women, apparently including prostitutes. The photographs would then be delivered in the morning by a Secret Service agent to the high-brow Mickelson Gallery, 10 blocks from the White House.

The owner, Sidney Mickelson, would measure the photograph for a frame, and then return the photograph to the agent. That evening, the same Secret Service agent would return with the photograph and wait as Mickelson framed it.

In 1996, Seymour Hersh tracked down a very reluctant Sidney Mickelson, then 70. In most of the photos, Mickelson recalled in *The Dark Side of Camelot,* the president and the others were wearing masks. One time the agent specifically pointed out JFK to him, Mickelson said, "and I had no reason to doubt it."

Mickelson told Hersh: "No other White House did this."

By the fall of 1963, even for JFK, the expenses of this double life were mounting to a level beyond his control. Preparing for the 1964 reelection campaign, the Kennedys were vacuuming up cash, and Kenny O'Donnell had begun skimming. He had been overheard by off-duty Secret Service agents badmouthing the Kennedys while drunk in Cape Cod bars.

The press was becoming another concern. Not all journalists were as compliant as Ben Bradlee and Hugh Sidey. Some were actually more interested in reporting the news than in having access to the endless vacations in Palm Beach and Palm Springs.

In London, the government of Harold Macmillan was being buffeted by a call-girl scandal involving John Profumo, a Conservative member of the House of Commons.

In Washington, JFK followed the daily developments from Great Britain with great interest, because before his inauguration, in New York he had enjoyed the services of some of the same hookers who were now in the middle of the Profumo affair.

In June 1963, with JFK in Europe, the Hearst-owned *New York Journal-American* ran a front-page story headlined:

"High U.S. Aide Implicated in V-Girl Scandal."

V Girl—an archaic World War II-era description for prostitute, but everyone got the reference to vice. However, the identity of the "High U.S. Aide" remained tantalizingly vague.

The story's lead:

"One of the biggest names in American politics—a man who holds 'a very high' elective office—has been injected in Britain's vice-security scandal."

June 1963: Bobby Kennedy got this story in the New York Journal-American *about his brother's hookers killed after one edition.*

In Washington, Bobby Kennedy immediately telephoned the Hearsts, and succeeded in having the story spiked after one edition. Two days later, the two reporters, neither of whom appeared to be starstruck by the glamor of the New Frontier, were flown to Washington on the Kennedys' private jet. They were brought directly to the Justice Department.

According to Hersh, RFK asked the two reporters who the "high U.S. aide" was.

"Your brother," one of the reporters told him.

But the problems were only going to get worse. Bobby Baker, the secretary of the Senate and one of LBJ's top fixers, operated a hideaway of sorts on Capitol Hill for connected Congressmen, high-rolling lobbyists and "V girls."

Investigations were already starting to swirl around Baker and his patron, LBJ. Hoover's G-men had dropped a bug into at least one of the hotel suites connected to Baker's so-called Carousel Club.

As all these events were unfolding in 1963, Baker was supplying JFK with the best hookers he could find.

One of them was Ellen Rometsch, the wife of an East German soldier attached to the consulate in DC. An Elizabeth Taylor–look alike, she was turning tricks to make ends meet.

Or she might have been a Communist spy.

The morning after Rometsch's first visit to the White House, JFK had telephoned Baker to thank him: "Mr. Baker, that was the best blow job I ever had!"

In retrospect, it was an ironic situation JFK found himself in. In 1941, he had first turned up on the FBI's radar screen when he began having sex with a European believed to be a Nazi spy. Now, 22 years later, at what no one yet knew would be the end of his life, he was embroiled with yet another beautiful European woman who was suspected of espionage for a different German regime.

Rometsch had to go. She and her husband were deported in August. As she was deported the Kennedys had paid her off, but they knew it wasn't enough.

By the fall of 1963, the rumors about JFK and the suspected Communist spy were circulating in official Washington. Clark Mollenhoff, a reporter for the *Des Moines Register*, had picked up rumblings from a Republican senator from Delaware about the scandal.

In late October 1963, Mollenhof's paper had broken the news with a front-page story. As the earlier *New York Journal-American* story, the president was only vaguely described as an "official."

The headline: "U.S. Expels Girl Linked to Officials/Is Sent to Germany After FBI Probe."

Once again, RFK had to scramble to keep the story from being picked up by the national wire services.

Once upon a time, the brothers could have counted on others to clean up their messes for them. Their father Joe was now an invalid in Hyannis Port. And Bill McEachern, the shadowy ex-FBI agent who had hushed up so many of JFK's earlier indiscretions (although Florence Kater had rejected his offer of an expensive painting in exchange for her photos and tapes) was likewise out of the picture. He had been killed in an automobile accident in May 1963.

U. S. EXPELS GIRL LINKED TO OFFICIALS

Is Sent to Germany
After FBI Probe

By Clark McDonald

Now the Kennedy boys were on their own. Bobby had to make a call to the man he so detested, J. Edgar Hoover, to ask him if could he intervene with Senate leadership to put a lid on the Delaware senator's plans to hold hearings on the Rometsch deportation. The director could, and did. Meeting privately with both the Democrat and Republican leaders of the Senate, the Director laid out the dirt he had collected on their members. They quickly agreed to cancel the hearing on Rometsch.

Front page headline from the Des Moines Register *Oct. 23, 1963 about certain unnamed "officials," i.e., President Kennedy.*

But there was a price to be paid—Hoover wanted Bobby to sign off, officially, in writing, on his plan to bug Dr. Martin Luther King Jr. What choice did Bobby have? It was a decision that would haunt him for the rest of his life.

Meanwhile, Jack had to engage his own deception. With the news of Ellen Rometsch now common knowledge in Washington, he had to portray himself as just another disinterested observer. Everyone understood his taste for gossip, how he loved to pass on juicy tidbits about others. As his brother and J. Edgar Hoover worked the phones, JFK pretended nothing was amiss. He whispered with a chuckle to Ben Bradlee how much "dirt" Hoover had on various senators, and how Rometsch had been charging "a couple of hundred dollars a night."

To the end of his life, Bradlee maintained his own pose—that of a journalistic Sgt. Schultz. He knew nothing!

The swearing in of LBJ on Air Force One. In the background is JFK trollop Pamela Turnure.

"We were always able to say we knew of no evidence," he wrote. "None."

For the Dallas trip in November 1963, Jackie decided to bring along Pamela Turnure. That Thursday afternoon, on November 21, they were working together in the front of Air Force One when a Secret Service agent approached and said that the president, in the back of the plane, needed Turnure to take some "dictation" for him. She was gone 45 minutes. It may have been JFK's final fornication.

A little more than 24 hours later, Pamela was back on Air Force One, as LBJ was sworn in as president with Jackie standing beside him in her bloodstained pink dress. In the famous photo of the transfer of power, with LBJ holding his right hand high, Pamela can be observed in the background, obscured by others, but her dark hair still visible. It somehow seems only appropriate—at least one of the "White House beauties" present at the end.

JFK's poon days were finally over.

CHAPTER SEVEN

"SOMETHING'S GOT TO GIVE"

THE DEATH OF MARILYN Monroe in 1962 could have been the first Chappaquiddick—a scandal involving the preventable death of a young woman sexually involved with the Kennedys.

And unlike the death of Mary Jo Kopechne, which brought down only one brother, the true story of Marilyn's mysterious, drug-fueled passing would have dragged down both the president and his attorney general in a frenzy of tabloid headlines.

But somehow the Kennedy brothers were able to cover up yet another scandal, with the help of their friends in law enforcement and the press.

Near the end of his life, in the grip of alcoholism and drug addiction, Peter Lawford claimed that he had taken photographs of his brother-in-law JFK and Marilyn Monroe—nude, in the tub in the onyx-and-marble bathroom off the guest bedroom of the Lawfords' Santa Monica beach cottage.

The photos, if they did exist, have never surfaced. Likewise, there is no evidence of Marilyn's rumored abortion of a child fathered by either JFK or his brother Bobby.

As the years have gone by, the stories about Marilyn Monroe and the Kennedy brothers have proliferated, and grown ever more outlandish.

How far back the affair between the two 20th-century American legends dates remains likewise a mystery. Sen. John F. Kennedy and Marilyn Monroe were definitely together at a Hollywood dinner party at the home of agent Charles Feldman in 1954, during her brief marriage to Joe DiMaggio. Kennedy got her phone number that night and called the next day. DiMaggio answered the phone and JFK quickly hung up.

But JFK may have encountered Marilyn earlier, as he was cutting a wide swath through Hollywood after World War II, when Marilyn was the brown-haired Norma Jean Mortenson and he had just been elected to Congress.

In his definitive book about Marilyn Monroe, *Goddess*, Anthony Summers quotes two sources as saying the future president knew her as early as 1951.

When JFK had himself hospitalized in 1954 in New York in order to avoid having to vote on the censure of Sen. Joe McCarthy, he had a popular poster of the day in his room—of Marilyn Monroe, in blue shorts, her legs spread. He attached the poster on the wall upside down. By the late 1950s, JFK and Marilyn were apparently in an off-again, on-again affair, including hookups at the Democratic national convention in Los Angeles in 1960.

At one convention party hosted by Lawford, JFK apparently used Sammy Davis Jr. as his beard—"I think they just asked him to bring Monroe in," Summers quoted one witness as saying.

Unlike so many others, Marilyn was not a one-night stand. She and JFK had sex in any number of places—at hot-sheet no-tell motels on Sunset Boulevard, at Bing Crosby's mansion in Palm Springs, at the Kennedy family suite in the Carlyle Hotel in New York, even, according to one source, at Hyannis Port.

(To the end of his life, one Boston newspaper photographer claimed that in the early 1960s, Marilyn pulled into a convenience store parking lot on Cape Cod and, after addressing the photographer and his brother as "Hi, boys!" asked for directions to the compound.)

She was smuggled at least once onto Air Force One in sunglasses and a scarf over her bleached-blonde locks, carrying a steno pad—just another secretary.

A few weeks before her death, at the behest of her psychiatrist, Marilyn sat down and spoke into a tape recorder in a stream-of-consciousness monologue that was later transcribed and given to Seymour Hersh. Some of the monologue concerned her deep love for the two brothers, especially "the President," as she called him.

"When he has finished his achievements he will take his place with Washington, Jefferson, Lincoln and Franklin Roosevelt as one of our great presidents," she said. "I'm glad he has Bobby. It's like the Navy—the president is the captain and Bobby is his executive officer. Bobby would do absolutely anything for his brother and so would I. I will never embarrass him. As long as I have memory, I have John Fitzgerald Kennedy."

By 1961, Marilyn was 35. On the set of her completed final movie, *The Misfits*, she had been almost impossible to work with. Her co-star, Clark Gable, an idol of her Depression-era youth, died of a heart attack shortly after the completion of the filming. She had no husband, only a white French poodle, a gift from Frank Sinatra that she named "Maf," short for "Mafia."

In 1961, she was briefly institutionalized at the Paine Webber psychiatric clinic in New York, thrown into a padded room. Panicked, frantic that she would end up like her mother, insane and destitute, she called her ex-husband, Joe DiMaggio. He flew to New York and threatened to take the hospital apart "brick by brick."

She was still in the presidential mix. George Smathers claimed to have seen her with Kennedy on board the presidential yacht on the Potomac; Chuck Spalding confirms the photographer's story that she visited Hyannis Port. She had the number of Kenny O'Donnell's private line in the White House. When she called, she identified herself as "Miss Green."

In February 1962 she flew to Miami, where she was ensconced in a suite in the Fontainebleau near the president. By then, she was in her final downward spiral. Later in February, she was the guest of honor at a fundraising party in New York for the president. She arrived two hours late. That evening JFK told her he was going to Palm Springs in March, without Jackie, and would she like to join him? This was to be his visit to Frank Sinatra, soon to be cancelled after J. Edgar Hoover's visit to the White House where he outlined the Mafia ties of another of JFK's steadier girlfriends, Judith Campbell.

The Palm Springs presidential party ended up instead at the home of Bing Crosby. According to some accounts, Monroe was flown to Palm Springs on Air Force One. However she got there, a Democrat politician from Los Angeles recalled seeing them together at Crosby's spread—"it was obvious they were intimate and they were staying there together for the night."

Marilyn had finally bought a home of her own, a small bungalow at 12305 Fifth Helena Drive in Brentwood. On the outside wall, an earlier owner had attached tiles with a few words in Latin—"Cursum Perficio."

In English, it meant, "I am finishing my journey."

Much of what transpired in the final months of Marilyn Monroe's tortured life remains unclear, the stuff of legend. But some facts are not in dispute. First, her relationship with JFK was coming apart. She was just too unstable, unable to accept Lawford's blunt assessment of her relationship to the president: "You're just another of Jack's fucks."

She was getting up there, in girlfriend terms, and the president made it clear to his pal Smathers that the affair was coming to an end. But she didn't take it well, so Bobby was assigned the duty of breaking it off. Decades later, in Kennedy family papers, a handwritten note turned up that Jean Kennedy Smith had written to Monroe in 1961 after Marilyn penned a letter to the now-paralyzed family patriarch.

"Dear Marilyn," it began, "Mother asked me to write and thank you for your sweet note to Daddy—he really enjoyed it and you were very cute to send it—Understand that you and Bobby are the new item! We all think you should come with him when he comes back East!"

RFK had his own reasons for an oc-casional visit to Los Angeles. As Warner

Bobby Kennedy got Marilyn on the rebound.

Bros. was shooting *PT 109*—a film that would bomb in 1963—Paramount was working on a screenplay for RFK's ghostwritten book about his work on the Rackets Committee, *The Enemy Within*. RFK would periodically fly out to LA and borrow the white convertible of the special agent in charge of the FBI office. Then he would rendezvous with Marilyn Monroe, usually in Malibu, at his brother-in-law's house. It quickly developed into an affair, Lawford told another of his later wives.

"From what Peter told me," Deborah Gould said of Bobby, "he fell head over heels."

Even in that very different era, such indiscretions among the rich and famous could not long remain unnoticed. At some point in late 1961, bugs were planted in the homes of both Lawford and Monroe. It's unclear who authorized the bugs, but among those who would have had great interest in monitoring those conversations was J. Edgar Hoover, the FBI director whom the Kennedys wished to rid themselves of. Then there was Jimmy Hoffa, the embattled president of the Teamsters Union, who despised RFK, and who was facing federal indictment.

One of the principals in the bugging operations was Fred Otash, a former LAPD detective who had become a private investigator for, among others, *Confidential* magazine, a Hollywood scandal sheet that was avidly read by millions, including JFK. Otash, who died at age 70 in 1992, would later claim that he was hired by the Teamsters, and that he brought in Bernard Spindel, one of the nation's top surveillance experts.

Even the CIA may have been involved. At least one CIA report from 1962 quoted bugged conversations of Marilyn.

In January 1962, less than seven months before her death, Marilyn attended a party at the Lawfords' house for RFK. Marilyn came on to RFK and taught him the hot new dance, the Twist. Finally, RFK called his father, who was incapacitated a month after his stroke in Palm Beach.

"Dad," he said, "guess who's standing next to me."

Then he put Marilyn on the phone.

In May 1962, the president was planning a huge 45th birthday party/fundraiser at Madison Square Garden. And who better to sing "Happy Birthday" than Marilyn Monroe? There was only one problem.

She had just begun shooting a new movie for Twentieth Century Fox, *Something's Got to Give*. It was already over budget and behind schedule. As she had been on set of *The Misfits*, Marilyn was being difficult, behaving like the diva that she was.

Her costar was Dean Martin, the member of the Rat Pack least enamored of President Kennedy. The suits at Fox refused to allow Monroe to blow off her shooting schedule, so the attorney general called Milton Gould, a New York lawyer who was basically running the company. RFK tried to convince Gould to give Marilyn a couple of days off, but Gould was adamant, as he recalled in a 1995 interview with Seymour Hersh.

RFK had his usual reaction to Gould's intransigence.

"He called me a 'Jew bastard' and hung up the phone on me."

Marilyn abruptly left the set of the film and was flown to New York. She had to be sewn into her tight-fitting gown. It became a running gag in the show, that once again she was a no-show at her own event. Peter Lawford, the master of ceremonies, repeatedly described her as "the late Marilyn Monroe." When she finally reached the stage, JFK watched from his private box, smoking a cigar, muttering to himself, "What an ass!"

Afterward, at the Carlyle Hotel, Marilyn was photographed with both brothers. Hearst columnist Dorothy Kilgallen reported that RFK danced with her five times, much to Ethel's chagrin. (Jackie was a no-show, back home in horse country in Virginia.) Many photographs were taken, but only a handful survive—a few days later, men with badges arrived at the major photographic agencies in New York demanding the negatives.

May 1962: Marilyn had to be sewn into her gown at Madison Square Garden.

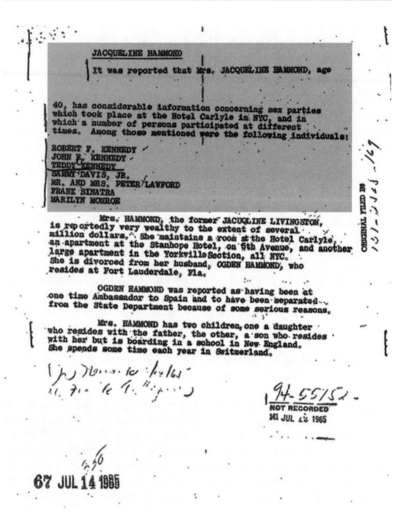

JACQUELINE HAMMOND

It was reported that Mrs. JACQUELINE HAMMOND, age

40, has considerable information concerning sex parties
which took place at the Hotel Carlyle in NYC, and in
which a number of persons participated at different
times. Among those mentioned were the following individuals:

ROBERT F. KENNEDY
JOHN F. KENNEDY
TEDDY KENNEDY
SAMMY DAVIS, JR.
MR. AND MRS. PETER LAWFORD
FRANK SINATRA
MARILYN MONROE

Mrs. HAMMOND, the former JACUQLINE LIVINGSTON,
is reportedly very wealthy to the extent of several
million dollars. She maintains a room at the Hotel Carlyle,
an apartment at the Stanhope Hotel, on 5th Avenue, and another
large apartment in the Yorkville Section, all NYC.
She is divorced from her husband, OGDEN HAMMOND, who
resides at Fort Lauderdale, Fla.

OGDEN HAMMOND was reported as having been at
one time Ambassador to Spain and to have been separated
from the State Department because of some serious reasons.

Mrs. HAMMOND has two children, one a daughter
who resides with the father, the other, a son who resides
with her but is boarding in a school in New England.
She spends some time each year in Switzerland.

1965 FBI report re: Kennedy family orgies with Marilyn Monroe at the Carlyle.

When she returned to Hollywood, Marilyn was fired from *Something's Got to Give*. Then she was rehired. Photographers were brought in for her last great shoot, swimming nude in a pool on the set. One of the photographers recalled one of Marilyn's hairdressers telling him that she had just had an abortion. Otash says it was performed by an American doctor in Tijuana. Like another of JFK's girlfriends, Mary Pinchot Meyer, Marilyn sought out Dr. Timothy Leary, looking for LSD, telling him that she was having problems with her boyfriend—"Only problem is, he's married right now. And he's famous, so we have to meet in secret."

Increasingly despondent, she called RFK at his home in Hickory Hill. He was irate. By June 25, she no longer had access to his private phone number at the Justice Department. She was reduced to calling the main switchboard number of the Justice Department—RE7-8200.

Marilyn was furious at Bobby, telling her confidante Robert Slatzer, "He's been ignoring me. I've been trying to reach him on the telephone, and I just can't reach him."

In late July, Marilyn flew to Lake Tahoe for a weekend at the Cal-Neva Lodge. It should have been a relaxing time; her old friend Peter Lawford was another guest. Instead, her life almost ended a week before she actually died. She was apparently drugged up and sexually abused by her hosts, chief among them Sam "Momo" Giancana, the Chicago gangster who had grown to despise the Kennedys.

According to FBI bugs, even Giancana's Outfit associates were taken aback by the brutality with which Momo treated Marilyn.

"You sure get your rocks off," Johnny Roselli told his boss on an FBI recording made at the Armory Lounge in suburban Chicago, "fucking the same broad as the brothers, don't you?"

Early Monday morning, Lawford flew back from Lake Tahoe to LA in a private plane, then got a lift from the pilot back to his beachfront home. About five minutes away from his house, at 5:40 a.m. Pacific time, Lawford asked the pilot to pull over at a public phone booth so he could make a call. The call was to the White House, and it lasted a half hour. Obviously, Brother-in-Lawford suspected that his house had been bugged, and his phones tapped. According to Otash, he was correct— four bugs had been placed in the apartment, and "numerous tapes (were) made of Marilyn and Jack in the act of love."

Hours later, Marilyn made her final call to the Justice Department. It lasted eight minutes. Later in the week, speaking from a pay phone, she called her confidant Slatzer. A few weeks earlier, she had shown him her diary, with mentions of what she'd been told by the Kennedys about Jimmy Hoffa, the Mob's plots to kill Fidel Castro, and Sinatra's ties to the Chicago Outfit. She told him she hadn't shown the diary to anyone.

"But I'm so angry I may just call a press conference and show it to the whole world," she said, "and let everybody know what the Kennedys are really like."

On Friday, in her Hearst gossip column, Dorothy Kilgallen wrote a teaser item, mentioning how Marilyn had of late "proved vastly alluring to a handsome gentleman who is a bigger name than Joe DiMaggio in his heyday. So don't write Marilyn off as finished."

That weekend, Bobby flew to San Francisco with Ethel and four of his children. He had a speech to deliver to a California bar association. On Saturday morning, at her home in Brentwood, Marilyn seemed haggard. She told a friend who stopped by that a woman had been calling her all night, yelling, "Leave Bobby alone, you tramp! Leave Bobby alone!" and then hanging up. Marilyn said she couldn't quite place the voice.

The official story has always been that RFK spent Saturday in the San Francisco area, but numerous witnesses later placed Bobby in Los Angeles—among them LA Mayor Sam Yorty, LAPD Chief of Detectives Thad Brown, Otash and Marilyn's maid Eunice Murray. RFK apparently arrived by helicopter on a lot at Paramount Pictures.

Lawford picked him up, and some of Marilyn's neighbors later said they saw RFK arrive at her house in the afternoon. Bobby's mission was to end her relationship with both brothers, once and for all. Deborah Gould, Lawford's third wife, said Lawford had told her that RFK "felt threatened that his enemies might get hold of information that could ruin his career. Peter mentioned 'gangster types.'"

Which presumably would have included Jimmy Hoffa.

In 1985, the maid Murray confirmed Otash's story that Marilyn and Bobby had a violent argument in the late afternoon.

"She was saying, 'I feel passed around! I feel used! I feel like a piece of meat!'" Otash told ABC News in a videotaped 1985 interview that was never aired at the behest of the Kennedy family.

In an interview with the *Los Angeles Times*, Otash described Kennedy grabbing Monroe in her bedroom and yelling, "Where is it? Where the hell is it? I have to have it! My family will pay you for it!" At the end, Otash recalled hearing a slap and then a door slamming. Awhile later, the bug recorded a phone ringing—apparently a call from RFK, who had returned to his sister's beach house.

"He tried to reason with her, and she angrily shouted, "Don't bother me. Leave me alone—stay out of my life."

She had only a few hours left to live. What happened next will probably never be known with any certainty. All the parties are long dead. There are almost as many different theories as there are books, and there are dozens of those. Among the suggestions: that Bobby murdered her, or that she deliberately took an overdose, expecting to be revived, but was left to die.

Another theory is that Marilyn accidentally overdosed and was found by somebody who called an ambulance, which arrived and was taking her to the hospital. But when it became clear that she was dead, her body was returned to her house in Brentwood to be found there. Another version is that she was killed with what Lawford told one of his later wives was "her last big enema," administered by an unknown physician. Or that she was killed, either accidentally or deliberately, in the ambulance.

Yet another theory is that after her body was discovered, the authorities were not notified until Bobby could be gotten out of town and all incriminating documents removed—which would explain why rigor mortis was already setting in by the time police arrived, just before dawn on Sunday.

According to Summers, early Sunday morning, after the two brothers-in-law had found the body, they fled back to Lawford's home. There, Lawford rented a helicopter, which landed on the beach in front of his house. RFK was flown to the airport in Los Angeles and caught a private flight back to San Francisco, where he attended Mass that morning with his family.

Shortly before her death, Monroe had been in her bedroom, nude, alone, trying to call JFK at the White House, but was told he was in

Hyannis Port. The Lawfords were hosting a small dinner party that evening, to which Marilyn had been invited. But apparently Monroe called at one point and in a slurred voice told Lawford, "Say good-bye to Jack, and say good-bye to yourself, because you're a good guy."

That was the version Lawford would recount for the press. Otash said Lawford told him of a much darker final conversation when he arrived at Otash's house, drunk, at 2 a.m. Sunday.

Otash said Marilyn spoke brusquely to Lawford: "Look, do me a favor. Tell the president I tried to reach him. Tell him good-bye for me. I think my purpose has been served." It was later reported that after that final call, Lawford called the White House.

According to the *Los Angeles Times*, "Lawford described Bobby as panicky and quoted him as saying, 'She's ranting and raving. I'm concerned about her and what may come out of this.'"

She would soon be dead. But even after her death that Sunday morning, there was still the matter of her diary, if it existed, as well as whatever other incriminating documents she might have on the brothers.

Which was why Lawford, still drunk from the party, then hired Otash to rush over to Marilyn's house and scrub it of any embarrassing material. Otash apparently did a good job. Deborah Gould said Lawford told her that Marilyn had left a suicide note, which was destroyed "to protect loved ones involved." Another version has Otash finding a "crumpled" piece of paper with a White House number on it. Otash and his operatives also apparently found the diary that RFK had been looking for, because the next day when Joe DiMaggio arrived, he tore the house apart futilely looking for what he called "a book."

As soon as news of Marilyn's death broke, reporters swarmed to the death house. Her personal flack, Pat Newcomb, arrived and began hysterically screaming at the photographers, "Keep shooting, vultures!"

Meanwhile, the race was on to find her telephone records. Joe Hyams, a reporter for the *New York Herald Tribune*, had sources at General Telephone who had in the past provided him with celebrities' phone logs—for cash. Summers reported that Hyams and his source quickly agreed on a price. But an hour later, the phone company employee called Hyams back from a pay phone, telling him that "all hell had broken loose here" and that the tapes had been removed by the Secret Service.

Another source told Summers that a General Telephone executive had told him that it was the FBI that had grabbed the phone records, but that he knew that Marilyn had placed a call to Washington in the final moments of her life.

The LAPD may have also been involved in the cover-up. Chief William Parker, a favorite of the Kennedys, assigned the head of his intelligence division, Capt. James Hamilton, to handle the Monroe matter. Hamilton was close to RFK, who had lauded him by name in *The Enemy Within*. Hamilton later bragged to at least one reporter that he had Marilyn's phone records from the last days of her life.

A year later Hamilton suddenly retired from the LAPD to take a much higher-paying job as head of security for the National Football League. Among those recommending him: Attorney General Robert F. Kennedy.

Chief Parker himself claimed to have the records in his possession. According to Marilyn biographer Donald H. Wolfe, Parker told one reporter that they were his guarantee of heading the FBI "when the Kennedys get rid of Hoover."

But that wasn't going to happen, not now. The Kennedys knew that one way or another, Hoover knew. On Monday, the day after Monroe's death, RFK visited the Seattle World's Fair, where at a press conference he went out of his way to laud the Director.

"I hope he will serve the country for many, many years to come," Kennedy said, directly contradicting what he had told his now-deceased girlfriend in Malibu seven months earlier.

Still, reporters kept digging. The rumors were just too salacious not to try to nail down. Armed with sourced information about Monroe's phone calls that Friday to the hotel where Kennedy was staying in San Francisco, Hyams filed a story to the *Herald Tribune*, even after receiving a phone message from Washington: "The Attorney General would appreciate it if you would not do the story."

An editor called Hyams to congratulate him on the story, but then told him it was being spiked because it was "a gratuitous slap" at the administration.

A couple of days later, the *New York Daily News* hinted in print about the "strange pressures" being applied to the LAPD, and reported that it was local cops who had grabbed the hard-copy records of Monroe's final outgoing calls.

Meanwhile, in his autopsy report, the coroner described her as a "36-year-old, well-developed, well-nourished Caucasian female weighing 117 pounds and measuring 65½ inches in length. The scalp is covered with bleach blonde hair. The eyes are blue."

The cause of death was listed as "acute barbiturate poisoning due to ingestion of overdoses." Under "mode of death," the coroner circled "Suicide," but then added above in his own handwriting, "Probable."

She was buried in what was then called the Mausoleum of Memories. Joe DiMaggio handled the arrangements, which included his pointed instructions—"no damn Kennedys." Frank Sinatra and the Rat Pack were likewise banned, although DiMaggio did send Marilyn's white French poodle, Maf, back to the Chairman of the Board. The only reporter allowed to attend the services was Walter Winchell.

The ghost of Marilyn Monroe would haunt RFK for the final 70 months of his life before his own murder in Los Angeles in 1968.

On August 20, 1962, FBI bugs recorded a conversation among three Mob kingpins complaining, as always, about what they considered Bobby Kennedy's double cross, vigorously prosecuting organized crime after their assistance to his brother in the 1960 presidential election.

"They will go for every name," one of the gangsters said of the Kennedys' campaign against them. "Unless the brother—it's big enough to cause a scandal against them. Would he like to see a headline about Marilyn Monroe come out? And him? How would he like it? Don't you know? . . . He has been in there plenty of times . . . Do you think it's a secret?"

It wasn't, obviously. On July 8, 1964, as Bobby Kennedy was preparing to run for the U.S. Senate from New York, J. Edgar Hoover gave him a heads-up that a right-wing author named Frank A. Capell was publishing a pamphlet: *The Strange Death of Marilyn Monroe.*

"Will make reference," Hoover wrote, "to your alleged friendship with Marilyn Monroe. Mr. Capell stated that he will indicate in his book that you and Miss Monroe were intimate, and that you were in Miss Monroe's home at the time of her death."

Its circulation may have been limited, but the pamphlet got Bobby's attention. Winchell wrote it up in his column. Soon Capell was being wiretapped—his name later appeared on a list of names President Richard M. Nixon released of those illegally monitored by the Kennedy administration. In a 1984 interview on *60 Minutes*, without mentioning Capell by name, former president Richard Nixon revealed that the Kennedys had also ordered an IRS audit of their foes, including one, he said, who had told the real story of Marilyn Monroe's death.

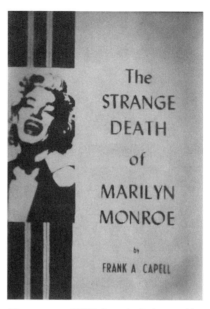

The STRANGE DEATH of MARILYN MONROE by FRANK A CAPELL

Hoover warned RFK about this little pamphlet.

In his pamphlet, Capell described certain unnamed "V.I.P.s" whom he called "ultra broad-minded" and "sex-depraved."

It wasn't hard to figure out who her boyfriend was: "His name has become one which no man may take in vain. A 'martyred' president whose whole career was built upon a public image very different from the real man has become the basis for deification of his whole family . . . a sacred name has been created which no one may speak against   "

Capell described Marilyn as someone who "came under the influence of many whom she allowed, in childish trust, to chart the course of her life and who led her to a premature grave."

All of Capell's accusations were dismissed as the rantings of a John Birch Society–affiliated paranoid with a history of dodgy behavior. What was more troubling to the Kennedys was the fact that, as Capell noted in his pamphlet, "there are person-to-person telephone calls, living witnesses, tape recordings and certain writings to attest to the closeness of their friendship."

The diary was gone—some have claimed that Chief Parker personally delivered it to Washington. In 1982, it was announced that the diary had been stolen from the LA County Coroner's office.

Other loose ends were quickly tied up as well. Pat Newcomb, Marilyn's friend and press agent, fled Los Angeles with the Lawfords. They all spent the day of Marilyn's funeral at the Kennedy compound in Hyannis Port. Then Newcomb was off on a six-month world cruise. When she returned to the United States, there was a GS-13 federal job awaiting her in DC. She'd been recommended by Robert F. Kennedy.

As for Joe DiMaggio, he would despise the Kennedys for the rest of his life. Late in the 1965 baseball season, the New York Yankees held a ceremony honoring Mickey Mantle. Naturally, DiMaggio would be there, a Hall of Famer to introduce the future Hall of Famer who replaced him in center field back in 1951.

Everything was going well until Sen. Bobby Kennedy unexpectedly appeared in the dugout. As Mantle, his family and assorted other Yankees, including DiMaggio, were taking bows around the pitcher's mound, Kennedy bolted onto the field and began working his way down the line of Yankee immortals.

In a magazine piece for *Esquire* in 1966, Gay Talese recounted what happened next: "DiMaggio saw him coming down the line and at the last second he backed away, casually, hardly anybody noticing it."

DiMaggio understood he could never go public with what he knew, but Bernard Spindel, the master wiretapper, was still out there. To protect Bobby's political career, the Kennedys desperately wanted whatever tapes he had made. Spindel had undoubtedly made copies of whatever evidence his bugs and wiretaps had produced, but Bobby needed to deliver him a message, just as he had to Capell with the wiretaps and the IRS audits.

One of RFK's most loyal allies in New York politics was Manhattan District Attorney Frank Hogan. In December 1966, a state grand jury in Manhattan indicted 28 people on charges of illegal wiretapping, one of whom was Spindel. Hogan's cops conducted a nine-hour raid on Spindel's upstate home, confiscating many of his wiretapping records in what Spindel told the *World Journal Tribune* was "a fishing expedition . . . they wanted to find out exactly what we have."

Later, Spindel filed suit in a New York state court, demanding return of his records. The charges in his complaint were so explosive that in late 1968, after RFK's murder, even the *New York Times* felt compelled to report on Spindel's sworn affidavit that "some of the seized material contained 'tapes and evidence concerning circumstances surrounding and causes of death of Marilyn Monroe, which strongly suggests that the officially reported circumstances of her demise are erroneous.'"

At the time of his death in 1971, Spindel was still trying unsuccessfully to get back his tapes. But copies had indeed been made. It was later reported that during the 1968 primary campaign, an automobile-industry executive was trying to buy the tapes, and had hired a retired military officer as the go-between. Negotiations on a price were underway when Bobby was murdered after the California primary in June 1968.

Another loose end: all the audio tapes of Marilyn's calls to the White House. Richard Burke, Ted Kennedy's aide who later wrote the tell-all book *The Senator,* said that he found transcripts of the Marilyn-JFK phone calls in Teddy's Senate desk. One of Burke's co-workers, he said, would spend weekends in Boston working on the tapes. One Monday, the other aide came into Teddy's office and said to Burke:

"We had to erase a couple of hours of tapes 'cause Marilyn was on the phone with the President. Boy, the things they talked about . . ."

The story, unlike the principals, refuses to die. Fast-forward to 1985. Anthony Summers was completing *Goddess* and he convinced the BBC to do a documentary, *Say Goodbye to the President.* In it, Summers included an interview with the maid, Eunice Murray, now over 80. After being asked whether RFK had been at the house the day Marilyn died, she was caught on videotape muttering to herself, "Why, at my age, do I still have to cover up this thing?"

ABC News decided to do a report on *20/20*, a TV newsmagazine. Among those assigned to the piece were Geraldo Rivera and Sylvia

Chase. In addition to interviewing the maid, ABC had interviews with ex-Sen. Smathers, who confirmed Marilyn's relationship with JFK, and with ex–LA Mayor Sam Yorty, who said that despite denials, RFK had been in the city the day she died.

The piece was budgeted for 26 minutes—an unusually long length. But then the problems started. From the beginning, ABC News had seemed a poor fit for a groundbreaking piece on Democrat corruption— then, as now, it was essentially run by Democrat operatives. In this case, the boss was someone from sports, journalism's "toy department," named Roone Arledge, who was known to have escorted RFK's widow, Ethel, to various high-profile events.

One of his top aides was an old Ted Kennedy hack from Boston named David Burke, and another employee was one Jeff Ruhe, who was at the time the husband of one of Bobby's daughters, Courtney. The network at the time also employed former JFK spokesman Pierre Salinger as a European "correspondent."

The *20/20* piece was quickly trimmed to 17 minutes, then 13. Finally, the story was killed, and replaced with a piece on police dogs. Arledge publicly denounced his own staffers' reporting as "a sleazy piece of journalism—gossip-column stuff."

The *20/20* staffers were outraged. In the end, Sylvia Chase quit the network and Geraldo Rivera was fired for insubordination.

Ten years later, in 1995, Geraldo had his own syndicated TV talk show, *Geraldo*. One of his guests was Kerry Kennedy McCarthy, Joe Kennedy's niece, the daughter of one of Joe's sisters.

"Quite honestly, Geraldo," she told the host, "you were a victim of the family . . . The family had become used to hearing the truth about Jack—but when it was Bobby . . ."

The *20/20* piece has never been aired. The tapes of Marilyn Monroe's last struggle with RFK are likewise gone. As for the photographs Peter Lawford claimed to have taken of JFK and Marilyn Monroe cavorting nude in his guest-room bathtub in Santa Monica—their whereabouts, if they still exist, or ever existed at all for that matter, are still unknown.

CHAPTER EIGHT

A HIGH-CLASS HOOKER

JUDITH CAMPBELL, FUTURE GIRLFRIEND of JFK, Frank Sinatra and Chicago Outfit boss Momo Giancana, had her first sexual experience in the late 1940s, when she was raped by a family friend in Pacific Palisades.

His name was Bob Hope.

Or so she claimed later. Her stories changed, over the years, depending on who she was talking to—her biographer Ovid Demaris, or Kitty Kelley or Seymour Hersh. But certain points in her life story remained constant. At age 18, she married an older C-list Hollywood actor named William Campbell, and the couple moved with a show-biz set that included A-listers Charlton Heston, Debbie Reynolds and Eddie Fisher, as well as B-listers Lloyd Bridges and Mike "Touch" Connors, future star of the TV series *Mannix*.

The marriage broke up, and in late 1959, she met Frank Sinatra at Puccini's, the restaurant he owned in Beverly Hills with, among others, Pete Lawford. Soon he had invited the beautiful Elizabeth Taylor look alike to join him on a brief jaunt to Hawaii. Another couple went along: Peter and Pat Kennedy Lawford.

Lawford and Sinatra spoke Rat Pack–ese, she reported in her autobiography *My Story*, sprinkling their conversation with words like "gas and gasser, clyde, cool, crazy, fink, mother, smashed, pissed, charley, and of course, ring-a-ding or ring-a-ding-ding, depending on the enthusiasm of the moment."

When it came to JFK's sister Pat, she recalled, Sinatra "was always careful about what he said to Pat, but he just pulverized Peter at will . . . I don't have an ounce of respect for Pete Lawford. I think he's an ass. He makes the best flunky in the world because it's important to Pete to be with important people."

She claimed her brief fling ended after Sinatra tried to bring a nude black woman into their bed—her refusal to join in threesomes would become another recurring theme in her various accounts

Judith Campbell Exner's publicity photo for her book, My Story.

of her life. She said Sinatra apologized profusely, and in early 1960 invited her to see his show in Las Vegas. He and the Rat Pack were filming the original *Oceans 11* by day, and honing their Rat Pack routine at the Sands Hotel by night. Sinatra alone was being paid $75,000 a week by the hotel.

"There was a barrel of talent up on that stage," Exner said in *My Story.* "They were all great ad-libbers. The only weak link was Lawford, the one with the least talent, and the least amount of respect from anybody."

On February 7, JFK's campaign plane, the *Caroline,* touched down in Vegas, and the frontrunner for the Democratic nomination checked into the Sands for a little R&R.

At 10 o'clock that evening, Judith stopped by Sinatra's table, where Jack and Teddy Kennedy were sitting. Lawford would later describe her as "a high-class hooker," the same description used by Secret Service agents. Sinatra's valet, George Jacobs, also said she was a prostitute, and that in 1958, she had been one of the whores that his boss had made

available to JFK's father when Joe was visiting Sinatra in Palm Springs—
"one of Mr. S's favorite call girls of all time, a wholesomely suburban
Irish Catholic dark beauty named Judy Campbell . . . the perfect Eisenhower era pinup of the girl next door."

She always claimed she was living off an inheritance from her grandmother, although as Jacobs pointed out in his book *Mr. S*, "Barbara
Hutton or Doris Duke could have barely afforded Judy's travel bills."

That first night at the Sands, it was Teddy Kennedy who made a pass
at her. Judith was unimpressed.

"He had nowhere near the charm and sophistication or just plain
likability of Jack."

Nonetheless, Teddy was able to sweet talk his way into her suite,
but she rebuffed him. In a very un-Kennedy-like fashion, he accepted
her rejection.

"All right," Teddy said on his way out the door. "But you can't blame
a guy for trying."

The next day, Judith huddled again with JFK and he called her out
by name during a press conference. None of the reporters mentioned
anything in their stories. Despite his campaign schedule, JFK kept in
touch with Judith almost daily until March 7, 1960, the night before
the New Hampshire primary. They met at the Plaza Hotel in New York,
that was when they consummated their relationship.

The next morning, a dozen red roses arrived at her suite with a note:
"Thinking of you . . . J."

A week later, Sinatra invited her to Miami to see his show at the Fontainebleau Hotel, and it was there that he introduced her to some of his
friends from the Chicago Outfit, including "Joe Fish" and "Sam Flood"—
Joe Fischetti, a cousin of Al Capone's, and Sam Momo Giancana, the boss.

She was still speaking almost daily with JFK, leaving messages with
his secretary, Evelyn Lincoln, which he would always return.

"Every time I would mention that I had seen him on television,"
she recalled, "Jack would invariably ask, 'How did I look? Did I come
across?' Sometimes he even asked me if I liked his suit. He was always
concerned about his appearance.

JFK secretary Evelyn Lincoln, who took the phone calls from her boss's whores.

During one of their conversations, she mentioned that she'd met "Sam Flood." In April, JFK invited her to visit him at his home in Georgetown. Jackie, pregnant with JFK Jr., was in Palm Beach.

"I wish I could show you the city," he told her. "But . . ."

Campbell understood, but she couldn't believe that he hadn't instructed the help to leave before her arrival.

"I worried about servants," she said, "of what they thought of my being there, and I couldn't quite understand how he could do that with the servants in the house."

There was a third person invited for dinner—the Florida lobbyist Bill Thompson, one of JFK's closest friends, and one of his procurers. They discussed the upcoming West Virginia primary. Finally, JFK mentioned "Sam Flood" to her and asked, "Could you quietly arrange a meeting with Sam for me?"

"Why?" she recounted to Kitty Kelley, in a *People* magazine story for which she was paid $50,000. "Or should I ask?"

"I think I may need his help in the campaign," JFK said.

Two days later, Judith met Giancana in Chicago, and a meeting between the gangster and the senator was arranged. It would be held in Miami Beach at the Fontainebleau on April 12. She was there at the hotel, but did not attend the meeting. Afterward, she recalled, JFK came by her suite.

"Jack told me that if he didn't get the nomination in July," she said, "he and his wife would get a divorce. He didn't say he was leaving her for me or for any other woman, or that Jackie was leaving him for any other man. He simply said that their marriage was unhappy and the divorce was a mutual decision between them."

Before he left, Kennedy handed her an envelope with two $1,000 bills inside.

That was the story she told Kitty Kelley. Interviewed by Seymour Hersh, she added that when she went to Chicago, she delivered a satchel to Giancana with $250,000 in one-hundred-dollar bills.

After the meeting in Miami Beach, and before the primary, Mafia money flowed freely into West Virginia. Much of the cash was funneled to the state's politically powerful sheriffs, many of whom had run up large gambling tabs in Atlantic City and in Greenbrier County. In May, JFK won the state primary with 61 percent of the vote.

Exner arranged more pre-election meetings between JFK and Giancana, including one at the Navarro Hotel in New York City. One evening on the campaign trail, after Kennedy finished a strategy session with his aides, he dismissed them while Campbell remained behind.

After a few minutes of foreplay, with the lights turned down, JFK went to the bathroom, opened the door and out stepped a "mousy-looking" secretary who had been at the earlier meeting. She was now nude.

As with Frank Sinatra earlier, Campbell again refused to take part in a threesome, or so she would say later. JFK profusely apologized, she told her biographers, and sent the other woman on her way.

Through Evelyn Lincoln, she got tickets to the inauguration in January 1961. And she continued visiting the president in the White House, not just as his lover, but also as the courier between JFK and the

Chicago mobsters, Giancana and his underboss, Johnny Roselli. The envelopes she carried back and forth, she said, were always sealed, and she never opened them.

The gangster and the president met at least twice during 1961, once in Chicago, after a political fundraiser in late April, the same month as the Bay of Pigs disaster, after which the Kennedys lost faith in the CIA's efforts to topple Castro. Campbell had a suite at the Ambassador East Hotel, where Giancana and Kennedy huddled briefly after the speech, with the Secret Service standing guard outside. There was no sex that evening.

According to Campbell's later stories, Giancana's final sit-down with the president took place in Washington on August 8, 1961. She was also in Washington that day, stopping by the White House. Her meeting went badly, she recalled in her memoirs, when JFK invited Dave Powers to lunch with them. The president began castigating her for allegedly spreading the story of the aborted threesome, during which JFK "implied that I was lending credence to a malicious story someone had invented."

That evening, Giancana stopped by her DC hotel room and told her he'd just come from his own sit-down with JFK. In his book, *The Dark Side of Camelot,* author Seymour Hersh turned up documentation showing that Giancana had applied for a passport that day in Washington, listing his occupation as "motel business."

That same evening, FBI agents again broke into Giancana's Chicago base, the Armory Lounge in Forest Park, to install another bug. Hoover was just following orders from RFK, but ironically, the bugs would provide him with enough blackmail material for him to keep his job, despite the Kennedys' abiding desire to fire him.

Campbell had apparently first turned up on the FBI radar screen the previous year, at the Sands Hotel, where a report noted that during JFK's visit, "show girls from all over the town were running in and out of the Senator's suite." In that same report, Sinatra was described as "a pawn of the hoodlum element." The agent also noted the presence with JFK of "a tall brunette UF (unidentified female)"—probably Judith.

She was spotted again by the FBI at the Democrat convention in July, in JFK's hideaway apartment, along with a procession of other women including Mafia-connected prostitutes and Marilyn Monroe. The FBI surveillance unit in LA was particularly shocked by Campbell's assignation with JFK—"the agents wanted to throw up," one of them later told Hersh.

After JFK's inauguration, Hoover may or may not have been wiretapping the White House phone lines, but he was definitely listening in on the phone calls she made from Sam Giancana's home. FBI agents recorded at least two calls she made from there to the White House.

Hoover's position as Director was increasingly precarious, which was why he wanted more dirt, any dirt, on the Kennedys.

Now he had the wiretaps and bugs from both Giancana's house and his lounge. And in all likelihood, Hoover also had access to the tapes that other parties were making at the West Coast homes of Marilyn Monroe and Peter Lawford—more ammunition for the master blackmailer.

Now he had evidence of JFK's affairs with both Monroe and Campbell, not to mention the Kennedys' ties to organized crime during the 1960 campaign. But Hoover didn't want to provoke a confrontation unless the Kennedys left him with no choice.

On January 6, 1962, columnist Drew Pearson, another of Hoover's enemies, made a prediction on his radio show:

"J. Edgar Hoover doesn't much like taking a seat, as he calls it, to a young kid like Bobby . . . and he'll be eased out of there if there is not too much of a furor."

Now it looked like Hoover wouldn't even make it to January 1, 1965–his 70th birthday, when he would reach the government's mandatory retirement age. On February 1, the wiretaps on Lawford's beach house confirmed Pearson's prediction. RFK was in Hollywood yet again, meeting Marilyn Monroe for the first time. Not wanting to appear to be a bimbo, she had prepared a list of questions for the attorney general, one of which involved what the brothers' plans were for J. Edgar Hoover.

"We'd like to get rid of him," RFK told Marilyn Monroe, "but we're not strong enough . . ."

Hoover knew he could wait no longer. To protect his job, he had to let the brothers know what he had on Judith Campbell. On February 27, he wrote memos to RFK and Kenny O'Donnell alerting them, as if they didn't know, that Campbell was an "associate" of both Roselli and Giancana, "a prominent Chicago underworld figure."

Four weeks later, on March 27, Hoover's limousine pulled up at 1600 Pennsylvania Avenue. It would be only his second—and his final—meeting at the White House with JFK as president. It lasted four hours. No audiotapes exist; nor did Hoover put a memo in his file, as he so often did. As they finished, Ted Sorensen and Arthur Schlesinger Jr. were waiting outside the Oval Office for their own scheduled meeting with the president.

JFK knew how much Hoover detested both men, and vice versa. So he told the Director to leave by the back door because, according to author Anthony Summers, he "did not want to upset Mr. Hoover too much."

Years later, O'Donnell recalled that at the end of the meeting, JFK whispered to him, "Get rid of that bastard. He's the biggest bore."

Later that afternoon, JFK called Campbell. He told her to go to her mother's home in suburban LA and call him at the White House from there.

"He was furious," Judy said. "You could feel his anger. He said that, at their meeting, Hoover had more or less tried to intimidate him with the information he had. He'd made it clear that he knew about my relationship with Jack, even that I'd been to the White House, that I was a friend of Sam and Johnny Roselli, and that Jack knew Sam, too. Jack knew exactly what Hoover was doing."

Hoover was covering his ass. He was protecting his job.

JFK's alcoholic aide Kenny O'Donnell took many of the calls from Marilyn Monroe and Judith Campbell.

Soon a new memo was inserted into the files by Hoover, asserting that he and RFK had only learned of the CIA's use of Giancana in the plots against Fidel Castro "with great astonishment." That memo could be used, if necessary, to show that the Kennedys had been out of the loop when the CIA botched the operations to take out Castro, up to and including the Bay of Pigs. The Kennedys now owed Hoover even more. Not only had he covered his own rear end, he had covered theirs as well.

The climactic four-hour White House meeting between the president and the FBI director claimed another casualty—Brother-in-Lawford. JFK had been planning a trip to Palm Springs, where he would stay at Frank Sinatra's mansion, which the singer had renovated at great personal expense, down to a new helicopter pad and a flag pole, for the president's visit.

After learning what Hoover knew about Campbell, Giancana and Sinatra, there was no possible way JFK could stay at the same place Giancana and his father had both frequented. RFK called Lawford and told him to break the news to Sinatra. Ol' Blue Eyes did not take the rejection kindly, going on a drunken rampage, destroying the renovations.

"Now I know what a whore feels like," he told his valet.

Heaping yet another indignity on the proud Sinatra, the presidential party was shifted to the estate of Bing Crosby, Sinatra's early rival crooner, and a Republican no less. (The Kennedys ended up throwing many of Crosby's clothes into the pool, destroying them, just as Sinatra had done days earlier with the clothes the Lawfords kept in the guest room he had reserved for them.)

After the snub, Lawford's show-biz career, at least as a member of the Rat Pack, was effectively over. He was written out of two upcoming Sinatra movies (and replaced in one by, of all people, Bing Crosby). Lawford's tailspin in alcoholism and drug addiction accelerated. Within two years, he would be divorced from Pat.

As for Campbell, when she was first outed as JFK's girlfriend in 1975, she claimed that she never spoke to JFK after the White House meeting with Hoover. In fact, she continued to call him, and perhaps meet with him, at least through the late summer of 1962. She felt compelled to speak to the president, at least in part, because she was now being tailed by FBI agents. JFK told her not to worry—"You know Sam works for us."

By the summer of 1962, she later told Hersh, she had been given another assignment by JFK—as a bagman, delivering payoffs to the White House from California defense contractors. By then, Campbell's relationship with the president had become known to the owners of General Dynamics, which was dueling with Boeing for a multi-billion-dollar contract for a new military plane called the TFX (Tactical Fighter Experimental), later known as the F-111.

General Dynamic's F-111 was not nearly the equal of Boeing's, but they had an ace in the hole—Campbell. Their director of security was I. B. Hale, a hulking ex-college football star at Texas Christian University who had long been an FBI agent, one of J. Edgar Hoover's favorites. He lived in Fort Worth, which was also the hometown of John Connally, the lawyer-fixer and LBJ confidante who would be elected governor of Texas in 1962.

In 1958, Hale's 17-year-old son Bobby, one of his twins, had eloped to Florida with Connally's 16-year-old daughter Kathleen. A month later, she was found shot to death in the apartment she shared with her teenage husband. At a coroner's inquest, young Hale testified that he had come home from looking for a job and found his wife pointing a gun at her head, and that when he tried to wrestle it away from her, the gun had gone off, killing her.

For years afterward, Bobby Hale tried to effect a reconciliation with his one-time father-in-law. But Connally refused to take his calls, as the Texas governor wrote in his autobiography.

In 1962, Campbell moved to an apartment in west Los Angeles. FBI agents trailed her wherever she went and had a 24-hour watch on her new home. One day in August, while she was out, the two-man FBI stakeout team observed a rented blue car with Texas plates pull up in front of her building.

Two young men got out, and climbed onto the second-floor balcony outside Campbell's apartment, then broke in. One of them was carrying a black bag, which could have contained surveillance equipment to be planted in the apartment. A few minutes later, they stealthily left. The FBI agents dutifully wrote up the break-in, but did not call the LAPD. It would have blown their stakeout.

The FBI quickly determined that the second-story men were the Hale twins, although Bobby denied it to the end of his life. However, Hoover decided not to have I. B. Hale interviewed about his sons' involvement in the break-in at the apartment of one of the president's girlfriends. He would have Miss Gandy put the reports in his private files, for future use, just in case . . .

In *The Dark Side of Camelot*, Seymour Hersh asked, "Was Jack Kennedy blackmailed by a desperate corporation?"

The answer seems obvious.

Three months later, the Kennedy administration shocked Washington and the defense establishment by selecting General Dynamics's flawed plane over Boeing's. Congressional hearings were scheduled, but after the assassination there was no interest in either party in heaping more dirt on JFK's grave.

The Navy finally cancelled its contract with General Dynamics in 1968, after the initial jets were built almost a ton over the weight limit for aircraft carriers. The Air Force had contracted to buy 2,400 F-111s, but ultimately didn't get even 600. The original price tag of $2.8 million per jet had ballooned to $22 million by 1970.

The sordid story remained unknown for 35 years, until Hersh's book, and is still an obscure footnote to the Camelot myth, so the price was small enough, at least for the Kennedys.

By the time of the Hale boys' black-bag job, Campbell was pregnant with JFK's baby, or so she said in one of her later interviews, with *Vanity Fair*. Like Inga Arvad before her, she claimed JFK impregnated her in their final assignation. She said she and the president agreed that she would abort the child, and that JFK then asked her:

"Would Sam help us?"

He would, and soon he too was sleeping with Campbell. Late in her life she claimed the Mafia boss even asked her to marry him.

The FBI continued tailing her in 1963; it was believed she would be subpoenaed to testify before a federal grand jury investigating organized crime. Johnny Roselli began moving her from hotel to hotel, hoping to keep her under wraps until the heat died down.

She was stashed in a hotel in Beverly Hills on November 22, 1963. That evening, Roselli called her room. There was no answer. He went to her suite and banged on the door. She refused to open it. Finally, he called the front desk and had a room clerk come up to unlock the door and let Roselli in to comfort her.

In the end, there would be no grand jury appearance for Campbell.

"I should have realized that there was no way the Justice Department would bring me before a grand jury," she said in *My Story*, "and risk the possibility that my relationship with Jack would be revealed . . . I didn't know it then, but I had diplomatic immunity."

A few months after the assassination, she made a half-hearted suicide attempt. In 1965, she gave birth to a son out of wedlock, whom she gave up for adoption. She cared for her parents until their deaths in the early 1970s. In 1975 she married Dan Exner, an aspiring professional golfer 12 years her junior.

Her friends in the Mafia had less luck staying out of trouble. Giancana was called before the same grand jury that she had feared. He refused to testify and was jailed for a year for contempt. After his release, Momo fled to Mexico, where he remained until he was deported back to Chicago in 1974.

The U.S. government tried to deport Roselli back to his native Italy, but Italy refused to take him. Eventually, in 1975, after revelations in the press about post-war U.S. intelligence operations, a Senate committee began an investigation.

Roselli was called to testify about the CIA's Operation Mongoose plots against Castro. His testimony led to a subpoena for Giancana, who at age 67 had returned to suburban Chicago. On the evening of June 19, 1975, the Oak Park police detail outside his house was abruptly pulled, and minutes later Giancana was shot to death in the basement of his home as he fried sausages and peppers.

Nine months later, Roselli was recalled by the Senate to testify about the assassination of JFK. He was about to be brought back to Washington when he went missing in Miami in July 1976. A few days later his decomposing body was discovered in a sealed 55-gallon oil drum floating off Miami.

By this time Campbell had been identified in the Senate assassination committee's initial report as a "close friend" of JFK, Giancana and Roselli. The *Washington Post* printed her name. Her old White House contacts—Kenny O'Donnell, Dave Powers and Evelyn Lincoln—all denied knowing her, despite incontrovertible proof on White House phone logs showing 70 calls between her and JFK.

Lincoln dismissed her as nothing more than a campaign worker. Powers said "the only Campbell I know is chunky vegetable soup."

So she released all the White House private phone numbers she had been given. She handed reporters copies of her plane reservations, her Washington and Miami hotel reservations, and her invitations and tickets to the 1961 inauguration. In the media firestorm that ensued, she was pretty much on her own; the lawyer she'd been assigned by the Senate committee was a member of Kennedy brother-in-law Sargent Shriver's law firm.

Finally, she held a press conference to deny the underworld ties she would later confirm for Seymour Hersh, Kitty Kelley and others. She was wearing huge sunglasses as she read a prepared statement with her younger husband sitting by her side.

"I can at this time emphatically state that my relationship with Jack Kennedy was of a close, personal nature," she read, "and did not involve conspiratorial shenanigans of any kind. My relationship with Sam Giancana and my friendship with Johnny Roselli were of a personal nature and in no way related to or affected my relationship with Jack Kennedy. Nor did I discuss either of them with the other."

Untrue, or so she would say later, after being diagnosed with metastatic cancer.

Near the end of her life, Judith Campbell Exner offered Hersh her assessment of both her boyfriend and his family.

"Jack didn't play by our rules," she said. "Jack had his own rules. I believe that all of the Kennedys play by their own rules. I don't think they conduct themselves the way we do. I think that's very sad."

She died of breast cancer at age 65 in September 1999. The *New York Times* ran her obituary September 27, complete with a headline that said she "Claimed Affair with Kennedy."

Claimed? The *New York Times*, keeper of the Kennedy flame after all these years, was still maintaining the long-discredited myths of Camelot. It was such an egregious falsehood that three days later the paper had to grudgingly run an "Editor's Note."

The *Times* mentioned the pro forma "Campbell's soup" denial by Dave Powers in the original piece, but then admitted that the earlier obituary "should also have reflected what is now the view of a number of respected historians and authors that the affair did in fact take place."

Small consolation for the late Judith Campbell Exner, but at least one of the leading propagators of the Kennedy myth had been embarrassed into telling the truth, however briefly.

CHAPTER NINE

ONE BRIEF SHINING MOMENT

I T WAS NOVEMBER 29, 1963. The president had been dead exactly a week when Jackie Kennedy called Theodore H. White at his home in New York.

Could the author of the worshipful best seller *The Making of the President 1960* come up to Hyannis Port? She knew he was working on a piece for the special assassination issue of *Life* magazine, which would have a circulation far above the weekly's usual millions, and she wanted to try to shape the piece with White before he filed his copy.

What could he say? How could he turn down the opportunity to have a one-on-one interview with the most beloved woman in the world? Plus, he was part of the Kennedy journalistic retinue—he'd gone to the same Boston high school as Joe Kennedy Sr., he'd graduated Harvard College in the same Class of 1937 with Joe Jr. And White had worked for many years for Time Inc., owned by Henry Luce, another loyal family retainer and ex-husband of Clare Boothe Luce, who had slept with one or more members of America's First Family.

The weather was miserable, he recalled in his memoirs, and his mother had just suffered a heart attack, but White immediately accepted Jackie's summons. He arrived at Hyannis Port the next evening and immediately sat down with Jackie.

She shared a few tidbits about November 22, but it quickly became clear that her main focus was the creation of a new myth—Camelot. The motif came from the legend of King Arthur and his Knights of the

Round Table, most recently reworked into the Broadway hit *Camelot* by Lerner and Loew. Alan Jay Lerner, of course, was JFK's classmate at Choate and Harvard. The only important thing, as far as Jackie was concerned, was to meld the "1,000 Days," as the Kennedy administration would soon be known, into a modern-day Camelot.

None of the president's aides had ever heard him speak of the play, but now Jackie told the loyal White how much her husband identified with the title song, especially these lines:

"Don't let it be forgot, that once there was a spot, for one brief shining moment that was Camelot."

The modern King Arthur and his queen, she told White, would often listen to the song in their private quarters in the White House before they retired for the evening—never mind that they slept in separate bedrooms.

"Jack had this hero view of history," she said, "the idealistic view."

She repeatedly used the "I" word—idealistic. White had known JFK well enough to understand that he was being spun, but as the newspaper editor in *The Man Who Shot Liberty Valance* says, "When the fact becomes legend, print the legend."

Jackie told White that the histories would be written by "bitter old men." But she said Jack was inspired by the likes of King Arthur and the Duke of Marlborough, the great 18th-century British general and statesman.

The special issue was about to go to press, but the editors in New York had moved the deadline, at great cost, to accommodate what no one else would have—an exclusive interview with the most famous woman in the world. After speaking to her, White retreated to another room in the house and banged out his piece in short order. Then he telephoned New York and began dictating it to the editors, as Jackie hovered nearby.

Surprisingly, the editors objected to the mawkish Camelot references, and wanted to excise them from the piece. As he recounted later in his memoirs, White looked at Jackie, who shook her head. Camelot had to remain in the story. The editors quickly relented, and a few days later, White's piece, "For President Kennedy: An Epilogue," was being read by millions. The legend of Camelot had been created.

"Quite inadvertently," White wrote 15 years later, "I was her instrument in labeling the myth."

And myth it was—Jack didn't much care for Broadway musicals, let alone *Camelot*. As for JFK's heroes, he had told many people—among them White's Time Inc. colleague Hugh Sidey—that his favorite historical work was David Cecil's *Lord Melbourne*, about a mediocre British prime minister who was a bounder in his personal life, a serial adulterer, with many more conquests in the boudoir than in the House of Commons.

But the myth-making had begun. Actually, it had begun almost as soon as JFK was declared dead at Parkland Memorial Hospital. The November 23 front page of the *New York Times* showed the incipient conflict between fact and fable. Next to the profile of Lee Harvey Oswald—headlined, "Leftist Accused/Figure in a Pro-Castro Group Is Charged"—was a piece by James "Scotty" Reston, the Times's Washington bureau chief. Its two-column headline: "Why America Weeps/ Kennedy Victim of Violent Streak He Sought to Curb in the Nation."

For a day or so, the more conservative newspapers resisted the national hysteria, stressing Oswald's Communist background on their front pages the next day.

The *New York Daily News:* "Leftist Jailed as Slayer."

The *Boston Record-American:* "Pro-Red Sniper Suspect Seized."

Despite those undisputed facts, by Sunday, a liberal Washington clergyman was comparing JFK to Jesus, telling his flock, "We have been present at a new crucifixion. All of us had a part in the slaying of the president."

An anti-Communist president had been slain, most likely by a Communist who had once defected to the Soviet Union, yet somehow the entire nation was to blame for JFK's murder. That was now the accepted wisdom.

The Soviet news agency chimed in, reporting that the president had been murdered by "racists, the Ku Klux Klan and Nazis"—an analysis not that much different from that of much of the American media.

The drumbeat of what would today be called "fake news" was so relentless that by December, Senator Milward Simpson of Wyoming, the father of Teddy Kennedy's future friend and colleague Alan Simpson, felt compelled to correct the record on the Senate floor.

It wasn't "hate" that killed JFK, Simpson pointed out. "Rightists and conservatives" were being blamed, he said, but the reality was that the murderer "was a single kill-crazy Communist."

Some of the deflection of blame away from a hard-core Communist who had actually defected to the Soviet Union was understandable. The new president, LBJ, was frantic when he learned of Oswald's visits to the Soviet and Cuban embassies in Mexico City earlier in the fall. He called J. Edgar Hoover. LBJ was concerned that if the assassination could be linked to the "Reds," as they were still called in newspaper headlines, then there would be calls for retaliation. As another *Times* columnist, C. L. Sulzberger, wrote: "It is essential in these restless days to remove the unfounded suspicions that could excite any latent jingo spirit."

There was a paroxysm of commemorations for the slain monarch of Camelot. Within a month, Idlewild Airport in New York would be renamed JFK. Cape Canaveral in Florida would likewise become Cape Kennedy. (The name would be changed back a decade later.) By January, the Benjamin Franklin half dollar had been replaced by a new JFK coin, but only because Mrs. Kennedy demurred when asked about her husband's likeness replacing George Washington's on the quarter.

And then there was the "Eternal Flame" at his gravesite at Arlington National Cemetery.

"The rhetoric has gone quite out of control," William F. Buckley Jr. noted in the *National Review*. "The symbol of our emotional, if not neurotic excess, is the Eternal Flame at Arlington, a few hundred yards from the shrines we built to the memories of George Washington (86 years after he died), Thomas Jefferson (117 years), and Abraham Lincoln (57 years); who have no eternal flames. The lovely and tormented Mrs. Kennedy needs a gentle hand lest in her understandable grief, she gives the air of the Pharaoh, specifying her own grief."

It was LBJ who came up with the idea of a special commission to investigate the assassination, chaired by Chief Justice Earl Warren, a nominal Republican, the former governor of California.

Record American

CLOUDY, COOLER FULL REPORT, SEE PAGE 4

(10c BEYOND 30 MILES) 8 Cents   Boston, Tuesday, November 3, 1964   52 Pages

PAYOFF

FINAL

"Now I Think That I Should Have Known That He Was Magic All Along. I Did Know It--But I Should Have Guessed It Could Not Last."

Jackie's Soulful Tribute to JFK

MRS. John F. Kennedy, in a touching tribute to her assassinated husband made public Monday, said: "I should have known that it was asking too much to dream that I might have grown old with him and see our children grow up together."

Mrs. Kennedy penned those words in connection with the approaching first anniversary of the death of President John F. Kennedy. They are contained in the "JFK Memorial Issue" of Look Magazine.

"Now I think that I should have known that he was magic all along," Mrs. Kennedy said. "I did know it—but I should have guessed it could not last."

"So now he is a legend when he would have preferred to be a man," the President's widow said.

She continued:

"It is nearly a year since he has been gone.

"On so many days—his birthday, an anniversary, watching his children running to the sea—I have thought, 'but this day last year was his last to see that.' He was so full of love and life on all those days. He seems so vulnerable now, when you think that each one was a last time.

"Soon the final day will come around again—as inexorably as it did last year. But expected this time.

"It will find some of us different people than we were a year ago. Learning to accept what was unthinkable when he was alive, changes you.

"I don't think there is any consolation. What was lost cannot be replaced.

"Someone who loved us this winter: 'The hero comes when he is needed.'

" 'When our belief gets pale and weak there comes a man out of that need who is shining—and everyone living reflects a little of that light—and stores some up against the time when he is gone.'

"Now I think that I should have known that he was magic all along. I did know it—but I should have guessed it could not last. I should have known that it was asking too much to dream that I might have grown old with him and see our children grow up together.

"So now he is a legend when he would have preferred to be a man. I must believe that he does not share our suffering now. I think, for him—at least he will never know whatever sadness might have lain ahead. He knew such a share of it in his life that it always made you so happy whenever you saw him enjoying himself. But now he will never know more—not age, nor stagnation, nor despair, nor crippling illness, nor loss of any more people he loved. His high noon kept all the freshness of the morning—and he died then, never knowing disillusionment.

" '. . . He has gone . . .

"Among the radiant, ever venturing on,

"Somewhere, with morning, as such spirits will.'

"He is free and we must live. Those who love him most know that 'the death you have dealt is more than the death which has swallowed you.' "

Mrs. Kennedy quoted from John Masefield's "On The Finish Of The Sailing Ship Race."

(United Press International)

Jacqueline Kennedy

Set MBTA Deficit for 78 Cities, Towns
STORY ON PAGE FOUR

Typical post-assassination front page.

Warren was already on record as blaming the assassination on "bigotry"—ironic, considering his own pivotal role as governor of California in the internment of thousands of Japanese-American citizens during World War II.

Before his election in 1942, Warren had denounced the incumbent Democrat governor as soft on "Japs," as Warren called them. They were the "Achilles' heel" of the U.S. war effort, he explained. With Caucasians, Warren explained, sounding as certain as a phrenologist discussing skulls, "we have methods that will test *The press printed countless photos like these commemorating "Camelot."*

loyalty . . . (but) when we deal with Japs we are in an entirely different field . . . (because of) their method of living."

By 1943, even some hard-liners were beginning to doubt the wisdom of the Nisei internment, but Warren insisted on maintaining the anti-Japanese policies of FDR and the national Democrats.

"If the Japs are released," Warren thundered at a national conference of governors in 1943, "no one will be able to tell a saboteur from any other Jap . . . We don't propose to have the Japs back in California during this war if there is any lawful means of preventing it."

Now, 20 years later, Warren reveled in presenting himself as the liberal conscience of America. The same media that were blaming right-wingers for the murder of JFK conveniently forgot his racist past. What could be more bipartisan than the selection of Earl Warren—a liberal Republican from California who would be denounced by both Republicans and conservative Southern Democrats still angry over *Brown v.*

Board of Education, the Supreme Court's school desegregation decision of 1954? Their attacks would just confirm the wisdom of LBJ's decision to appoint him chairman . . . if only he would agree to take the thankless task.

But Warren initially refused the job, so Johnson asked him to come to the White House. The president used all of his legendary powers of persuasion, and the chief justice finally relented.

"I pulled out what Hoover told me about a little incident in Mexico City," LBJ would later tell Sen. Richard Russell of Georgia, one of his political mentors, when he pitched Russell to join the Commission.

LBJ told Russell that at their Oval Office meeting, Warren began weeping, but finally agreed.

"Well, I won't turn you down," the chief justice told the president. "I'll just do whatever you say."

In other words, he understood what he was being asked to do— whatever he was told to do. It was an equally unappealing assignment to Sen. Russell, especially considering his low personal opinion of the preening Warren.

"I don't like that man," he told LBJ.

Once again, LBJ wouldn't take no for an answer.

"We've got to take this out of the arena where they're testifying that Khrushchev and Castro did this and did that and kicking us into a war that can kill 40 million Americans in an hour."

Against his better judgment, Russell agreed to serve.

Bobby Kennedy had suspected a conspiracy from the moment he got the news about his brother's assassination from J. Edgar Hoover— "he told me with the same emotion he would have used if he'd found a Communist on the faculty of the Howard University law school."

Bobby asked Allen Dulles, the former CIA director, if his spooks had done it. No, Dulles said. In fact, the CIA was embarrassed. It had dropped the ball on Oswald's visits to the Cuban and Soviet embassies in Mexico City that had so alarmed the new president.

Next RFK called an Outfit expert in Chicago and asked him to poke around.

But Bobby too had his reasons not to want to dig too deeply. There was his brother's legacy to consider, not to mention his own political ambitions. The Cubans, the Soviets, the Mafia—if a conspiracy of any sort were uncovered, the Kennedys' complicity in all sorts of unsavory, if not illegal, activities would be splashed across the front pages. In 1971, shortly before his death, talking about the Kennedys, LBJ would blurt out to a reporter, "They were running a damn Murder Incorporated down there in the Caribbean."

For years, nobody understood what LBJ was talking about.

For once, LBJ and RFK had a common goal: keeping a lid on all the administration's dirty little secrets. Obviously, there was only one solution for all concerned—J. Edgar Hoover. And he too had good reason to want to selectively manage the dissemination of some, but not all, of the facts.

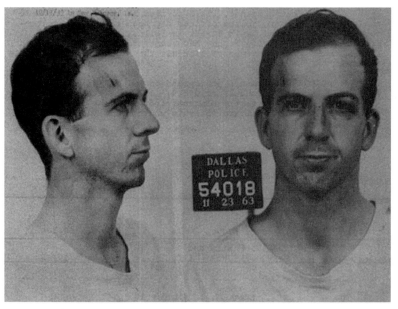

Lee Harvey Oswald mugshot.

First of all, his agents in Dallas had been in contact with Oswald. Oswald had even left a threatening note at the FBI office in Dallas for the agent who had questioned his Russian wife. (It was quietly destroyed the weekend of the assassination.)

Equally ominous, at least from Hoover's perspective, were Oswald's ties to New Orleans. Hoover knew how much Mafia boss Carlos Marcello hated the Kennedys; he had the tapes and the informants' statements to prove it. His New Orleans agents had always kept Marcello at arm's length; he was dismissively described in one FBI report as a "tomato salesman."

The fact that Oswald's uncle had once been a low-level operative in Marcello's gambling organizations was not helpful either. Then there was Rose Cheramie, a 34-year-old heroin addict who had been picked up on a Louisiana highway Wednesday, November 20. She had ended up in a state hospital in Louisiana in Eunice, babbling to doctors and nurses before the assassination that the president was about to be murdered in Dallas.

Another problem: the eyewitness accounts of the people who had actually been there in Dealey Plaza that day. Many of them said they heard shots coming not from Oswald's perch in the Texas School Book Depository, but from the "grassy knoll" in front of the limousine. Among the witnesses initially telling that story: JFK's closest aides, Kenny O'Donnell and Dave Powers, who had been the car behind the president's open limousine. (They changed later their testimony at the family's behest.)

Then there was Abraham Zapruder's 26-second film of the assassination. It clearly showed that the final, fatal shot, which literally blew his brains out, had come from the front of the limousine. How else to explain JFK's head being thrown back just after he yelled his final words, "My God! I'm hit!"

So many loose ends—while the media spun the Dallas hate narrative, Lee Harvey Oswald made the clenched-fist salute as he was moved between cells in the Dallas jail, shouting out to reporters, "I'm just a patsy!" With his one allowed phone call, he tried to reach the lawyer for the Communist Party USA.

On Sunday morning, the problem of Lee Harvey Oswald was solved once and for all when he was shot and killed in the basement of the Dallas police headquarters by Jack Ruby, a fast-talking 52-year-old nightclub owner.

But that just created a whole new set of loose ends—Ruby (birth name: Jacob Rubinstein) had ties back to the Chicago Outfit and had vacationed in Cuba in 1959 as the guest of a mobbed-up gambler. He knew Tampa Mafia boss Santo Trafficante. The evening before the assassination, he had dined at a Dallas restaurant owned by a businessman with ties to the Marcello organization.

Justice in Texas in those days was neither delayed nor denied. By March, Ruby had been convicted of Oswald's murder. He had said that he killed Oswald to spare Mrs. Kennedy the trauma of having to endure Oswald's own murder trial, but that seemed far too pat.

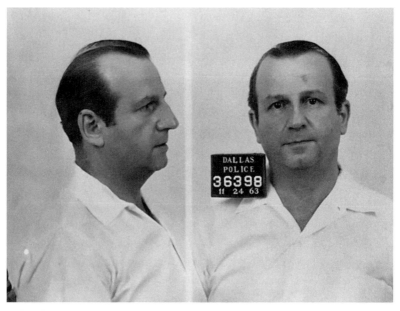

Jack Ruby mugshot.

On the other hand, as the world learned more about him, Jack Ruby seemed an unlikely linchpin for a conspiracy vast enough to murder the most powerful man on the planet. He was garrulous, until very recently he had been in deep financial trouble, and he hadn't tried to cover any of his pre-November 24 tracks.

The Warren Commission began working furiously to complete its report. Johnson had stacked it, with help from Bobby Kennedy, still deep in grief. On behalf of the Kennedys, Bobby tapped Allen Dulles, the former CIA director who had plenty of reasons of his own not to rock the boat, not the least of which were the CIA's ties to the Mafia in the series of aborted attempts to depose Castro.

RFK's second choice was another family loyalist, New York corporate lawyer John McCloy, a Rockefeller Republican. McCloy, an assistant secretary of war during World War II, had like Warren been directly involved in the internment of Japanese-Americans in 1942.

From Congress, LBJ picked two Republicans. The first was Sen. John Sherman Cooper, a social friend of JFK. Cooper was married to the first wife of Thomas Shevlin, who had wed Durie Malcolm six months after JFK's secret wedding to her in Palm Beach in early 1947.

LBJ's other Republican was Rep. Gerald Ford of Michigan, the future president. Ford too would be a team player. His wife Betty was already a victim of the alcoholism that she would parlay into a late-life career as a substance-abuse counselor. In search of female companionship, Ford had often visited Bobby Baker's Quorum Club, where JFK's East German girlfriend Ellen Rometsch plied her trade. Ford also frequented lobbyist Fred Black's suite in the Sheraton-Carlton Hotel, where Hoover had installed bugs.

"So he had this tape," Bobby Baker recalled in 2009, "where Jerry Ford was having oral sex with Ellen Rometsch . . . Hoover blackmailed . . . Ford to tell him what they were doing."

Ford had long been one of Hoover's fair-haired boys in Congress. One of his first speeches in the House in the 1940s had been in favor of a pay raise for the FBI director. William Sullivan, the former FBI assistant director, agreed that the future president was "our man, our informant on the Warren Commission."

The second Congressional Democrat on the Commission after Russell was Rep. T. Hale Boggs of New Orleans. He was a product of the Democratic machine in the Crescent City, Marcello's hometown. And he was in the Democratic leadership in the House. He was on the speaker's track, behind John McCormack and Carl Albert. Boggs too had every reason to go along, to get along.

Hoover was able to direct the assassination investigation as he—and almost everyone else in Washington, including the Kennedys– wanted it to proceed. At one point, a Commission investigator began asking questions about why, after the assassination, Oswald appeared to be headed toward Jack Ruby's apartment.

To stop that line of investigation, Hoover called Ford and leaked him background information about the impertinent staffer's long-ago Communist connections. Ford raised the issue, and although Warren was able to block the man's firing, he quickly came to understand the reality of the investigation.

As far as J. Edgar Hoover was concerned, some matters, say, the provenance of Oswald's rifle, were more important than others—like Jack Ruby's voluminous long-distance telephone records of calls to organized crime figures in Chicago and Las Vegas, and his sudden spate of deposits into his bank accounts in the days leading up to November 22.

Perhaps the most memorable moment of the "investigation" occurred in June 1964. Reluctantly, Warren agreed to meet with Jack Ruby in the Dallas city jail. With him Warren brought the staff and Rep. Gerald Ford. Ruby immediately begged Warren to bring him back to Washington, so that he could speak freely.

Ruby: "If you request me to go back to Washington with you right now, that couldn't be done, could it?"

Warren: "No, it could not be done . . . There are a good many things involved in that, Mr. Ruby."

Ruby: "Gentlemen, my life is in danger here . . . Do I sound sober enough to you as I say this?"

Warren: "You do. You sound entirely sober."

Warren tried to assure Ruby that there was no need for him to make the journey to Washington, that the Commission had interviewed between 200 and 300 people in Dallas "without going to Washington."

"Yes," said Ruby, "but those people weren't Jack Ruby."

"No," agreed Warren, "they weren't."

Ford asked him if there was anything he could tell them in Washington that he couldn't say in Dallas.

"I want to tell the truth," he said, "and I can't tell it here."

He continued his plea to Warren: "I am in a tough spot, and I don't know what the solution can be to save me . . . I won't be around for you to come and question me again . . . I won't be living long now."

And he wasn't. He was granted a new trial, but before it could begin, he was diagnosed with lung cancer, months after he began telling his guards that he was going to be injected with cancer cells. He died at Parkland Memorial Hospital in Dallas in January 1967.

One of Ruby's final interviews was with Dorothy Kilgallen, the Hearst newspaper gossip columnist and longtime panelist on the popular CBS quiz show, *What's My Line?* She returned to New York claiming she was going to break the real story of the JFK assassination, but on November 8, 1965, she was found dead on her bed, fully clothed. No notes of her interview with Ruby were ever found.

Two days later, her good friend and newspaper colleague, JFK's longtime girlfriend Florence Pritchett Smith, died in New York at the age of 45. She reportedly was suffering from leukemia.

JFK's grandmother Mary Fitzgerald died at age 98 in 1964, never knowing that her grandson had been murdered.

The Warren Commission report was issued in September 1964. Lee Harvey Oswald was described as the "lone gunman." Jack Ruby had likewise acted alone, the Commission declared. Among the seven Commission members, only Sen. Richard Russell refused to sign the final report.

"I don't believe it," he told LBJ in the wired Oval Office.

"I don't either," LBJ replied.

In 1969, after leaving office, LBJ sat down for an interview with Walter Cronkite. He was asked about the Warren Commission. After saying that "they did the best they could," LBJ again mentioned his own doubts about their conclusions.

"I can't honestly say I've never been completely relieved of the fact that there might have been international connections," LBJ said. "I have not completely discounted it."

At LBJ's request, that part of the interview was excised from the final CBS broadcast.

Meanwhile, as the Warren Commission tried to craft its version of the assassination, the president's widow was continuing her quest to shape her husband's legacy. She seemed to resent anyone writing about JFK. She continued to employ JFK's girlfriend, Pamela Turnure, who sometimes read the early drafts of the memorial books that were now being churned out in bulk. Paul Fay, JFK's Navy buddy, was ordered by Jackie to cut one-third of his book, *The Pleasure of His Company.* Apparently even the hagiographies weren't adoring enough.

Arthur Schlesinger Jr. wrote more than 1,000 pages in his tome, *A Thousand Days: John F. Kennedy in the White House,* without once mentioning Oswald by name. He spent more than a page on the "hate" in Dallas. Yet Jackie still wasn't pleased with the book.

The Kennedys, namely Jackie and Bobby, decided that they needed their own authorized account of November 22. They wanted to head off Jim Bishop, the syndicated columnist, a onetime Hearst tabloid writer who had hit pay dirt with a best-selling 1955 potboiler, *The Day Lincoln Was Shot.* Now he was going to write *The Day Kennedy Was Shot.* Jackie was appalled, considering him a "hack." When she tried to

JFK gal pal Pamela Turnure, right, continued working for Jackie post-November 22.

shut off access to him, Bishop angrily said, "She's trying to copyright the assassination."

To write their version, the Kennedys settled on William Manchester, who had already written one sycophantic book on the president in 1962, *Portrait of a President.* Like Ben Bradlee and the Bundys, he was of old New England Yankee stock, a few years younger than JFK and totally enthralled by him.

In 1964, Jackie spent hours being interviewed by Manchester, always after dark—apparently, she still couldn't bear to talk about the assassination in the daylight hours that somehow reminded her of Dallas. She guzzled daiquiris and chain-smoked L&M cigarettes as she talked to Manchester.

He finished writing *The Death of a President* in 1966 and sent a copy of the manuscript to Jackie. She didn't read it; that task went to Pamela Turnure, who was appalled at the revelations, including the fact that Jackie smoked cigarettes. Turnure also objected to Manchester reporting that JFK sometimes wandered the halls of the White House at night in his underwear. For his part, Manchester was shocked that he was being critiqued by . . . a girlfriend, on behalf of the widow.

Jackie wanted to stop publication of the book, or at least its serialization in *Look* magazine. She summoned Manchester to Hyannis Port, where she told him, "It's us against them. Anyone who is against me will look like a rat, unless I run off with Eddie Fisher."

In November 1966, Jackie filed suit in New York, seeking an injunction against Manchester and his publication of the book.

"Because she assisted him," the complaint read, "she therefore has an absolute right to decide what may or may not appear therein."

For the first time since the assassination, the Kennedys looked like the heavies. RFK's poll numbers suffered.

"Why am I being dragged into this?" Bobby reportedly complained.

In the end, Manchester cut 1,600 words out of the magazine serialization, and seven of the book's 654 pages. The book sold more than a million copies, with profits going to the JFK Library. The Kennedys should have been happy, but they weren't. They have since allowed the book to go out of print.

For the record, to the end of his life, Manchester agreed with the Warren Commission: Oswald was the lone gunman.

"Those who desperately want to believe that President Kennedy was the victim of a conspiracy have my sympathy," he wrote in a collection of essays. "You want to add something weightier to Oswald. It would invest the President's death with meaning, endowing him with martyrdom. He would have died for *something*."

Or, as Fred Kaplan put it in *Slate* in 2013: "It makes for a neater fit, a more intelligible universe, to believe that a consequential figure like John Kennedy was taken down by an equally consequential entity, like the CIA, the Mafia, the Soviets, Castro . . . take your pick."

Rita Dallas was the head nurse for Joe Kennedy, paralyzed and speechless. Rose always addressed her formally as "Mrs. Dallas"—at least until November 22. In her book, *The Kennedy Case,* Dallas said that after the assassination, it was at least six months before Rose could call her by name Mrs. Dallas. The word "Dallas" was just too painful.

But Lee Harvey Oswald was an even greater insult than Dallas. He was, as Jackie put it, "a silly little man." And faced with the reality of the silly little man's deed, or at least the inability of anyone to conclusively prove or disprove his guilt, the family and its retainers could only work ever more diligently to burnish the myth of Camelot. They began turning out an endless stream of books like *Johnny We Hardly Knew Ye,* published three years later by JFK aides Kenny O'Donnell and Dave Powers. O'Donnell was the main narrator.

While the book does have its compelling moments, it's essentially the definitive whitewash by two of the late president's aides and part-time pimps.

Scores are settled, the record "corrected" over and over again. On *Profiles in Courage,* "Jack worked on the book day and night." At the 1960 convention in Los Angeles, his hideaway apartment was not a trick pad where he could rendezvous with assorted girlfriends and hookers, but a place where he "would be able to sleep and eat a quiet breakfast." About his plans to dump LBJ from the Democratic ticket and replace him with North Carolina Gov. Terry Sanford—"baseless."

As for the decision not to stay at Frank Sinatra's place in Palm Springs, O'Donnell wrote that "the Sinatra misunderstanding was my fault, not the President's."

(Considering that when O'Donnell wrote those words, no one had yet heard of Judith Campbell, or knew of her ties to the Kennedys and the Mafia, it appears he was doing proactive damage control.)

O'Donnell recounted the story of how the presidential party was moved to Bing Crosby's home. No mention was made of how the abrupt change destroyed Peter Lawford's career, only that "Lawford called me and said, 'Don't you realize Bing Crosby is a Republican?' I said, "I don't care if he's a Red Chinaman—the Secret Service liked his place better than Sinatra's place and that's it."

It would be a few more years before the truth of the Kennedy years would come out, in the Congressional hearings of the mid-1970s. But even then, as the girlfriends were dragged out of the shadows and as the Mafia permanently silenced the Sam Giancanas and the Johnny Rosellis, the Kennedy family loyalists would continue to toe the line.

Damage control. Something King Arthur never had to concern himself while ruling over the original Camelot.

CHAPTER TEN

JACKIE AND BOBBY AND ARI

ARISTOTLE ONASSIS, A GNOME-LIKE, ugly little man, was a collector—of oil tankers, jewelry, airlines, sparkling islands in the Aegean Sea, but most of all, of glamorous women, like Greta Garbo and world-famous opera singer Maria Callas.

And after the assassinations of, first, her husband, and then her brother-in-law who was also her lover, Ari would finally capture the most fabulous prize of all, Jacqueline Bouvier Kennedy. It was a triumph he would come to regret almost immediately.

Jackie Kennedy post-assassination: Glamorous and beloved.

"I thought I was buying a prize cow when I married Jackie," he would later say. "How could I know the cow would cost me $50 million?"

His courtship of Jackie would take years, mostly because the former First Lady, the most admired woman in the world in the mid-sixties—"the Widder," as her own sisters-in-law disparagingly called her—was madly in love with her brother-in-law, Bobby Kennedy. After JFK's death,

Bobby took his place, as Peter Lawford archly told his wife Pat, "in every department."

Not that either Jackie or Bobby were faithful to each other in the four-plus years he had to live after his brother's murder in Dallas. Her paramours included, among others, Marlon Brando, Warren Beatty, Paul Newman, a white-shoe New York lawyer and even, very likely, Peter Lawford, on a vacation to Hawaii with their children. But Bobby and Jackie shared a special bond. They were in love, or as much in love as any two such narcissists could ever hope to be.

As her relative Gore Vidal once said, "The only man Jackie ever loved . . . was Robert Kennedy."

"Jackie and Bobby were as close as you could get," said Charles Spalding, one of JFK's closest friends. "What do I mean by that? Just anything you want to make of it."

So Onassis would have to bide his time. Still, even the thought of his bedding Jackie appalled not just her Kennedy in-laws, but also the American public, most of whom seemed to wholeheartedly believe in the newly created myth of Camelot.

Despite his fabulous wealth, Aristotle Onassis was unspeakably *de classe*. As one of Jackie's gay friends later put it, "He bestrode the world like a maître d'."

Not that such jibes bothered Onassis.

"Everybody here knows three things about Aristotle Onassis," he once explained of the snide remarks from Jackie's Social Register set. "I'm fucking Maria Callas. I'm fucking Jacqueline Kennedy. And I'm fucking rich."

Onassis and the Kennedys had been circling each other warily since at least the early 1950s. Onassis had already made several fortunes, in tobacco, whaling, investments in Monaco. His biggest windfall came in 1946, when, at the age of 40, he had married the 17-year-old daughter of the richest Greek shipping magnate.

In the early 1950s, as an aide to Sen. Joe McCarthy, Bobby Kennedy had immersed himself in an investigation into Greek shipping families who were trading with Communist China. The probe turned up evidence, unrelated to the original investigation, that Onassis had been acquiring American tankers through strawmen, and then illegally using them to transport Saudi oil.

Onassis was indicted by a federal grand jury in New York. He was fingerprinted and forced to pose for a mugshot. He was finally tossed into a holding cell with common criminals, including male prostitutes, muggers and some of the Puerto Rican terrorists who had just shot up Congress.

Ari eventually paid a $7 million fine, which he called a "ransom," and he blamed the 27-year-old Bobby for his humiliation.

"Nobody gave a shit about who owned those tankers until Kennedy started shooting off his big Irish mouth," he told an associate.

Years later, when JFK was planning to run for president in 1960, he keenly realized that one of the major political problems he had to surmount was his father's appeasement of the Nazis while serving as ambassador to London in the late 1930s. He reached out to Winston Churchill, the wartime prime minister of Great Britain. JFK wanted to put to rest any lingering ill will dating back to those years. A meeting between JFK and Churchill was arranged—on Aristotle Onassis's fabulous 325-foot yacht, the *Christina*, named after his beloved daughter.

Onassis, more interested in women than politics, let Churchill and Kennedy talk while he escorted Jackie around the *Christina*, a vessel known not just for its size, but also its breathtaking opulence. If there was any single possession that Onassis owned that indicated the enormity of his wealth, it was the *Christina*, and Jackie was always one to appreciate the smell of money.

Onassis was likewise taken by the 29-year-old future First Lady. He would tell an aide, "There's something damned willful about her, there's something provocative about that lady. She's got a carnal soul."

Three years later, JFK was president. He was planning his second trip to Europe as president. Before joining him, Jackie would be visiting Greece alone. So JFK summoned to the Oval Office the Secret Service who would be handling advance work for the First Lady. It was Clint Hill who, on November 22, 1963, would be climbing onto the trunk of the presidential limousine in Dealey Plaza in Dallas as the president was fatally shot.

On this day, Hill was ushered in to speak to the president and his brother, the attorney general.

"The attorney general and I want to make one thing clear," JFK said, "and that is, whatever you do in Greece, do not let Mrs. Kennedy cross paths with Aristotle Onassis."

"Yes sir, Mr. President," Hill said.

In 1962, Jackie was in Europe again, traveling to the Amalfi Coast of Italy. Again, the president's instructions to Hill were direct:

"I don't want to see photos of her at luncheons with eight different wines in full view of jet-set types lolling around in bikinis. Do what you can to remind her of that. Above all, no nightclub pictures."

In fact, Jack Kennedy's blunt instructions to Hill were tacit proof that Aristotle Onassis's intuitions about Jackie's "carnal soul" were on target. Long before the assassination, she had been frustrated and embarrassed by her husband's prolific philandering and neglect. In the late 1950s Jackie hooked up with Academy Award–winning actor William Holden, whom she met at a party at the home of Hollywood producer Charles Feldman.

Holden had famously starred alongside Gloria Swanson, Joe Kennedy's former mistress, in *Sunset Boulevard*. Holden later revealed to Feldman that he "had to teach Jackie how to [have oral sex]. She told me that Jack had never insisted on that. At first she was very reluctant, but once she got the rhythm of it she couldn't get enough."

Holden added, "If she goes back to Washington and works her magic with Kennedy, he will owe me one."

In 1963, Jackie was pregnant once more. She cancelled her official engagements and forbade White House photographers from shooting her in maternity clothes, believing them to be undignified. Nevertheless, the nation was excited at the prospect of the first baby to be born to the wife of a sitting president in 70 years.

In August, Jackie gave birth prematurely to a son, Patrick Bouvier Kennedy. The infant had serious respiratory problems and was soon transported from Cape Cod to Children's Hospital in Boston. JFK slept on a cot near his newborn son, hoping that the infant would pull through. But the baby slipped into a coma and died the next day.

The president was overcome with grief and appeared closer to his wife than ever before, not that that was saying a lot. The two were photographed holding hands as Jackie left the hospital, and there was talk of a rekindled romance between the pair. But that didn't stop him from making a cross-country trip the next month with Mary Pinchot Meyer, one of his favorite mistresses.

Meanwhile, Jackie was called by her younger sister, Lee Radziwill, who had spent the summer in Greece vacationing with Aristotle Onassis. Though married at the time to a Polish prince, Radziwill had designs on an annulment from her husband in order to marry the far wealthier Onassis.

Gold digging ran deep in the Bouvier genes.

During dinner with Ari, Lee told him how despondent her sister was over the death of her infant son. Sensing the opportunity he'd been waiting for, Ari offered the First Lady the use of his yacht *Christina*.

This time, JFK allowed his wife to join Onassis, though not without some trepidation.

"It's so dicey," he said, referring to Onassis's scandalous relationship with Maria Callas.

In order to quell any perception problems, the president asked Franklin Delano Roosevelt Jr. and his wife to accompany Jackie.

"Your presence will add a little respectability to the whole thing," Jack told FDR's son, who was a former congressman from New York.

The trip lasted two weeks, and was covered intensely by the press. Jackie and Ari were photographed walking hand-in-hand in Smyrna, the Turkish city where he had been born in 1906, and on Onassis's private island, Skorpios. He showered her with extravagant gifts—including a diamond and jewel-encrusted necklace.

When she returned to the States, JFK met her at the airport, children in tow. He seemed to be trying to reconcile with her, as best he could. He asked her to do something she seldom did—accompany him on a political trip, to Dallas.

After JFK was assassinated, Jackie's sister, Lee, invited Onassis to stay at the White House over the weekend before the funeral, as part of her official party. He was one of only a handful of people outside the family who stayed at 1600 Pennsylvania Avenue that bleak weekend when Bobby and Jackie were inseparable. On Sunday night, with the funeral only a few hours off, they all sat down together for one final dinner in the White House.

After a few drinks, Bobby began badgering Ari, as one of his biographers later put it, about his immense wealth. Finally, RFK wrote out an impromptu contract stipulating that Onassis divest himself of half his wealth to help the poor of South America. Bemused by the joke, Onassis signed the document—in Greek.

"Bobby did everything he could to humiliate me," Onassis told a friend, "but I didn't take the bait . . . the more I smiled, the madder he got."

For the moment, Jackie would be Bobby's woman.

In 1964, Jackie moved to New York, buying a 14-room apartment on Fifth Avenue for $200,000. After LBJ refused to make Bobby his running mate, RFK decided to run for the Senate from New York. So he too had to establish a legal residence in the Empire State. Ethel and the always-growing brood mostly remained behind at Hickory Hill and, in the summer, at Hyannis Port.

Bobby bought a large spread on Long Island, but spent most of his time in the family's favorite Manhattan digs, the Carlyle. Secret Service logs would later show Bobby and Jackie occasionally spending the night together at 950 Fifth Avenue—the home of Steve and Jean Kennedy Smith. Jackie and

Bobby and Ethel Kennedy.

Bobby vacationed together in Jamaica, at Montego Bay. They only needed one bedroom.

Kennedy family confidantes, including Pierre Salinger, Arthur Schlesinger, Jack Newfield, Gore Vidal, Truman Capote and Morton Downey Jr. all confirmed that there was a passionate affair between JFK's widow and his grieving brother.

Trusted JFK aide and biographer Schlesinger recalled that during a May 1964 dinner cruise on the presidential yacht, the USS *Sequoia*, RFK and Jackie "exchanged poignant glances" then disappeared below deck, leaving Bobby's wife Ethel upstairs.

"When they returned, they looked as chummy and relaxed as a pair of Cheshire cats," he said.

FDR Jr., the same man who was trusted by JFK to chaperone his wife on her visit to Greece, told C. David Heymann for his book *Bobby and Jackie: A Love Story*:

"Everybody knew about the affair. [RFK and Jackie] carried on like a pair of lovesick teenagers. I suspect Bobby would've liked to dump Ethel and marry Jackie, but of course that wasn't possible."

Ethel implored family friends to urge Bobby to end the affair, but to no avail. It was no surprise that Ethel was aware of the relationship. After all, close family friend Chuck Spalding said "You had to be deaf, dumb, and blind not to see it."

FBI Director J. Edgar Hoover understood the situation. In 1963, in return for Hoover's assistance in ending any Senate investigations of JFK's East German girlfriend, Ellen Rometsch, RFK had signed off on the FBI director's proposal to wiretap and bug civil rights leader Martin Luther King Jr.

Knowing of the attorney general's distaste for the plan, Hoover deliberately kept Bobby uninformed about his findings—until February 22, 1964, when the feds recorded King and several of his cronies in a Los Angeles hotel, boisterously drinking and partying.

At one point, King drunkenly recalled JFK's funeral a few months earlier, and how Jackie had leaned over and kissed the middle of his casket.

"That's what she's going to miss the most!" King told his fellow clergymen.

William Sullivan, Hoover's deputy who later left the Bureau after breaking with the Director, wrote a memoir about his years at the FBI. In his initial book proposal, Sullivan mentioned how King, like Fred Otash and Truman Capote, had questioned the size of JFK's manhood, although he did have some admiration for JFK:

"I believe that man got more poontang than even me!"

Sullivan's publishers did not allow him to include such stories in his book. And there is no way to know if King actually did make such statements, because the FBI's transcripts of the King conversations remain under seal until at the earliest 2027—his 100th birthday.

What is known is that Hoover immediately sent a transcript of the bug to Bobby, who passed it on to Jackie. A few months later, in an oral history of JFK made public in 2011, she told the interviewer, "I just can't see a picture of Martin Luther King without thinking, you know, that man's terrible."

By almost all standards, Jackie remained fabulously wealthy. She inherited about $10 million in two of JFK's trust funds, which threw off about $175,000 a year. Then there was the presidential widow's pension—$10,000 a year, not an inconsiderable sum in 1964.

But it wasn't nearly enough, given her extravagant spending. In the White House years, she spent all of her husband's presidential salary, and then some, on clothes. Only half-facetiously, JFK had asked aides if there was a 12-step program called "Shoppers Anonymous." Now she continued to send many of her outstanding bills to the Kennedy family offices on Park Avenue, and no eyebrows were raised—not yet anyway.

Everyone knew of her relationship with Bobby, including Onassis, who devoted considerable resources into gathering intelligence on matters that were important to him. He began subsidizing Jackie's opulent lifestyle, and at some point, seduced her. But she refused to break off her relationship with Bobby, which infuriated Ari. He was used to getting his way. He once even threatened to "bring down" Bobby by going public about his affair with his widowed sister-in-law.

"I could bury that sucker," he said, "although I'd lose Jackie in the process."

Eventually, he decided that Jackie was worth waiting for. Onassis decided not to leak what he knew to the press.

Despite her apparent love for Bobby, Jackie made no pretense of an exclusive relationship with him. In 1964 she bedded Marlon Brando. In an unpublished first draft of his 1994 memoir *Songs My Mother Taught Me*, Brando recounted how, after a night of much dancing and even more drinking, Jackie seduced him.

"From all I'd read and heard about her," he wrote, "Jacqueline Kennedy seemed coquettish and sensual but not particularly sexual. If anything, I pictured her as more voyeur than player. But that wasn't the case. She kept waiting for me to try to get her into bed. When I failed to make a move, she took matters into her own hands and popped the magic question. 'Would you like to spend the night?' And I said, 'I thought you'd never ask.'"

A week later, the two again rendezvoused at a friend's apartment. Brando described Jackie as having "boyish hips" and a "muscular frame."

"I'm not sure she knew what she was doing sexually, but she did it well."

During RFK's 1968 run for the White House, Jackie used her sexual allure to seduce Paul Newman in an ill-fated attempt to win him over to the Kennedy side. The seduction worked, but the political maneuvering failed. Newman never wavered in his support for Eugene McCarthy.

But her torrid parallel affairs with Bobby Kennedy and Aristotle Onassis dominated her life leading up to 1968, when RFK decided to seek the presidency. Bobby's decision to run came after much debate, and some speculate that the specter of having to give up Jackie weighed on his decision.

Finally, on March 16, 1968, Bobby announced his bid for the Democrat nomination to the White House. The following morning, a "morose" RFK called one of his best friends, *New York Post* columnist Jack Newfield from Jackie's apartment.

October 1967: Sens. Ted and Bobby Kennedy with their father at the World Series in Fenway Park.

"If I had to hazard a guess," Newfield recalled, "I'd say this must have been their last romantic occasion together."

Jackie had inherited JFK's cottage in the family compound at Hyannis Port. In April, during that final campaign, she and Bobby and the rest of the family had gathered for a rare weekend off the trail. That Sunday, Bobby went to early Mass, and returned with the Sunday papers. He gathered the family together and read them the stories about how the polls seemed to be turning in his favor.

"Looks like we're going to make it!" he announced, and the assembled Kennedys began cheering.

"Oh Bobby!" Jackie cooed. "Won't it be wonderful when we get back in the White House!"

Ethel, the scorned woman, fixed her with an icy glare.

"What do you mean, 'we?'" she said.

In her memoirs, Joe Kennedy's nurse Rita Dallas recalled, "Jacqueline Kennedy looked as if she'd been struck. She flinched as though a blow had actually stung her cheek. I'll always remember the look of pain in Jackie's eyes."

After Bobby apparently broke off his physical relationship with Jackie as too risky, Aristotle Onassis sensed that his time had finally come. He was soon looming over Jackie, proposing marriage. But the Kennedy family went to work to convince her that even the announcement of such an engagement would be devastating to RFK's already long-shot prospects.

A delegation of Kennedy women, led incredibly by Ethel, as well as Joan Kennedy, pleaded with Jackie not to irreparably damage the Kennedy brand. Then Bobby arrived to make his own pitch:

"For God's sake, Jackie," he told her, "this could cost me five states."

Jackie relented and promised not to marry Onassis until after the election.

RFK wasn't just concerned over the ramifications for his campaign. He was jealous.

"She'll marry that man over my dead body," he told Pierre Salinger.

Like so many, Jackie had a premonition of what lay ahead.

"Do you know what will happen to Bobby?" she asked Arthur Schlesinger Jr. "The same thing that happened to Jack."

On June 5, 1968, after winning the California primary, Bobby Kennedy ducked out of a ballroom at the Ambassador Hotel in Los Angeles. He was on his way to a victory party at Peter Lawford's trendy new nightspot, the Factory.

But a Palestinian immigrant was waiting for him. Sirhan Sirhan fired six shots at Bobby at point-blank range. Brain dead, RFK was kept on life support as the family rushed to his beside. When Jackie arrived, Ethel allowed them time alone together.

Ari Onassis waited for bulletins from his suite at the Pierre Hotel in New York.

"Someone was going to fix the little bastard sooner or later," he reportedly said. He also ordered his aide Johnny Meyer to provide him with updates about Kennedy's condition.

In his biography of Ari, Peter Evans wrote: "Onassis told him to call as soon as Kennedy was dead—'as if he wanted to know the result of the four o'clock race at Santa Anita,' Meyer later said."

"He ain't gonna make it, Ari," Meyer reported.

"Call me the minute he don't," the tycoon replied.

Two days later, it was Jackie, not his wife or surviving brother Ted, who signed the legal documents to end RFK's life support.

"I guess the kid had everything but the luck," Onassis told Meyer.

Bobby's assassination sent Jackie into another tailspin. She told Pierre Salinger "I hate this country . . . I despise America and I don't want my children to live here anymore. If they're killing Kennedys, my kids are number one targets. I want to get out."

According to Roswell Gilpatric, who served in the Kennedy Administration and also dated Jackie, "She had just lost the source of her safety and strength. Within less than five years, she'd lost her husband and then the man who very possibly had been the love of her life."

Onassis saw it a different way: "At last, Jackie's free of the Kennedys."

Onassis provided Jackie with the opportunity to immediately have the three things she wanted most: money, security for her children, and an escape from the United States. Just four months after the murder of Bobby, she married the Greek magnate. But the preparations didn't go smoothly.

One problem was that Onassis's beloved children, Christina and Alexander, didn't like Jackie. They regarded her as nothing more than a gold digger.

"It's a perfect match," Alexander said. "My father likes names and Jackie likes money."

Once Jackie remarried, she would automatically lose the money she received from the Kennedy family trust. She would also forfeit her widow's pension from the federal government. So suitable financial arrangements had to be worked out before Onassis could claim the ultimate trophy.

The person to whom Jackie turned to iron out the dollars-and-cents deal was her brother-in-law Ted.

Ted's role in the negotiations was particularly ironic, given that, according to most accounts, he was the third of the Kennedy brothers to bed Jackie. Jackie's distant relative, Gore Vidal, remarked that after Bobby was murdered, Ted and Jackie had a sexual relationship and "made a bond sealed not with blood, but with something even more personal—sex. I call it the devil's pact. It involved the ongoing promotion of the legend of Camelot, not the reality of the Kennedy administration."

Teddy arrived on Onassis's Skorpios Island to negotiate the financial terms of the marriage. Seeing him up close for the first time, Christina Onassis was disgusted.

She saw Teddy's mission for what it was. He was negotiating the purchase price for Jackie. Christina was also repulsed by Ted's "heavy drinking and girl-grabbing revels."

Whereas once the Kennedy and Auchincloss families would have been appalled at Ari's philistine ways, it was now the Onassis family noting the unseemly behavior of the Kennedys.

Aristotle Onassis was on his best behavior as he prepared for his meeting with the Kennedy delegation.

"It was obviously one of Onassis' best-staged evenings of his life," a leading Greek journalist told the BBC. "And the purpose of the glamour was that he was in love with the idea of stealing the first lady of the United States."

That same journalist briefly imagined he had a major scoop when he photographed Teddy with an attractive young blonde woman who was definitely not Joan. Somebody on the *Christina* told the journalist that Onassis had flown in the blonde from Sweden "as a gift" for him.

Ari had obviously done his research—he understood the Kennedys' fondness for whores. But the story and the photographs never appeared in print. Onassis's security staff had the reporter detained for a night at the local police station. When he was released in the morning, the journalist discovered that both his office and his apartment had been ransacked.

All his photographs of Ted had disappeared. Though his newspaper published his article detailing the romance between Onassis and Jackie Kennedy, all references to Ted Kennedy had been excised.

A year later, after Chappaquiddick, the Nixon White House would ask J. Edgar Hoover to check out rumors that Teddy had been accompanied to Greece by Mary Jo Kopechne. For once, the rumors apparently turned out not to be true.

Two months later, in October 1968, following prolonged prenuptial negotiations, Jacqueline Kennedy married Aristotle Onassis on Skorpios. Jackie's take was a premarital contract that awarded her $3 million in tax-free bonds. Meanwhile, her wedding gift to her new husband was considered by many to be either tasteless or bizarre: a watch that had once belonged to JFK. It was as if Onassis was collecting the late president's personal possessions as a dowry.

Not only was the marriage upsetting to the Onassis children, it caused a rift between Jackie and her sister Lee Radziwill. Though she was aware of Lee's desire to leave her husband for Onassis, Jackie had kept her engagement to Ari secret from her sister. Radziwill learned of it not from Jackie, but from Ari.

"How could she do this to me?" she reportedly asked Truman Capote.

Public reaction was no better. There were rumors that Jackie would be excommunicated from the Roman Catholic Church. Richard Cardinal Cushing of Boston, that great friend of the family, rushed to her defense, creating such a stir among the faithful in Massachusetts that he was forced to retire two years early.

The pairing seemed unusual at best—a young, beautiful, stylish woman escorted by a rumpled, swarthy, uncouth, dodgy foreigner. She was 39, he was 62. Even without high heels, she towered over him. It was the ultimate trophy-wife scenario played out while the nation was still reeling from the murders of two Kennedy brothers in less than five years.

Even though the family knew the marriage was in the works, it still came as a shock.

"Oh shit," sighed her brother-in-law, Steve Smith.

The only Kennedy in favor of the union was Rose Kennedy, because, as George Smathers pointed out, "She was tired of paying all those bills!"

It wouldn't take long for the ruthless shipping baron to realize his folly. Just 48 hours after marrying her, he told former Olympic Airways chairman and close friend Yannis Georgakis, "I've made some terrible mistakes in my life, but marrying Jackie might take the biscuit."

Finances and fame aside, the couple was a poor match. Jackie told her jet-set pals that Ari was a "loner." In fact he did have friends, oilmen mostly. It was just that Jackie considered them parvenus, philistines. They were boring, she said.

Columnist Jack Anderson reported that when a top executive of the British Petroleum oil company brought his wife to vacation on Skorpios, Mrs. Onassis ignored them and instead watched movies by herself every night. When a Mobil Oil executive came to dinner, she refused to go, inventing an illness for JFK Jr. that kept her away.

According to Anderson, Jackie complained frequently about her new husband, and thought his tastes "vulgar." On one occasion, she was wearing an ostentatious diamond Ari had given her when one of the Beautiful People she counted as among her closest friends arrived.

"What is *that?*" her friend hooted.

Jackie was accustomed to being worshipped for her sense of style. Her friend's reaction left her "mortified."

Ari was now seeing Jackie in a different light. Things that he had overlooked during their mad courtship suddenly grated, now that she was his wife, and they were living together, sort of. He was appalled at the way Jackie was raising her children. Too permissive, he thought. And their clothes—trashy!

Worse, Onassis found Jackie's friends too effete and jaded for his tastes. Anderson reported that he would often refer to them as "faggots," loudly, with little concern about who overheard him.

Jackie finally had the financial security she had always dreamed of. It went to her head. Back in New York, she hired and fired household help on a whim—19 chefs alone in four years, one of whom only lasted four days at her co-op at 1040 Park Avenue. Onassis's biographer reported this exchange between Jackie and her housekeeper.

"That new maid, get rid of her."

"But why, Mrs. Onassis? She seems efficient."

"She has a sad face," Jackie said. "She depresses me."

What grated most on Aristotle Onassis was Jackie's prodigal spending. In a single shopping expedition, she bought 200 pairs of shoes at a cost of $60,000. At first, Ari tolerated her lavish lifestyle.

"God knows Jackie has had her years of sorrow," Onassis once said. "If she enjoys it, let her buy to her heart's content."

But Onassis vastly underestimated what her heart's content would cost him. In her biography, *Jackie O!*, Kitty Kelley reported that Jackie's face served as her credit card. She simply had to present goods at any haute couture salon and all bills would be sent directly to Onassis. At one point, it was estimated that she was spending up to $3,000 per minute on some of her shopping sprees.

Onassis was stunned. He told friends he never saw his new wife wearing anything except jeans. At age 39, Jackie had begun taking birth-control pills, but she was wearing flannel nightclothes to bed. Finally, Ari demanded that she at least wear some sexier lingerie. She sent a bra and panties to the designer Halston and asked him to work his magic.

Halston recalled the conversation.

"I said, 'Something very Marilyn Monroe?' Remember, at the time none of us knew anything about Jack Kennedy and Marilyn Monroe. There was this silence, and then she said, 'She didn't wear any.'"

In the end, Halston billed Ari $5,000 for the custom-made satin lingerie.

While Onassis disapproved of Jackie's handling of her own children, he was also displeased with the lack of effort that she put into establishing a strong bond with his two children, who still continued to resent her expensive intrusion into their father's life.

In early 1973, their relationship would deteriorate still further when Ari lost his beloved son Alexander in a private plane crash at the Athens airport.

Alexander's death plunged Onassis into a deep depression. He began to brood that the crash was not an accident. He came to believe that his enemies had had a hand in the death of his only son.

Ari's grief was too real for his trophy wife to assuage, so he turned to the woman who was in fact his true love, Maria Callas. More and more, she would be photographed with him. Unlike Jackie, she didn't seem to have a problem with the paparazzi. They were even photographed kissing under a tree.

Comforted by the presence of Callas but haunted by the loss of Alexander, Ari grew ever more disenchanted with Jackie. More than ever, her extravagant spending became a major issue. He cut her budget by 33 percent and became enraged when she pushed him to build a house in Acapulco.

On one occasion, after seeing ledgers and bills for the clothes that Jackie had purchased from the swankiest design houses in Paris, he complained, "What does she do with all those clothes?"

In fact, in many instances, she was sending the clothes back to New York to be sold at second-hand shops, consignment stores and auction houses in Manhattan. She was pocketing the cash, sometimes as much as a million dollars a year, tax free.

It was an obsession of hers. She had a phobia about ending up like so many of her Bouvier kin—destitute, or close to it.

Living hand to mouth like her relatives in a dilapidated old mansion in Newport, with whole wings shut off to save on heating and electricity—it was just too horrible a fate even to contemplate. So she would buy another $200,000 worth of gowns in Paris, ship them back to New York and net another $100,000.

At least at first, divorce seemed out of the question. Ari had his ways of getting back at her. In November 1972, he arranged for the paparazzi to be in place in the waters off Skorpios as Jackie sunbathed in the nude. The photos, with their full-frontal nudity, ran in men's magazines around the world.

In Italy, one headline read: "THE BILLION DOLLAR BUSH."

"The Widder," as the Kennedy women still called her, was no longer above reproach. She became involved in an acrimonious lawsuit with one of the paparazzi, Ron Galella. It was a no-win situation, particularly after she presented Ari with legal bills of $400,000.

More ominously, in 1973 the *New York Times* ran a front-page expose of Dr. Max Jacobson, "Dr. Feelgood," who had continued to supply her with illicit drugs all these years.

Frantic, she called Chuck Spalding, Jack's old friend who had introduced both of them to his magic elixirs. Spalding escorted Dr. Feelgood to 1040 Park Avenue, then excused himself. Jacobson told her he was broke, and reminded her that JFK had always promised to take care of him. She assured Jacobson that the check would be in the mail, and he left feeling relieved. The money never arrived, and his medical license was revoked in April 1975. But he never went public about his most glamorous client.

In November 1973, Jackie was a guest at the wedding in Georgetown of Bobby's oldest daughter, Kathleen, to David Townsend. On her way out, she shot "an icy glare" in the direction of another glamorous guest, Angie Dickinson, her husband's late-night date on Inauguration Day 12 years earlier.

By then, Ari had had enough. They argued about everything, including their children. Jackie fretted that her son might become a "fruit," a concern Truman Capote later described as her "homosexual panic." She informed Ari that he had passed on his boorish manners onto his sole surviving child, Christina.

"No man finds a fat girl with food on her chin attractive," she said. "No matter how rich she is."

Ari now described her behavior to anyone who would listen as "bloodletting." He decided to file for divorce. His choice for an attorney to handle the matter was Joe McCarthy's pit bull, Roy Cohn, who had had such an acrimonious relationship with Bobby Kennedy in Washington two decades earlier. His health already in steep decline, Onassis asked Cohn what Jackie's silence might cost him.

"That's going to depend," Cohn said, "on what you want her to be silent about."

Kathleen Kennedy, goddaughter of Sen. Joe McCarthy, at Peabody City Hall in 1972. Left is Cong. Mike Harrington of Salem, another scandal-plagued Massachusetts Democrat.

"Well," said Ari with a sigh, "I've lived an interesting life."

Cohn plotted a preemptive strike. He called the columnist Jack Anderson and offered to provide him with evidence of Jackie's multimillion-dollar designer-clothes grift. Cohn, Anderson and Ari had lunch in Manhattan, then repaired to Ari's new 51-story Olympic Airlines Towers on Fifth Avenue, where Onassis showed Anderson the stacks and stacks of bills.

"I was shocked," Anderson said.

But before Anderson could get the story into print, Onassis was dead. When he was hospitalized in Paris, on his deathbed, Jackie spent a final 10 minutes with him, then rushed out to the salon of Emanuel Ungaro to buy more gowns, which she had shipped back to New York for immediate resale.

Ari died on March 15, 1975. Jackie's first call was to Teddy—he would be negotiating her final payout, her severance, so to speak. The second call was to Valentino, the designer. She needed a black funeral gown, and this one she would have to wear before reselling it.

Ari was buried on his beloved island of Skorpios. In the funeral procession, Teddy rode in the same limousine as Christina Onassis. Booze on his breath as always, Teddy leaned over and told her, "Now it's time to take care of Jackie."

Christina began screaming at the driver to stop the car. She jumped out and ran up ahead to the limousine carrying her grieving aunts.

"I didn't need that big walrus sloshing around in my pool and telling me to do right by Jackie," she said later of Teddy.

A day later, Jackie was photographed at one of Paris's most exclusive hair salons, laughing. A few months later, her former brother-in-law, Stas Radziwill, died in London. Jackie was photographed at his funeral, this time with a look of real grief, not relief, etched on her face.

By that time Teddy had negotiated the final settlement—about $26 million, according to most accounts. That August, Jackie would have her first date with Maurice Tempelsman, the wealthy married diamond merchant who would so adroitly manage the millions she had taken from her second husband during their six unhappy years together.

No one who knew Jackie well was really surprised by what had happened. She had never made a secret of her lust for cash. It was one of the reasons she had gotten along so well with her father-in-law Joe Kennedy.

Years earlier, he had told her how he had given each of his children a million dollars on their 21st birthdays.

"I did this," he told her, "so they could be independent and turn around and tell me to go to hell, if they want."

"Do you know what I would tell you if you gave me a million dollars" she asked her father-in-law. "I would tell you to give me another million."

CHAPTER ELEVEN

"HAS ANYONE SEEN TED'S PANTS?"

THE KENNEDYS ARE NOTORIOUSLY thin-skinned. In the 1980s, as Ted Kennedy's weight ballooned, one columnist for the Rupert Murdoch–owned *Boston Herald* began referring to him in print as "Fat Boy." It was the last straw for Kennedy, who had long been vexed by Murdoch's media.

A few months later, in a late-night Senate session, Teddy had one of his Democrat colleagues attach a rider to a budget bill. It was designed to force the Australian press baron to divest himself of either the *Herald* and the *New York Post,* or his two TV stations in Boston and New York. (He sold the Boston TV station and the *Post,* both of which he eventually bought back.)

Over the years, however, the Kennedys have sometimes been required to make jokes about themselves. In 1957, running for the presidency, JFK was invited to speak at the National Press Club's annual dinner. His father convened a panel of DC insiders to write Jack's material.

His most memorable line came when he pulled a "telegram" from his breast pocket that JFK explained had come from his father. He read instructions to buy the election, but not a landslide. Joe's purported line was to spend enough to win—"but not a penny more."

That mild joke was recounted endlessly in the run-up to the 1960 election, perhaps because the junior senator was not known, at least until the posthumous hagiographies began appearing, for his humor.

Indeed, the family was better known for its cantankerous relationship with anyone who dared question their place in the political pantheon.

But the Kennedys had little to worry about, either from probing journalists or from comedians. It was a different, more worshipful era. So it was quite a surprise in 1962 when a 26-year-old standup comic with roots in both Massachusetts and Maine put out a gently mocking record album called *The First Family*.

The comic's name was Vaughn Meader, and within two weeks in the fall of 1962, he had sold 1.2 million records, with radio stations playing his bits about JFK's rocking chairs, touch football and other such harmless, mild subjects. How bad could it have been—he was invited onto the TV variety show of Kennedy family retainer Andy Williams, and he filmed an episode of the sitcom starring Joey Bishop—one of the lesser members of the Rat Pack.

JFK had different reactions at different times, but Jackie Kennedy instantly detested Vaughn Meader. At one point, Arthur Schlesinger, the administration's token egghead, was given the assignment of seeing what could be done to make him go away.

By November 22, 1963, sales of *The First Family* were up to 7.5 million, and the follow-up album had climbed as high as number four on the album charts. But the assassination ended Meader's career as certainly as it ended JFK's life.

That night, comedian Lenny Bruce, who himself had less than two years to live, refused to cancel his performance. He went on stage and his first words were, "Boy, is Vaughn Meader fucked!"

Indeed he was.

The Joey Bishop episode in which Vaughn Meader appeared was not just filed away, the film was actually destroyed. All copies of both albums were recalled, and it was impossible to buy a new copy until a double CD was issued in 1999. Vaughn Meader attempted other showbiz ventures, but nothing ever clicked for him again.

He eventually retreated back to Maine, dying in 2004 at age 70.

In the first few years after JFK's assassination, the family was off limits for comedy and satire, or even moderately critical reporting.

That worshipful coverage began to change with the controversy over William Manchester's authorized book about the assassination. Jackie demanded wholesale deletions of what she considered unflattering references to herself, her husband and the family, dragging RFK into the fray.

As the war in Vietnam escalated, and as the draft loomed more and more ominously for young American males, a "counterculture" developed, complete with an alternative press that did not share the mainstream media's reverence for the powers that be, or had been.

One such new medium was a weekly called *The Realist*, published by Paul Krassner, a self-described "investigative satirist." As the leaks detailing the excised portions of Manchester's book continued, Krassner decided to go with his own front-page story, headlined "The Parts That Were Left Out of the Kennedy Book."

To establish a faux credibility, Krassner resurrected some of JFK's semi-forgotten, now unmentionable scandals (such as the photos of him fleeing his girlfriend Pamela Turnure's apartment in 1958). At the very end of the piece Krassner dropped his made-up bombshell, although he distanced himself a bit from it, attributing these words to "Manchester":

"This writer conceives (it) to be delirium, but (this is what) Mrs. Kennedy insists she actually saw."

Today it would be called "fake news." In 1967, however, many believed that Jackie was actually being quoted in *The Realist* about what she saw LBJ doing in Air Force One on the flight from Dallas back to Washington:

"That man was crouching over the corpse . . . And I realized—there is only one way to say this—he was literally fucking my husband in the throat. In the bullet wound in the front of the throat. He reached a climax and dismounted. I froze. The next thing I remember he was being sworn in as the new President."

Then Krassner included, in italics, "marginal author's notes: Check with (Warren Commission counsel Lee) Rankin: did secret autopsy show semen in throat wound?"

The shit hit the fan. In Cambridge, police confiscated copies of *The Realist*. Lawsuits were threatened. Many people, even in government, apparently believed the story—"maybe because I just wanted to believe it so badly," Krassner quoted Daniel Ellsberg as telling him.

A San Francisco talk-show host asked Krassner why he'd done it.

"To separate the men from the boys," he answered.

Not even RFK's assassination could restore the family's Teflon image. Jackie's marriage that fall to Aristotle Onassis led to a torrent of shocked headlines, and then the next summer came Chappaquiddick. Suddenly nothing was off limits.

Comedian Bob Hope was reported to have cracked up Vice President Spiro T. Agnew with a joke about RFK's last words to his younger brother Ted: "Mary Jo Kopechne fucks!"

After Chappaquiddick, the monthly magazine *National Lampoon*, a slicker countercultural vehicle than *The Realist*, ran a full-page parody of a Volkswagen magazine ad pointing out the Beetle's waterproof manufacture.

Only the headline on the ad copy had been changed: "If Ted Kennedy drove a Volkswagen, he'd be president today."

Volkswagen threatened to sue. *National Lampoon* pulled the issue from the shelves.

In 1982, Teddy was running for his fourth full term, just two years after his disastrous presidential run. Republicans smelled blood. They produced a comic book attacking Teddy, "Every Family Has One," meaning, a black sheep. Teddy had been expecting a TV onslaught like the one that came from the National Conservative PAC (NCPAC), which in 1980

Volkswagen threatened to sue the National Lampoon *over this parody ad that spoofed* Chappaquiddick.

helped Republicans take over the
U.S. Senate for the first time since
1954. His representatives had indi-
rectly threatened to sue TV stations
running any such spots, but they
never anticipated . . . a comic book.

It came out of DC, produced
by veteran conservative cartoon-
ist Dick Hafer under the auspices
of "Citizens Organized to Replace
Kennedy"—CORK. More than
a million black-and-white copies
were distributed in Massachusetts.

*Satirical 1982 comic book about Teddy's
scandalous record.*

"Every Family Has One" was
quite well done, with Teddy alter-
nately portrayed as the black sheep,
or a rotund, florid, lecherous old hack. Every charge against him was
footnoted. The comic book asked embarrassing questions about, among
other things, his driving record, his support of forced busing in Boston,
and government-controlled health care: "Would your license have been
revoked? . . . Have Teddy's children gone to public schools? . . . Would
Teddy's family go down to the government clinic and take a number?
And wait their turn? After you?"

With the usual assist from the *Boston Globe,* which revealed that
his businessman opponent had once been a member of the John Birch
Society, Teddy was reelected easily, but the satire genie couldn't be put
back in the bottle.

After JFK's White House liaisons with Marilyn Monroe and Judith
Campbell Exner came to light in the 1970s, even the late president was
no longer off limits.

Sam Kinison, a latter-day Lenny Bruce (like Bruce, he would die
at age 39, in 1992), developed a bit that was for a time a staple on FM
rock radio, heavily edited, to adhere to the FCC's ban on certain pro-
scribed words:

"My favorite president, John F. Kennedy," Kinison's routine began. "Charming guy, great president. Fucked Marilyn Monroe. President of the United States and fucked Marilyn Monroe. What do you want?!... You'd have been just like JFK... lookin' out at the Washington Monument going, 'You know, it doesn't get much better than this, does it? President of the United States. Dick in Marilyn Monroe. My finger on the fucking button, telling the fucking Russians to get their missiles out of Cuba in 12 hours. It doesn't get any better than this!'"

Teddy tried to keep the Camelot myth alive, but his own behavior increasingly belied it. In a memorable *Saturday Night Live* skit just before the 1988 election, "Ted Kennedy" made a cameo appearance, trying to pick up the wife of the Democratic presidential nominee, Mike Dukakis.

But it wasn't until 1991, after the sordid details of the family drinking binges in Palm Beach that ended with the indictment of William

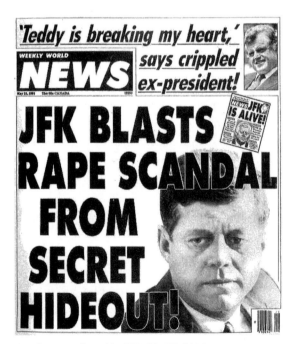

Spoof supermarket tabloid Weekly World News, *1991.*

Kennedy Smith for rape, that the Kennedys became a full-fledged national laughing-stock.

Some of the most devastating material came from David Letterman's, *Late Show* on CBS. For weeks, Letterman used the torrent of information coming out of the courthouse in West Palm Beach as source material of his Top 10 lists. The more embarrassing the information—the booze, Teddy's pants (or lack thereof)—the more likely it was to become a recurring Letterman theme.

On April 30, 1991, the Top 10 topic was "Good Things About Ted Kennedy."

"10. Not the kind of guy who snobbishly insists on wearing pants."

"6. Ate his own weight in McRibs before limited time offer expired."

"1. Every time he gets away with something, it drives Nixon nuts."

On May 24, Letterman unveiled "Ted Kennedy's Top 10 Party Tips."

"7. Make sure cocktail napkins have liability waivers on back."

"5. Mix Chivas & Slim-Fast—get drunk and lose weight."

"2. Billy Dee Williams was right. Colt 45."

"1. Take off pants. Mingle."

On July 23, it was time for "Top 10 Things Overheard at Rose Kennedy's 101st Birthday Party."

"6. 'Anybody seen Ted's pants?'"

"2. The Chivas truck is here!"

Teddy probably hoped his marriage to Victoria Reggie might take at least some of the heat off. Instead, it provided more fodder. On March 17, 1992, Letterman ran with the "Top 10 Reasons Ted Kennedy Will Make a Good Husband."

"1. Has phone numbers of hundreds of babysitters."

By 1995, Teddy had faded a bit from the headlines. Yet he could always make a cameo appearance on one of Letterman's lists, like "Top 10 Reasons You Know You're on a Bad Date."

"No. 2: He's drunk, he's all hands and he brags about beating Mitt Romney."

Until his final illness, Ted would remain a staple of late-night comics. A long droning State of the Union Address? "Halfway through, Ted Kennedy sent drinks over to the Bush twins." (Letterman)

Ted endorses John Kerry for president. "I'm wondering, do you really want the endorsement of a guy with a Bloody Mary mustache." (Letterman)

The *National Enquirer* reports (and later retracts) that Ted has a 21-year-old "love child" on Cape Cod. "Apparently, Kennedy isn't denying the report, but the kid is." (Conan O'Brien)

Kennedy calls for the resignation of Defense Secretary Donald Rumsfeld. "This marks the first time Kennedy has ever come out against anything with rum in it." (O'Brien)

President George W. Bush attends ceremony renaming the U.S. Justice Department building after Robert F. Kennedy. "Then he went around the corner and named a strip club after Ted." (Jay Leno)

"Declassified papers report that John Kennedy was taking eight different medications a day. He was so wasted, his Secret Service code name was Ted Kennedy." (Craig Kilborn)

During the Supreme Court confirmation hearings for Samuel Alito, Teddy attacked the conservative jurist (getting his name wrong, naturally, apparently confusing him with a former mayor of San Francisco named Alioto). One of Ted's accusations was that "Alioto" had once belonged to a club that didn't allow women.

Jay Leno on *The Tonight Show* cracked: "(Then) it was discovered that Sen. Kennedy also once belonged to a club that wouldn't allow women. Of course, with Kennedy those were club rules in place purely for the safety of women."

Q. "Why does a Kennedy always have red eyes after sex?"

A. "Mace."

In the late 1990s, as the lives of Bobby's older sons unraveled, a series of ice cream jokes made the rounds in Boston. One recalled how Joe Kennedy had paralyzed Pam Kelley in that 1973 Jeep accident on Nantucket.

Q. What is Joe Kennedy's favorite ice cream?

A. Fudge cripple.

In those days, Patrick Kennedy was unmarried. His favorite ice cream flavor was said to be "Tutti Frutti."

Michael Kennedy was being investigated for having sex with his underage babysitter. The joke was that he preferred a scoop of "statutory grape."

Sometimes scandals could be melded together. In 1997, Joe Kennedy badly burned one of his twins with illegal fireworks. So what was Michael Kennedy's favorite type of fireworks?

A cherry bomb.

Even as the scandal faded into the past, Chappaquiddick remained the ultimate punchline for Kennedy jokes. When the anti-nuke movement gathered strength after Three Mile Island, this bumper sticker appeared: "More People Have Died in Ted Kennedy's Car Than in Nuclear Accidents."

When Vice President Dick Cheney wounded another hunter on a 2006 quail hunt, another variation on the Chappaquiddick joke appeared: "I'd Rather Go Hunting with Dick Cheney Than Driving with Ted Kennedy."

Teddy died in 2009, and seven years later a Hollywood producer announced that he was going to make a film about Chappaquiddick, from the point of view not of Mary Jo, but of Ted.

"You'll see," the producer said, "what he had to go through."

He wasn't the first to express interest in such a Chappaquiddick project, but none of them have ever come to fruition. This time, on at least one talk radio show in Boston, listeners were asked to come up with their own titles for the new Chappaquiddick film. Many reworked titles associated with his older brother Jack. *PT 109* would become *PT 9-1-1*. From *Profiles in Courage* to *Profiles in Cognac*. The death car was a 1967 Oldsmobile Delmont, so one caller suggested *The Full Delmonty*. Since Martha's Vineyard is in Dukes County, another offered, *The Bridges of Dukes County*.

Here are a few more of the suggested titles for the Chappaquiddick movie:

- *Dude, Where's My Car?*
- *The Man from C.H.I.V.A.S.*
- *Ice Cube Station Zebra*
- *The Drowning Fool*
- *Sponge Ted No Pants*
- *A Bridge Too Far (possible sequel: A Bridge Au Bar)*

- *20,000 Beers Under the Sea*
- *Drowning Miss Daisy*
- *Grumpy Olds Man*
- *He's Just Not That into You*
- *Dial T for Murder*
- *In Golden Tidal Pond*

Meanwhile, on the anniversary of Ted Kennedy's death every August 25, hundreds if not thousands of tweets go out along the same lines: "Ted Kennedy celebrates his (fill in the blank) year of sobriety."

CHAPTER TWELVE

THE OTHER KENNEDYS

F ROM 1954 TO 1960, the junior senator from Massachusetts was John F. Kennedy of Boston.

From 1953 to 1960, the elected treasurer of the Commonwealth of Massachusetts was John F. Kennedy of Boston.

The difference: The senator was John Fitzgerald Kennedy, the treasurer was John Francis Kennedy.

There was another difference: John Fitzgerald Kennedy's next job was president of the United States. John Francis Kennedy's next job after leaving office was as the live-in manager of an apartment building in St. Petersburg, FL.

The other JFK is almost totally forgotten now. But the lesson of his political career is that having the last name Kennedy is a good thing in Massachusetts politics, even if you're not a "real" Kennedy.

John Francis Kennedy won three two-year terms as the treasurer and receiver general of the Commonwealth of Massachusetts. Not bad for a guy whose previous employment was in the stock room of the Gillette razor factory in South Boston.

State Treasurer and Receiver General John F. Kennedy.

But he had the right name. John Francis Kennedy, as George Washington Plunkitt of Tammany Hall would have said, seen his opportunities and he took 'em.

When the real JFK was beginning his political career in 1945, Mayor James Michael Curley pronounced his verdict.

"How can he lose? Two of the great names—Kennedy and Fitzgerald."

John Fitzgerald Kennedy. But almost as good was . . . John Francis Kennedy. He won three statewide elections, the same number as John Fitzgerald Kennedy.

Down through the decades, the name Kennedy has paid off for a number of winners in the lucky-surname lottery in Massachusetts. And the farther down the ballot the name appears, the more likely it is that the Massachusetts voters will be fooled.

Of course, history has shown that it doesn't take much to baffle a Massachusetts voter. Just look at the office of state treasurer even before John Francis Kennedy's first election in 1954.

In 1920, the incumbent Republican treasurer, someone named Burrill, resigned. To replace him, the legislature elected a state rep named Burrell.

Then came the Hurleys. Democrat Charles Hurley was elected in 1930, and re-elected to two more two-year terms. Term-limited, he ran for governor and won. Charles Hurley was succeeded as treasurer by a Republican named William Hurley, who defeated a Democrat named James Hurley.

Republican Hurley served six years and was succeeded by Francis X. Hurley, who served his three terms and was in turn succeeded in 1944 by John Hurley.

By 1952, the last of the Hurleys had resigned to become a court clerk (no term limits to worry about there). John Fitzgerald Kennedy was running for the Senate, so John Francis Kennedy figured his time had come.

He lost that first time out, but then, in 1954, the office was open again, and John Francis Kennedy won.

John Francis Kennedy bragged that he never spent more than $200 on a campaign. He insisted, apparently with a straight face, that "not more than 5 percent" of the population confused him with the other JFK.

But in 1960, he was term-limited, like all those Hurleys before him. So John F. Kennedy ran for governor in the same year John F. Kennedy ran for president.

He finished third in the Democrat primary. Another lesson: you can fool some of the people all of the time, but you can't fool all of the people all of the time. Even in Massachusetts.

Running to succeed John F. Kennedy as treasurer were John M. Kennedy of Boston and John B. Kennedy of Boston. But they were defeated by a state rep from Dorchester named John Driscoll.

Two years later, in 1962, John F. Kennedy attempted to win back his old job. John B. Kennedy ran again as well, meaning that there were two John Kennedys on the ballot for treasurer. But incumbent John

Treasurer Kennedy, right, with Attorney General Edward McCormack. In the middle is Governor's Councilor Iron Mike Favulli, who would later go to prison.

Driscoll prevailed, meaning that he has the distinction of being the only politician in Massachusetts to have defeated three different John Kennedys, four times.

In 1966, there was a new treasurer, Robert Q. Crane. He had gotten his former colleagues in the legislature to remove the three-term limit, and had also had the two-year terms changed to four years. Suddenly, the job was even more attractive than when John F. Kennedy had held it.

The temptation was too great. John Francis Kennedy ran for treasurer for the sixth time. But now he was really pushing his luck—John Fitzgerald Kennedy had been dead almost three years. He lost, again, giving him a lifetime 3–3 record running for treasurer.

That was when John F. Kennedy decided to move to Florida.

One thing about the "real" Kennedys, though: once they win an office, they consider that it is their own personal property. They may allow someone else to hold it as a seat-warmer for a while, but eventually, one of them will very likely circle back around to claim it for himself once more.

Before his stroke, Joe Kennedy insisted that Teddy run for Jack Kennedy's old Senate seat in 1962—"that's our seat, I paid for it!"

Even though Ted was a "real" Kennedy, the fact that he was running on his name alone infuriated his main opponent, Attorney General Eddie McCormack. That McCormack himself was the beneficiary of the same surname as the Speaker of the U.S. House, his uncle John McCormack, did not seem to register with him. Of course, he had served both as AG and earlier on the Boston City Council.

In their televised primary debate, McCormack lost his temper and began pointing at Teddy, sternly telling him, "If your name were Edward Moore, your candidacy would be a joke!"

Which was true of course. But it didn't matter. Teddy defeated McCormack easily, and then defeated a Republican named George Lodge, the son and grandson of Republican senators from Massachusetts. But their names no longer counted for as much as "Kennedy," as Ted's campaign slogan that year made clear:

"He Can Do More for Massachusetts."

Edward McCormack: "If your name were Edward Moore, your candidacy would be a joke . . ."

Teddy's 1962 slogan: "He Can Do More for Massachusetts."

Congressman John F. Kennedy was succeeded in 1952 by Massachusetts House Speaker Thomas P. "Tip" O'Neill. Thirty-four years later, Tip was retiring as speaker of the U.S. House, and suddenly Joseph P. Kennedy II, Bobby's oldest son, decided to reclaim what he believed was the family's birthright.

Joe Kennedy didn't live in the district. He didn't even know which communities were in the district—in the beginning, he campaigned in the North End of Boston, unaware that Tip had shorn it, and its Italian voters, from the district that JFK had represented so long ago.

Still, Joe Kennedy won easily. In fact, on primary election day 1986, in Medford, which was not in the Tip O'Neill/Joe Kennedy district, old ladies looked over their ballots, saw that Joe Kennedy's name was not on it, and then angrily asked the wardens why they couldn't vote for that nice young man whose ads they'd been watching on television.

"They were yelling," recalled one Medford poll watcher. "Ed Markey had been their congressman for 10 years, and they had no idea who he was. They just wanted to vote for a Kennedy, any Kennedy."

Actually, the first job Joe Kennedy had eyed was the other John F. Kennedy's old statewide office—treasurer. By 1976, it was a much more powerful position than it had been in the 1950s. Over the years, Bob Crane had continued to amass more power. Among other things, he now ran the state lottery commission.

Crane was a loyal Kennedy hand. In the 1960s, he'd campaigned out of state for both JFK and RFK. But at age 24, Joe Kennedy needed a job, a springboard to higher office. Teddy demanded a meeting at the State House with Crane and brought Joe along. Teddy told Crane he was all done.

"Teddy looked at me like I wasn't there," Crane recalled years later.

A tough World War II combat veteran, a sergeant in the Marine Corps at age 19, Crane wasn't about to give up his dream job for . . . Joe Kennedy. For once, the Kennedys backed down.

The larger problem was, Joe just wasn't very bright. Even his grandmother Rose recognized his limitations.

"He's so handsome," she told Barbara Gibson. "It's a shame he isn't smarter."

So a "nonprofit," Citizens Energy, was set up to give him some experience of sorts. He would get into the oil-importing business, buying heating oil cheap from the Venezuelan government and then re-selling to the hard-pressed residents of Massachusetts. And since it was a "nonprofit," Citizens Energy—and Joe—would get free TV spots, public service announcements (PSAs) to inform the public of its offerings. The Citizens Energy gambit worked—after six years of free PSAs on TV, everyone knew Joe and his toll-free number, Joe 4 Oil.

He was elected to "Jack's seat" in 1986.

Middlesex County is, or was, one of the largest counties in the United States, encompassing most of the suburbs west and north of the city of Boston. In 1988, the courthouse gang that had run the county for years was worried about losing control of the three-member county commission.

They needed a "straw" candidate to drain enough votes to defeat the reform candidate. What to do?

Actually, it was an easy decision. In 1988 Sen. Edward M. Kennedy would be running for reelection on the statewide ballot. And his nephew Joe would likewise be running for reelection in his district, which included some of Middlesex County.

So why not run another Edward Kennedy for county commissioner— specifically, former Lowell city councilor Ed Kennedy. Surely he could drain enough votes from the reform candidate in liberal communities like Cambridge and Newton to ensure the reformer's defeat.

What could possibly go wrong?

Edward Kennedy spent even less money on his race than John Francis Kennedy had on his 30 years earlier—zero. That was also the number of endorsements he received. He had no campaign literature.

On primary election night, when the returns started trickling in, Edward Kennedy quickly opened an insurmountable lead across the county, not only on the liberal incumbent, but also on the candidate backed by the regulars.

In Lowell, the leader of the hack cabal, incumbent Commissioner Mike McLaughlin, quickly realized his disastrous mistake.

McLaughlin, who is now in federal prison for illegally inflating his public-sector salary by more than $200,000, saw that he would soon be serving with the other Edward Kennedy. Kennedy's neighbor, Marty Meehan, the future congressman whom Ted Kennedy would call "Andy Meehan" four years later, went over to give Kennedy the unexpected news.

Another election, another Kennedy victory.

The *New York Times* even did a story, quoting one of the defeated candidates:

"People think he's Teddy Jr. When our people were calling town halls for results, they all thought he was some nephew or something."

The legislature finally dissolved the cesspool that was Middlesex County government. But that didn't stop Edward Kennedy—the other Edward Kennedy, that is. Years later he decided to run once more for the Lowell City Council. Eventually he was elected mayor.

Robert Kennedy likewise had a good run on his surname. In addition to the Lowell City Council, he was elected as a state representative and as governor's councilor. In 1972, Robert Kennedy failed to win the Democratic nomination for Congress in the Fifth District, losing out to John Forbes Kerry, who liked to stress his initials—JFK.

After the real Edward Kennedy's death in 2009, a special election was called to fill his Senate seat. A Libertarian candidate suddenly entered the fight—perfect to drain off votes from the GOP standard bearer, state Sen. Scott Brown. This third candidate came out of nowhere, but he wasn't exactly an unknown, or at least his name wasn't.

Joe Kennedy.

"I'm not going to be delusional," Joe Kennedy said. "There will be hard-core Kennedy

2010: Yet another Joe Kennedy, running for Ted Kennedy's Senate seat.

voters who will pull the wrong lever."

The hapless Democratic candidate, Martha Coakley, insisted that Kennedy be included in all the televised debates, so obviously the party organization figured that as a Libertarian, Joe Kennedy would take more Republican votes from Brown than "hard-core Kennedy" votes from Coakley.

Despite his name, the Joe Kennedy of 2010 could only manage 1 percent of the vote. Joe Kennedy's political career was over, at least until 2012, when Joe Kennedy was elected to an open seat in Congress.

Joseph P. Kennedy III runs for the U.S. House seat once held by Barney Frank, 2012.

Of course, this was a different Joe Kennedy, a "real" Joe Kennedy. This Joe Kennedy was Joe Kennedy II's son, and Joe Kennedy Sr.'s great-grandson, and Joe Kennedy Jr.'s great nephew.

But he was no relation to Joe Kennedy . . . of 2010.

CHAPTER THIRTEEN

CHAPPAQUIDDICK

Ted Kennedy didn't even know Mary Jo's last name.

On the morning of July 19, 1969, the assistant majority leader of the U.S. Senate sat in the office of Edgartown police chief Dominic Arena and handwrote his report of the incident at the Dike Bridge on Chappaquiddick Island.

"There was one passenger with me, one Mary Jo—" He left a blank space to fill in her last name, once he learned it—"a former secretary of my brother Sen. Robert Kennedy. The car turned over and sank into the water and landed with the roof resting on the bottom."

Mary Jo Kopechne was not what she seemed in those first news stories. She was 28, about to turn 29, 5'4", 110 pounds. The associate medical examiner described her as a "well-developed, well-nourished very attractive young woman." On her death certificate, she was listed as "being maiden."

Everything about her screamed "Kennedy girlfriend," including the fact that at the time of her death, she had not been wearing underwear.

Mary Jo Kopechne: Kennedy boiler-room girl, died not wearing underwear.

She had been one of Bobby Kennedy's "boiler-room girls" in his doomed 1968 campaign, but she went much further back with the Kennedys. In 1963, a year after graduating from a woman's college in New Jersey, she had gone to work in the Senate office of Sen. George Smathers, JFK's old "pussy posse" buddy.

In DC, she had first lived in a house owned by Bobby Baker, the corrupt protégé and crony of LBJ who also procured women for JFK, among them Ellen Rometsch, the suspected East German spy deported in August 1963. Kopechne's roommate was Baker's girlfriend, who died in a plane crash near her boyfriend's motel in Ocean City, Maryland, in May 1965.

When Bobby was elected to the Senate in 1964, Mary Jo got a job in his office, then went to work in 1968 for his presidential campaign. At the time of her death, she was working in Washington for a political consulting firm run by one of RFK's old Justice Department hands, Joe Dolan.

This was a mess, worse even than Marilyn Monroe. The Kennedys didn't have the same resources they could have once deployed—JFK and RFK were dead, their father Joe was an invalid. Mary Jo's parents were naturally distraught and distant enough, in New Jersey, not to feel bound by the usual Kennedy family *omerta*. The money her parents had been saving for their only child's wedding—now it would be used for her funeral. Fortunately for Ted, they were opposed first to an autopsy and later to an exhumation of the body. Months later Gwen Kopechne would tell reporters she didn't want "my little girl's body dug up—my tiny, lovely baby."

Joseph and Gwen Kopechne: They just wanted to protect their only child's reputation.

Teddy likewise opposed any autopsy, and later, an exhumation of her body from its grave in Pennsylvania—"I hope there will be no more grief for the girl's family."

That Saturday the corpse would be rushed off the island at the direction of another Kennedy intimate, K. Dun Gifford. Amid the haste and the secrecy, rumors were bound to spread—that she was pregnant. But Mrs. Kopechne would explain that Mary Jo had just finished her period three days before she drowned.

"I know she wasn't pregnant," Mrs. Kopechne said.

As for the "shabby rumors," as District Attorney Edmund Dinis put it, Teddy himself would deny them in a televised speech from Hyannis Port a few days later:

"There is no truth whatever to the widely circulated suspicions of immoral conduct that have been leveled at my behavior and hers regarding that evening . . . Nor was I driving under the influence of liquor."

One of the shabbier rumors, never confirmed, was that when RFK had been forced to break off his sexual relationship with Jackie Kennedy in March 1968 as he began his presidential campaign, he had turned to, among others, Mary Jo Kopechne.

Within hours, Ethel Kennedy issued a statement from the family compound in Hyannis Port. There was no mention of the circumstances of her death, only Ethel's description of Mary Jo as a "sweet, wonderful girl . . . She often came out to the house (Hickory Hill) and she was the one who stayed up all night typing Bobby's speech on Vietnam. She was a wonderful person."

Her mother's statements to the contrary notwithstanding, some have claimed that Mary Jo was pregnant at the time of her death. Paul David Pope, in his 2010 history of his family's ownership of the *National Enquirer,* said that his father Gene Pope Jr. once bought a Chappaquiddick story from Maxine Cheshire, the gossip columnist of the *Washington Post.* The 1980 piece laid out the facts of the accident, the pregnancy and the coverup.

"The story named names," Pope wrote, "none of them lacking attribution, and included no anonymous quotes. There were dates, times, places and supporting documents . . . But it never ran . . . Gene had bought the story to kill it."

Supposedly, in return for spiking the story, publisher Pope hoped to gain greater access to the "Holy Grail" of supermarket tabloids—Jackie and her children. In retrospect, it seems a poor choice, if that indeed is what it was. A hundred puff pieces never sell as many copies as a photograph of, say, Elvis Presley lying in his casket, or a titillating story about the "love child" of a Sen. John Edwards or a Rev. Jesse Jackson. Printing such a story about Chappaquiddick would have established the *Enquirer's* credentials as a real newspaper, once and for all.

"Once people read it," young Pope wrote, "there'd be no way that Ted Kennedy could ever run for president, maybe not even dogcatcher in Massachusetts."

Mary Jo was the oldest of the Bobby boiler-room girls who had gathered on Martha's Vineyard that weekend. The others ranged in age from 23 to 27—the most loyal of the Kennedys' devoted female aides. As Esther Newberg, later a New York literary agent, said, "We all revere the Kennedys. We all had a special feeling. We all were in college when President Kennedy was in the White House. We all came to Washington hoping to work for some of them."

The surviving Kennedy brother had been a wreck since his brother's assassination in June 1968. In his authoritative book on Chappaquiddick, *Senatorial Privilege,* Leo Damore quoted an anonymous friend of Teddy's as saying, "It's inaccurate to say he was drunk most of the time. It's also inaccurate to say he wasn't drunk at all."

Teddy himself told friends, "I know I'm going to get my ass shot off . . . and I don't want to."

In April 1969, after a trip to Alaska, he had gotten drunk on the return flight, running up and down the aisles, throwing pillows at reporters and aides, screaming, "Es-ki-mo Power!" Despite the witnesses, a number of whom were reporters, no accounts of Teddy's tirade appeared in print.

The gathering on Martha's Vineyard in July 1969 was not the first post–RFK assassination reunion of the boiler–room girls. The first one, a year earlier on Nantucket, had been attended by Joan. This one was timed to coincide with the annual regatta of the Edgartown Yacht Club,

which had become a tradition of bad
behavior for Teddy. One year he de-
molished a rental cottage at Katama
Beach. Another summer he began an
affair with a young woman that lasted
a couple of years.

The arrangements had been left
to Joe Gargan, Teddy's cousin on his
mother's side. After his mother's death,
Gargan had been raised with the Kennedys, but he and his sister were always
treated more like the help than kin.
Gargan, a lawyer, had wanted to rent a
cottage on South Beach in Edgartown,
but by May everything was gone. He
had to settle for a cottage on the little
undeveloped island of Chappaquiddick.

Joe Gargan, Kennedy cousin, refused to say he was driving.

Eight women were invited; six accepted.
Joan Kennedy, pregnant with her fourth child,
due in February, was not invited. The women
would stay at a motel in Edgartown; some of
the men would stay at the cottage, while Gargan and Kennedy booked a room at the Shiretown Inn in Edgartown.

It was a mixed group. Among the men
was Jack Crimmins, Ted's sometime driver, a
heavy-drinking, grumpy 67-year-old political hand from South Boston. He bought the
booze for the party at a package store in South
Boston—three half-gallons of vodka, four fifths
of Scotch, two bottles of rum and two cases of
beer. Another guest was Paul Markham, the former U.S. attorney for Boston—another hard-
drinking Kennedy operative.

Paul Markham, former US attorney, tried to save Mary Jo.

That Friday, Teddy raced his brother's boat, the *Victura,* finishing a poor ninth. Afterward he went to a party on another yacht and had three rum and Cokes. Then he returned to the Shiretown Inn, where Gargan had a six-pack of Heinekens sent up. After they took the ferry over to the party on Chappaquiddick, Teddy gulped at least one more rum and Coke. In all, there were six women and four men at the cottage.

Up to this point, the facts are not in dispute. Later, Teddy said he and Mary Jo left the party around 11:15, in his mother's 1967 Oldsmobile Delmont. He was driving her to the dock, he said, so that she could catch the last ferry back to Edgartown. To return to the ferry dock, he should have turned left. Instead he turned right and drove onto the Dike Bridge.

According to his statement to the police, "The car went off the side of the bridge . . . The car turned over and sank into the water and landed with the roof resting on the bottom. I attempted to open the door and the window of the car but have no recollection of how I got out of the car. I came to the surface and repeatedly dove down to the car in an attempt to see if the passenger was still in the car. I was unsuccessful in that attempt."

The timing, however, appears in doubt. A deputy sheriff who lived on Chappaquiddick had been working a paid detail at the regatta dance in Edgartown. The ferry to Chappaquiddick shut down at midnight, so he'd gotten a boat ride back to the island. He was walking home around 12:45 a.m. when he saw a dark car parked on the side of the road. Suddenly the car took off, headed for the bridge. It was later speculated that when Ted saw the deputy in uniform, he panicked and fled.

After swimming to safety, the soaking wet Teddy trudged past four cottages where he could have sought assistance. Instead, he kept walking, back to the rented cottage, where he told his cousin he needed to speak privately to him. Gargan came outside into the driveway with Markham. The three lawyers hopped into a white Valiant outside and drove back to the bridge. According to Teddy, it was now 12:20 a.m.—almost a half hour before the deputy saw the dark car speeding toward the bridge.

At the inquest in January, 1970, Teddy was asked how he knew it was 12:20.

"I believe that I looked at the Valiant's clock," he replied, under oath.

But that Valiant model did not have a dashboard clock. Confronted with that fact by a *Boston Globe* reporter in 1974, Kennedy said, "I made a mistake about a clock being in the Valiant that wasn't there."

The conversation among the three men on the way back to the bridge was later recounted by Damore in *Senatorial Privilege*. Teddy was in the backseat.

Kennedy: "I don't believe this could happen to me. I don't understand it. I don't know how it could happen."

Markham: "Well, it has happened."

Kennedy: "What am I going to do? What can I do?"

Markham: "There's nothing you can do."

From the backseat, Teddy kept asking his cousin, "Do you believe it, Joe? Do you believe it happened?"

At this point in Damore's account, he stops quoting Kennedy directly. Teddy reportedly asked, in so many words, "Why couldn't Mary Jo have been driving the car? Why couldn't she have let me off, and driven to the ferry herself and made a wrong turn?"

After which, Teddy speculated that he could say he somehow made his way back to Edgartown, which would leave it to Gargan to "discover" the submerged Oldsmobile. Gargan, a graduate of Notre Dame and Georgetown Law, was nobody's fool. He pointed out that they didn't even know if Mary Jo could drive, or had a license. Then Gargan pointedly told his cousin, "You told me you were driving."

Gargan and Markham drove Teddy back to the dock, where he impulsively dove in and swam the 200 yards back to Edgartown in a moderately swift current. Soaking wet, he walked back to his hotel room. At 2:30 a.m., he telephoned downstairs to the front desk, ostensibly to complain about noise but more likely to establish his presence in Edgartown. In his televised statement, he would say that he spent the night in bed "tossing and turning."

"I had not given up hope all night long that, by some miracle, Mary Jo would have escaped from the car."

Could Mary Jo have been saved? Yes, said John Farrah, the diver who recovered her body the next day. He found scratch marks on the backseat ceiling of the car, which would have been the last part of the vehicle to be flooded with sea water.

"She was definitely holding herself in a position," he testified, "to avail herself of the last remaining air that had to be trapped in the car."

If someone had called the authorities earlier, he said, "there was a good chance the girl could have been saved."

On Saturday morning, about 7:30 a.m. the senior senator turned up at the Inn's front desk. In true Kennedy-family fashion, Teddy said he had no cash and asked to borrow a dime from the room clerk.

He used the dime to make a collect call to one of his mistresses, Helga Wagner. He wanted to get the phone number of his brother-in-law, Steven Smith, the family fixer.

Teddy would later say he was "in shock" after the accident, but it would soon be reported that he had made 17 long-distance calls prior to reporting the accident, including five "before midnight." The first was to Hyannis Port, for 21 minutes, the next two to Ted Sorensen, then one to Burke Marshall, one of the better legal minds in the family retinue. Altogether, Teddy made 12 calls from the Shiretown Inn.

As Markham arrived in Edgartown the next morning, he was shocked when Kennedy sheepishly admitted that he hadn't reported the accident, and that he was still considering whether to tell the police that Mary Jo had been driving. Finally, the two walked together to the police station. By then, the accident had been reported, and the Olds was being pulled out by a tow truck from the Depot Corner Garage.

On the side of the truck were the words, "You Wreck 'Em—We Fetch 'Em."

At the station, Teddy and Markham introduced themselves to Chief Arena. Teddy immediately admitted that he had been driving the car that was now being pulled out of the tidal pond.

"We must do what is right," Teddy told him, "or we'll both be criticized for it."

Arena asked for his driver's license. Teddy said he'd misplaced his wallet. In fact, his driver's license had expired on his 37th birthday, February 22, almost five months earlier, and he had never bothered to renew it. Word was spreading quickly now, and two inspectors from the state Registry of Motor Vehicles soon arrived. Following protocol, they read Ted his Miranda rights. One of them then asked a question, and Ted replied:

"I have nothing more to say. I have no comment."

Gargan took the next ferry back to Chappaquiddick to break the news to the younger boiler-room girls, who had slept over in the cottage after missing the last ferry back to Edgartown. They too were shocked by their friend's death but unshaken in their loyalty to the Kennedys. One of them, Nancy Lyons, asked if "somebody else" could have been the driver. Gargan shook his head.

"I don't know why she couldn't be driving the car," Lyons persisted. "Can't somebody else take the blame?"

Somebody not named Kennedy. After all, once there was a spot, for one brief shining moment that was known as Camelot . . .

But all that was over now.

Mary Jo's body had already been pulled from the vehicle.

Inside the car, police found the wallet of the youngest of the women, Rosemary Keough, age 23. This led to another theory—that Mary Jo had drunk too much and had gone out to the Oldsmobile to sleep it off. Later Keough and Kennedy left together, this scenario went, and when the car went off the bridge, they swam to safety, not even knowing that Mary Jo was in the backseat, passed out.

"A ridiculous untruth," Keough said in a later statement. "I was not in the car at the time."

She said she'd apparently left her purse in the car when she went out to the Oldsmobile to get a transistor radio for the party.

The women were taken back to Edgartown where they gathered their belongings, checked out of the motel and fled. The Boston FBI office had already reported to J. Edgar Hoover that Kennedy had been the driver of the death car. Another theory was that FBI agents had been keeping a tail on Teddy, either for the Director or perhaps at the behest of the new president, Richard M. Nixon, who feared that Teddy would be running against him in 1972.

That Saturday afternoon Kennedy flew back to Cape Cod in a private plane, still in a state of shock, mumbling to himself: "Oh my God, what has happened? What has happened?"

Ethel Kennedy had already arrived at Hyannis Port, after calling Robert McNamara, JFK's former secretary of defense.

"Come up here Bob," Ethel said to McNamara. "There's nobody here but women."

Now Teddy had to do what he most dreaded—call the Kopechnes, Joseph and Gwen, at their modest home in Berkeley Heights, New Jersey.

Mrs. Kopechne picked up the phone and Teddy blurted out: "Mary Jo was in an accident."

Later, Gwen Kopechne recalled, "He just told me what happened and I broke down. I remember screaming, 'I'm alone here!' From then on, I don't remember anything. I must have let out some awful noises."

Teddy never got around to telling Mrs. Kopechne that he'd been driving the car in which her only child had drowned.

"That kind of upset us," Mary Jo's father Joe Kopechne said later.

Then it was time for another grim duty. Ted had to tell his incapacitated, 81-year-old father. That spring, after the death of President Dwight Eisenhower, Joe had watched Ike's funeral on television and gone into hysterics, thinking that now Teddy had been murdered.

In her book about her duties as Joe's nurse, *The Kennedy Case,* Rita Dallas recalls that Saturday afternoon in Hyannis Port when Teddy came upstairs to his father's room and put his hand on his shoulder.

"Dad, I'm in some trouble," she quotes Teddy as saying. "There's been an accident, and you're going to hear all sorts of things about me from now on. Terrible things. But Dad, I want you to know that they're not true. It was an accident. I'm telling you the truth Dad, it was an accident."

The old man took his surviving son's hand and clutched it to his chest. "Dad, a girl was drowned . . . I left the scene of the accident, and things aren't good because of that. But I want you to know that I'm telling you the truth."

Dallas wrote that Joe Kennedy nodded "weakly" and patted Teddy on the hand. His eyes closed.

The usual media fell into the usual lockstep behind their hero. Nothing to see here, folks, move along. The *New York Times*, whose Washington columnist James "Scotty" Reston, a summer Vineyard resident, had been among the first reporters there, knew more than he could report. The Paper of Record lamented the tragedy befalling the "doomhaunted Kennedy family."

The *Boston Globe* described Teddy as "the only surviving brother in a family pursued by tragedy." A front-page headline said, "Senator Wandered in Daze for Hours."

Boston Sunday Globe: *Teddy "wandered in daze for hours."*

The regatta, it continued, was supposed to be an event "of great personal pride for Sen. Kennedy. Instead, he was being forced by tragedy and controversy to remain cloistered in Hyannis Port, reported by aides under a doctor's care."

At the compound, the so-called wise men were gathering—Burke Marshall, Arthur Goldberg, Arthur Schlesinger Jr., Richard Goodwin, Ted Sorensen. A father-and-son team of local attorneys specializing in Massachusetts motor-vehicle law were added to the team. Jackie Onassis soon arrived from Greece, and her house was turned into a makeshift headquarters for the defense team. Teddy was there, in body if not in mind, as he "walked around in a stupor," as Dallas put it.

Joe Gargan and Paul Markham were shunned; somehow, what had happened was their fault, not Teddy's. Finally, one of Kennedy's attorneys approached them and told them that since they were both attorneys, Teddy felt that they all shared attorney-client privilege, so they should say nothing about the events of the evening.

Also cut out of the loop was Kenny O'Donnell, at home in Jamaica Plain, preparing to run for governor of Massachusetts for a second time. All weekend he waited by the phone for a call, but none came. He had been drinking heavily of late, too much apparently, despite his lengthy record of service in Kennedy scandal coverups.

On Sunday, Teddy again telephoned the Kopechnes. This time he spoke to Mary Jo's father Joe.

"He said he wished he had died in the accident instead of Mary Jo," Joe recalled later.

On Monday morning, the *Manchester Union-Leader* in New Hampshire ran a front-page editorial. Everyone is asking questions, publisher William Loeb wrote in his usual blunt style, about "a married man driving a young secretary around the countryside at midnight."

Loeb then addressed Teddy directly: "Had you been drinking and was that the reason why you drove off the road into the pond?"

And why didn't the senator immediately call the police "to see if the girl's life could still be saved. Don't you think you ought to resign immediately?"

Another day went by with no statement from the compound. That afternoon, Teddy went to Cape Cod Hospital for X-rays. He was found to be suffering from no serious injuries.

Mary Jo Kopechne's funeral was the next morning in Pennsylvania. Teddy flew to Scranton/Wilkes-Barre in a private DC-3 owned by Great Lakes Carbon Corp., the company owned by the family of Ethel Skakel Kennedy. Wearing a neck brace despite his clean bill of health, Teddy was accompanied by his pregnant wife Joan and his law-school classmate, John Tunney, now a congressman from California.

After the funeral Mass, when he returned to Cape Cod, Teddy was met at the airport by reporters demanding a statement. He told them it was not appropriate for him to comment on the day of Mary Jo's funeral. He returned to Hyannis Port, where he had to run another gauntlet of reporters.

Steve Smith, watching the commotion, turned to McNamara and said, "Well, Bob, you handled the Bay of Pigs and Vietnam. Now let's see what you can do with this one."

Even some of the Kennedys' most loyal media were having a hard time carrying the water for the Kennedys this time. *Life* magazine, which had printed the first stories about "Camelot," was appalled, describing Chappaquiddick as a parody of the Cuban missile crisis.

"All the surviving New Frontiersmen scheming to extract their man from the scandal of an accident . . . the classic rich kid's stunt—running away from an accident that Dad can fix with the judge."

The FBI agent on scene, James Handley, telephoned a report to Washington on Wednesday, saying that Chief Arena "suspects the possibility exists that Kennedy may have been too loaded to report the matter immediately . . . The police department is being deluged with letters from all over the world, 90% of which are against Kennedy and urging them to be thorough in this investigation so Kennedy can be convicted of the worst."

But the fix was already in. It was Massachusetts, where in the halls of justice, the only justice is in the halls. Especially for a Kennedy. Teddy would waive his initial hearing and plead guilty to leaving the scene of an accident. In return, his 20-day jail sentence would be suspended.

On a foggy Friday morning, six days after Mary Jo's death, Teddy, Joan and Stephen Smith boarded the Kennedy family yacht, the *Marlin*, in Hyannis Port. After more than an hour in rough seas, the *Marlin* docked at Oak Bluffs on Martha's Vineyard. Teddy was wearing a dark suit, but no neck brace.

His local lawyer, Richard McCarron, met them at the dock. He told Teddy he was concerned about the mandatory 20-day sentence for leaving the scene of an accident with personal injury, but Teddy reassured him. The judge was going to broom it.

"Don't worry about it," Teddy said, "He's already made up his mind."

The judge was James Boyle, a Republican and what Joe Kennedy's generation called "a left-footed Irishman"—a Protestant. As Kennedy walked to the courthouse, the Associated Press wire was moving a story on Teddy's driving record in Virginia during law school little more than a decade earlier—speeding, "racing with an officer," no license, etc. A deputy sheriff was quoted as saying, "That boy had a heavy foot and a mental block against the color red."

The case, *Commonwealth v. Edward M. Kennedy,* was first on the docket. The clerk read the charges and asked Sen. Kennedy how he pleaded. A pause. Finally, Ted stammered out, "Guilty." It was barely audible, so after gulping, Teddy repeated, "Guilty."

Arena read a partial statement of facts, and then Boyle asked him if there had been "a deliberate attempt to conceal the identity of the defendant."

"Not to my knowledge, Your Honor," Arena answered before hurrying from the witness stand. Then Boyle turned to the defense table. This was the moment of truth. Would Boyle ask Teddy why he hadn't reported the accident for all those hours?

He didn't ask.

"I should be glad to hear you gentlemen on disposition," the judge said.

McCarron started to answer, but Boyle wisely cut him off.

"On a plea of guilty that's a confession. I don't think you should argue there are legal defenses."

McCarron and his client had been saved by the judge. McCarron asked that Teddy's sentence be suspended because "I believe his character is known to the world." The prosecutor, future judge Walter Steele, agreed. The judge turned to the chief probation officer, Helen Tye, and asked if Teddy had a record of driving infractions.

"None, Your Honor," she replied, oblivious to the AP story that was even now being set into type in thousands of evening newspapers across the United States.

Imposing sentence, Boyle mentioned Teddy's "unblemished record" and added that he will "continue to be punished far beyond anything this court can impose." Then the judge imposed the minimum jail sentence, suspended—"assuming the defendant accept the suspension."

"The defendant will accept the suspension, Your Honor," said the defendant's lawyer.

The entire proceeding had taken seven minutes. Teddy was escorted down the back stairs by state troopers into a sea of reporters waiting in a light rain on the courthouse steps. Teddy began:

Teddy and Joan leave the courthouse after he pleads guilty to "leaving the scene" of an accident.

"I have made my plea and I have requested time on the networks tonight to speak to the people of Massachusetts and the nation . . ."

He flew back to Hyannis on a chartered plane. That night he delivered his televised address from the compound. All three network affiliates in Boston had given him 15 minutes at 7:30. The feed would be handled by Channel 5, WHDH-TV. It was another inside job— Harold Clancy, the station general manager and publisher of the *Boston Herald-Traveler*, was a former employee of Joe Kennedy's. Teddy would be introduced by Jack Hynes, a Channel 5 anchor. Hynes's father and namesake John B. Hynes was a former mayor of Boston. It was Hynes who in 1949 had finally vanquished James Michael Curley, who 36 years earlier had ended Honey Fitz's political career.

Teddy insisted that he be allowed to deliver the statement without any family watching. It had been cobbled together by Ted Sorensen,

Teddy on TV: "Suspicions of immoral conduct."

who had carefully questioned Gargan and Markham, to make sure that his account would include no lies. Gargan would later say, "It was made up, all of it, including thoughts and emotions."

After being introduced by Hynes, Teddy appeared on screen, clutching his script. He described taking his 16-year-old nephew Joe with him on Bobby's yacht, and how Mary Jo Kopechne had been heartbroken by RFK's murder.

"For this reason and because she was such a gentle, kind and idealistic person, all of us tried to help her feel that she still had a home with the Kennedy family."

Then he denied the "suspicions of immoral conduct" and that he had been "under the influence of liquor."

He described the accident improbably and then said, "My conduct and conversation during the next several hours, to the extent that I can remember them, made no sense to me at all. Although my doctors inform me that I suffered a cerebral concussion as well as shock . . ."

Not true.

Teddy then recounted his flight to the cottage, then returning with Gargan and Markham to the bridge, where they tried to rescue Mary Jo "at some risk to their own lives."

Then he really laid it on thick.

"All kinds of scrambled thoughts . . . went through my mind during this period. They were reflected in the various inexplicable, inconsistent and inconclusive things I said and did, including such questions as . . . whether some awful curse actually did hang over all the Kennedys . . ."

Finally, Teddy put aside the text he had been reading from. He folded his hands, paused, looked directly into the camera and appeared to begin speaking extemporaneously. But he wasn't. Cousin Joe Gargan had been temporarily recalled from exile to hold up cue cards.

Teddy began to speak about how his actions and guilty plea earlier in the day "raises the question in my mind of whether my standing among the people of my state has been so impaired that I should resign my seat . . ."

He reeled off a list of distinguished members of Congress from Massachusetts, including two future presidents, John Quincy Adams and his own brother, describing them as "men who inspire the utmost confidence. For this reason, I would understand full well why some might think it right for me to resign . . . And so I ask you tonight, the people of Massachusetts, to think this through with me. In facing this decision, I seek your advice and opinion. In making it, I seek your prayers. For this is a decision I will have to finally make on my own."

Then he quoted from *Profiles in Courage*, not by actual citation, saying with false familial modesty that "It has been written."

He repeated his brother's words, as massaged, at the very least, by Ted Sorensen, who had also written the very speech Teddy had just delivered:

"'A man must do what he must . . . Each man must decide for himself the course he will follow. The stories of past courage cannot supply courage itself. For this each man must look into his own soul.'"

Now he turned from the words Sorensen had written for his brother to another set of words that Sorensen had written for him:

"I pray that I can have the courage to make the right decision. Whatever is decided, whatever the future holds for me, I hope I shall be able to put this most recent tragedy behind me and make some future contribution to our state and mankind whether it be in public or private life. Thank you and good night."

Teddy then went upstairs to speak to his father. Joe hadn't watched the speech, just as he hadn't watched or read any of the coverage over the preceding days. According to nurse Rita Dallas, all he said to Joe after the speech was, "Dad, I've done the best I can. I'm sorry."

Dallas wrote: "From that point on Mr. Kennedy failed rapidly, and a pall fell over the compound, for we all knew that it was only a matter of time . . . "

An hour after the speech, Gwen Kopechne went out onto a neighbor's front porch to read a hand-written statement that began: "I am satisfied with the Senator's statement and do hope he decides to stay on in the Senate."

But it wasn't over. Kennedy's office claimed the mail was "over-whelming" in his favor, but the press reaction was brutal. *Time* magazine said, "There was nothing heroic about fencing with half-truths, false-hoods, omissions, rumors and insinuations of cowardice . . . He asked to shoulder the blame for what happened, at the same time he was obviously begging to be excused."

David Halberstam wrote: "The speech was of such cheapness and bathos as to be a rejection of everything the Kennedys had stood for in candor and style."

Humiliated by the reaction to the speech he had written for Ted, Sorensen fled the compound and returned to New York to work on the galleys of his new book, *The Kennedy Legacy.* He methodically deleted every reference to any possible future presidential campaigns by Teddy.

That Sunday, Teddy attended Mass at St. Francis Xavier Church in Hyannis. At the end of the service the congregation sang "America

"Youth for Truth" demonstrate against Teddy in Hyannis.

the Beautiful," as the monsignor explained to the press, "in tribute to Sen. Kennedy."

But nearby, at the post office, a group of young people calling themselves "Youth for Truth" was circling about carrying signs saying "Swim, don't run in '72."

That evening, in Boston, the Massachusetts Registry of Motor Vehicles announced it was revoking Teddy's license.

The pressure was too much for the district attorney, Edmund Dinis. He began researching the possibility of holding an inquest, a rare event in Massachusetts. The state attorney general, a former House speaker from Dorchester named Bob Quinn, toed the Democrat party line, saying he had no interest in any further investigations of Teddy.

"Let us hope," Quinn said, "that in the deep resources of his human capabilities, he can again redouble his efforts in service to the people."

Jack Anderson was taking over the Washington-Merry-Go-Round column that had vexed both Jack and Bobby Kennedy. Now, quoting "Kennedy intimates," Anderson spun out a bizarre tale about how Teddy had used a rowboat to get from Chappaquiddick to Edgartown after the accident. But Anderson did get one fact out there for the first time, that Kennedy had tried to "ask his cousin, Joe Gargan, to take the rap for him." For the first time, Anderson revealed Gargan's status in the family: "Although a lawyer, he was more a handyman who ran the errands."

On August 28, Joan Kennedy miscarried, for the third and final time. It was left to one of Ted's Senate staffers to issue a statement denying that the "strain" of Chappaquiddick had been a factor in Joan's miscarriage.

As the summer turned into fall, Dinis continued his attempts to conduct an inquest into Kopechne's drowning. He sent lawyers to Pennsylvania, asking for an order to exhume Kopechne's body. The judge, who had a bust of JFK in his chambers, was not sympathetic. Back in Massachusetts, on October 30 the Supreme Judicial Court issued a decision barring the press from the inquest, which was now scheduled for early January.

On November 18, Joe Kennedy died, surrounded by his family, including Jackie Onassis.

On December 1, the judge in Pennsylvania denied the motion to exhume Mary Jo's body.

It was almost anticlimactic when the inquest finally got under way on January 5, 1970. Judge Boyle was again presiding. Teddy was the first witness. He denied "any personal relationship" with the woman, and then Boyle asked him if he were under the influence of alcohol.

"Absolutely not," Teddy replied.

Teddy was asked about his telephone calls before he went to the police station in Edgartown. He mentioned that to get his brother-in-law Smith's number he had to call "a party that I felt would know the number." He did not mention that the party was his mistress, and Boyle again asked no follow-up question.

During the run-up to the inquest, the Kennedy lawyers had developed sources who were familiar with the district attorney's evidence. Teddy knew that the two men he had had three rum-and-Cokes with before heading to Chappaquiddick would not be testifying. That meant no evidence would be presented of how much alcohol Kennedy had consumed earlier that evening.

At the end of Boyle's desultory questioning, Ted realized he hadn't had a chance to get on the record how many drinks he'd had. So he brought up the subject himself, he said, "since the alcoholic intake is relevant."

He then carefully told the judge how many drinks he had consumed on July 18—omitting the first three post-race rum and Cokes. It was, as Damore put it, "a gratuitous falsehood." Later that day the two yachtsmen he had been drinking with, who had been summoned to court but weren't called to testify, decided to stop by the compound. One later told Damore that they spent no more than two or three minutes on the front porch, and that Teddy didn't invite them inside, leaving one of the two men "very offended."

"He'd come all the way from Florida and hired an attorney. He'd spent time and money to make sure Ted didn't get bagged for drunk driving. And all the thanks he got was a fast brush off."

In other words, they treated him like a Gargan.

In January, Kennedy would be stripped of his leadership position in the Senate, replaced by a former Ku Klux Klansman from West Virginia named Robert Byrd. On May 27, 1970, the Registry of Motor Vehicles revoked his driver's license for another six months. He had the right to appeal but didn't, and less than three weeks later was stopped by the State Police while driving, unlicensed, from Boston to Haverhill.

The Kopechnes eventually received a wrongful-death payment of $140,923, including $50,000 from the Kennedy family. In a statement announcing the settlement, Kennedy only mentioned the $90,923 from the insurance company. That fall, District Attorney Edmund Dinis was defeated for reelection, an outcome that puzzled him.

"The girl died," he said, "and I got defeated?"

Ted Kennedy, of course, was reelected to the Senate by a wide margin in 1970, and would be six more times. But he would never reach the White House. In his one race for president, in 1980, he could never escape the shadow of Chappaquiddick.

In March 1980, after delivering what was billed as an important foreign-policy speech at Columbia University, his limousine was headed downtown when suddenly, on 114th Street, loudspeakers in a fraternity house began blaring out Simon & Garfunkel's famous song:

"Bridge Over Troubled Waters."

As late as 1994, on the 25th anniversary of Chappaquiddick, rather than face the inevitable questions from reporters, Teddy had his Senate office issue a statement to the press:

"I bear full responsibility for the tragedy, and I always will. I have expressed my remorse to my family, the Kopechne family, and the people of Massachusetts. I only wish I had the power to do more to ease the continuing pain I feel and that Mr. and Mrs. Kophechne feel for Mary Jo's loss."

It was duly noted in some newspapers that he expressed remorse first to his own family, not Mary Jo's, and that he first mentioned the "continuing pain" that he felt, rather than the Kopechnes. And this was in an election year.

Several of the boiler-room girls would go on to law school, but they all remained silent about the events of that weekend on Martha's Vineyard. But in 1974, on the fifth anniversary, Rosemary Keough did issue a statement that did not exactly exonerate Ted Kennedy.

"My friend Mary Jo," she said, "just happened to be in the wrong car at the wrong time with the wrong people."

CHAPTER FOURTEEN

THE LOST BOYS

IN THE BLEAK AFTERMATH of his father's murder, Michael Kennedy took to answering the family phone at Hickory Hill with one word: "Chaos!"

There was no longer even a semblance of adult supervision for the Kennedy kids. No one remained to remind them, "Kennedys don't cry!" At the time of Bobby's death, Ethel had been three months pregnant with their 11th child. According to family tradition, a new Kennedy should be named after a deceased family member (Joe, Kathleen), a loyal family retainer (Edward Moore) or a military hero (Maxwell Taylor, Douglas MacArthur).

That tradition too had now gone by the wayside. Bobby's final child would be named "Rory," because, Ethel said, "It sounds like Bobby."

Paralyzed with grief, Ethel neglected almost all her duties as a mother, but a week after Rory's birth, she did manage to take the infant to visit her father—at Arlington National Cemetery.

Bobby's kids were now in and out of trouble, mostly in, especially during summers on Cape Cod. They would dart into the gridlocked, rubbernecking tourist traffic around the compound, bang the rear bumper of an out-of-state car and then sprawl to the pavement as their siblings yelled, "You've killed a Kennedy!" Another longtime family tradition was not to pay for anything, through the simple expedient of not carrying cash. Now some of them shoplifted as well. Their supply of fireworks (illegal in Massachusetts) seemed limitless; after dark the compound often sounded like a military practice range.

More than 40 years later, now-elderly neighbors still recall the Kennedy "kids" pouring sugar into the gas tanks of their cars.

Most of the time such mindless hooliganism could be hushed up with cash payments to the victims. No police reports, no headlines. The reservoir of sympathy for the family in the general public remained high, but patience quickly wore thin among the neighbors. How many times could a stoned, bucktoothed Kennedy youth sneer, "Do you know who I am?" at some harried shop clerk or auxiliary cop before the pushback started?

Finally, in 1970, they started getting arrested. The first pinch—of Bobby Jr. and his cousin Bobby Shriver—was for marijuana. But soon the cops began lugging them with more serious controlled substances— prescription drugs, cocaine, finally heroin.

Next came the periodic school transfers—always to an institution less prestigious than the last. Bobby Jr. attended four high schools before

August 1970: Bobby Kennedy Jr. enters Barnstable courthouse with Teddy and Ethel after his first arrest for drug possession.

graduating, although he was of course accepted at Harvard College. His older brother Joe could not even manage that.

The cousins were bonding, in a manner of speaking. They would panhandle at the New York Port Authority bus terminal on 42nd Street together—a rejection of sorts of what would later be called white privilege. Next it would be trips uptown to Harlem to score drugs, followed by the inevitable rehab stints at McLean Hospital in Belmont and finally the treks to wooden churches for AA meetings.

But early on, what united them was the shared hatred and resentment they shared for their elders. Bobby told Michael Skakel how Ethel beat him with a hairbrush. Michael Skakel told him that his father, Rushton, Ethel's brother, beat him with a hairbrush too. There were so many family traditions . . .

No matter how consumed he was with politics, RFK Sr. had always tried to schedule one white-water rafting expedition with the younger family members every summer. After he was gone, the grief-stricken

July 1972: Teddy and the family children on a family outing.

adults gamely tried to continue his beloved tradition in the Grand Canyon. Now, however, they were less interested in the children, and more interested in assuaging their own grief, with the aid of massive amounts of vodka. The long-awaited trek turned out to be a disaster.

Back at Hickory Hill, Ethel ran through an endless stream of employees—nannies, cooks, drivers, etc. She had a particular problem with nonwhites. In his 1994 book, *The Other Mrs. Kennedy*, Jerry Oppenheimer quoted one of her secretaries as saying, "She would say things like, 'Those black people are stupid.' . . . I really don't think she liked blacks or Hispanics. She couldn't stand it if they didn't speak English."

One day, according to a *New York Post* story in September 2015, Ethel flew into a rage when she noticed a new black maid tidying up, throwing out scrap paper.

"You stupid nigger!" she screamed. "Don't you know what you're doing. You're destroying history. Get out of my sight. You're fired!"

To care for the younger children, she hired one polite, well-bred young woman after another. They never lasted long. Many were products of the same type of elite East Coast finishing schools as Miss Porter's, whose graduates had proven so alluring to JFK.

Again, the family traditions continued. Sen. Kennedy occasionally stopped by to check in on his brother's unruly brood. One afternoon in the summer of 1973, he arrived at Hickory Hill drunk, as he so often was.

One of Ethel's young summer hires—an attractive Southern blonde about 20 years old—found herself in one of the sprawling home's basements that were accessible only through a secluded outside door. She was searching in the darkened room for a toy for the younger children, when she suddenly heard a rustling behind her.

She turned to see Ted Kennedy, a glazed look in his eyes. In one hand he held a drink, in the other, his erect penis. His Bermuda shorts were around his ankles. He stared at her blankly, saying nothing.

Horrified, the young woman ran past him out of the basement and immediately fled, never to return.

It was only a matter of time until the next disaster. This one would involve Joseph P. Kennedy II, Bobby's oldest son. He had literally begun his life as a campaign prop—he was born in late October 1952, in the midst of his bachelor uncle JFK's tough Senate campaign against incumbent Republican Sen. Henry Cabot Lodge.

The next day, the *Boston Post,* to which his grandfather had just "loaned" $500,000, ran a front-page photo of the beaming young family—infant Joe, his parents, his baby sister Kathleen (herself named for another dead sibling) and of course his uncle, Cong. John F. Kennedy.

Jackie wouldn't be in the picture for another 10 months or so, so baby Joe would have to do, to establish Jack's family bona fides.

Fifteen years later, on his father's funeral train, Joe had gone car to car, working the narrow aisles, shaking the hands of the old men, kissing the cheeks of their plump, perfumed wives, an impressive debut that prompted his mother Ethel to turn to her own sisters-in-law and say, "He's got it! He's got it!"

In fact, he didn't. Even by third-generation Kennedy standards, Joe wasn't the sharpest knife in the drawer. He *looked* great—barrel chest, curly blond hair, perfect teeth, an easy swagger as he walked. The lights were on, as the old saying goes, but nobody was home. If he'd been a baseball pitcher, the scouting report would have read, "Million-dollar arm, ten-cent head."

He briefly attended Milton Academy, his uncle Ted's prep-school alma mater. He also put in time at the Manter Hall School in Cambridge, for generations a fallback destination for the three-watt-bulb scions of rich, inbred Boston families.

(The joke was that when they were trying to pick up girls, Manter Hall students, as dim as they tended to be, at least knew enough to brag to their new acquaintances, "I go to school in Cambridge," not specifying which one, for obvious reasons. Joe didn't have to worry about that; his last name was usually enough to pique the interest of the opposite sex.)

Just as old man Joe in his frustration had shipped Rosemary off to live with Edward Moore and his family, Ethel began farming out her rebellious children as soon as they were old enough to fend for themselves. Joe ended up briefly across the country in Berkeley, fantasizing about becoming a drug smuggler, enrolling in, and then never attending, classes at the university, wrecking a car or two—the usual m.o. for his generation of Kennedys.

The summer of 1973 should have been a happy one for the Kennedys. In January, the military draft had finally ended, removing that lingering question mark for any of the male cousins. Much more significant for these Kennedys, though, was a small change in Massachusetts law that spring—the drinking age was lowered from 21 to 18. The older boys—Joe, Bobby Jr., Michael, Chris Lawford, Bobby Shriver—could finally put away their fake IDs once and for all.

On the national scene, less than a year after his 49-state presidential landslide, the old family bogeyman Richard Nixon was being pummeled in the Watergate hearings. Suddenly it seemed like half the cars in the state carried a bumper sticker that said, "Don't Blame Me, I'm from Massachusetts."

That August, Joe was on Nantucket, partying as usual. He would soon be enrolling in yet another new school—the University of Massachusetts. He reached out to his younger brother David, and invited him to join his crew for the weekend. David, a shy kid who sometimes felt like the odd man out in his boisterous family, was ecstatic at being included. David brought with him to the island his new girlfriend, Pam Kelley, a Hyannis Port neighbor whose sister Kim dated Bobby Jr.

The plan was to return to the mainland by ferry Monday morning. But Joe figured they had time for one more swim, so he borrowed a Toyota jeep and rounded everybody up—his brother David and Pam and Kim Kelley, as well as one other local girl.

As usual, Joe was driving recklessly. He had learned nothing from his recent accident in California. His squealing passengers held on to the roll bar of the jeep as Joe showed off behind the wheel.

"Joe was cutting through the woods, spinning the jeep in circles," Pam later recalled to authors Peter Collier and David Horowitz. ". . . there was a rest area on the other side of the highway and Joe started to cross over to it. He didn't see this station wagon heading toward us until the last minute."

He swerved to avoid the station wagon, jerking the jeep left but hitting a ditch with the vehicle's right-side tires. The impact broke the jeep's axle and hurled the occupants into the air. Joe and Bobby's girlfriend Kim quickly got up and dusted themselves off. The third girl in the jeep was transported to the hospital with fractures to her pelvis and femur.

Like his big brother, David gamely tried to wave off his injuries. But he was in such obvious pain that he agreed to go to Cape Cod Hospital. X-rays quickly showed fractured vertebrae. After admission, he was administered large doses of pain medication.

For David's new girlfriend Pam, the news was even worse. She would later recall flying through in the air and hitting the ground, seeing David's face alongside hers. After impact, she tried to pull herself up, but couldn't move her legs. She was paralyzed from the waist down.

Pam was airlifted to Cape Cod Hospital's intensive care unit where surgeons worked to repair the damage to her spine, using ice to ease the spasms that were now racking her. But the damage had been done. Pam Kelley would never walk again.

Joseph P. Kennedy II was cited by police for reckless driving and ordered to appear in Nantucket District Court. Accompanied by his mother Ethel and his uncle Ted, Joe's demeanor at the hearing was described by the press as "outwardly impassive." As always, the Kennedys imported a connected, heavy hitter as lead counsel. For this mop-up operation, Uncle Ted selected the son of a former Illinois senator as well as an old RFK hand in the Justice Department.

Another family tradition, of course, was to have the actual nuts-and-bolts defense managed by a townie type more familiar with the local district

Joe Kennedy was fined $100 for paralyzing Pam Kelley.

court, its customs and its denizens. But the facts left little wiggle room. The investigating Nantucket cop testified that "the accident was entirely [Kennedy's] fault." The driver of the other vehicle recalled Kennedy "coming at me in my lane."

In other words, Joe was guilty beyond a reasonable doubt. But in yet another Kennedy family tradition, the judge turned out to be a dear family friend. He had graduated from Harvard College in 1937 with Joe's uncle and namesake. And, like Joe's father Bobby, the judge had worked at one time in Washington for Sen. Joseph McCarthy.

When time came to impose a sentence, the star-struck family retainer asked Joe to rise.

"You had a great father and you have a great mother," the judge said. "Use your illustrious name as an asset instead of coming into court like this."

The judge then asked Joe if he believed a jail sentence would serve as a deterrent for highway offenses.

"No," said Joe, wisely.

The judge nodded in agreement. For putting Pam Kelley in a wheelchair for the rest of her life, Joe Kennedy was fined $100.

As Joe headed off to his new college, Pam Kelley remained in intensive care. Occasionally Rose and Ted would stop by, sometimes with new movies and a projector, which the staff seemed to enjoy more than Pam, who used the films as an excuse to sneak out of her room in her new wheelchair and smoke a cigarette.

Actually, Ethel was Pam's most frequent visitor from the family. Ethel had never cared much for Pam, but now they too had a bond of sorts—they were both victims, in one way or another. Ethel would often show up to putter around Pam Kelley's increasingly cluttered room and tidy it up. The visits continued until Pam reached a settlement with the insurance company—just under a million dollars, according to authors Collier and Horowitz.

After that, the Kennedys largely faded out of Pam Kelley's new, constricted life, which was marked by bouts with depression and

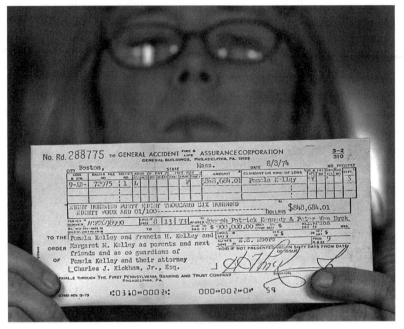

Pam Kelley received $848,684.01 from the Kennedys for her paralysis.

battles with alcohol and drugs. But she persevered. She was married for a time and in 1989 gave birth to a daughter. She eventually became an executive with a nonprofit agency that promoted disabled rights.

"What happened to me stinks," Pam Kelley told the *Cape Cod Times* in 1999. "But I made something decent out of it."

As for David Kennedy, as he recuperated in another room at Cape Cod Hospital, for days no one bothered to tell him that his new girlfriend was now paralyzed. The whole weekend on Nantucket was like a microcosm of David's brief life—a promising start, ending in disaster.

Pam Kelley: "I made something decent out of it."

Of all the Kennedys of his snake-bit generation, David may have lived the most tragic life. In June of 1968, at the age of 12, he had accompanied his father to California for the make-or-break primary against Sen. Eugene McCarthy.

On election day, his father had accepted an invitation to Hollywood director John Frankenheimer's beachfront estate in Malibu. Waiting for the polls to close, father and son decided to go for a swim in the ocean. Always slight, like his father, David was caught in an undertow and nearly drowned before Bobby rescued him from the pounding surf.

A few hours later, still shaken from his brush with death earlier in the day, David was watching the election returns by himself in his room at the Ambassador Hotel as his father finished his victory speech in the ballroom downstairs. Then Bobby ducked into a serving pantry for a quick getaway to the raucous victory party that was already well underway at Brother-in-Lawford's trendy new West Hollywood nightclub, The Factory.

Suddenly shots rang out—again—as the cameras recorded the gruesome scene, the screams and the gasps.

"Get the gun Rafer!" someone yelled at former Olympian Rafer Johnson, one of Bobby's bodyguards.

Another supporter also leaned over to hand Bobby some rosary beads. A Mexican busboy, wracked with grief, stood over Bobby's sprawled body.

David watched it all, alone, in silence.

In the chaos, David was forgotten. Finally, author Theodore White, that most loyal of family retainers, realized that David was by himself. White raced to David's room in an attempt to prevent David from seeing a replay on TV of what had just happened, but it was too late. Helpless to do anything else, White called room service and ordered chocolate for the boy. David didn't speak for days.

More trauma came as the funeral train carrying David and his family made its way across the country. David and his closest friend in the family, Chris Lawford, were watching out the window as a train on another track struck a group of mourners. It was a gruesome scene, with two dead. One of the victims was disemboweled.

It has been reported that David became addicted to the opioids Demerol and Percodan, as well as the sedative Mellaril, as he was laid up in the hospital after the Nantucket jeep accident. But his drug use had actually begun years earlier. His fellow students at the tony Middlesex School in Concord, where so many of the cousins came and went over the years, noted that he smoked marijuana each morning and dropped acid on a weekly basis.

By the age of 15, he had spent time panhandling in New York City with his cousin Chris Lawford, who had also become a heavy drug user as a teenager. It was in New York City that the boys were first introduced to heroin, although they would insist to Collier and Horowitz that they only snorted it.

It wasn't until after his hospital stay on Cape Cod for his fractured vertebrae that David began injecting heroin. At the age of 17, David became the first member of the Kennedy family to become a junkie. He would not be the last.

By 1977, David's behavior had made him persona non grata in Hyannis Port, and Ted Kennedy, of all people, took on the task of keeping tabs on him. Ted ordered David to his home in McLean, Virginia.

But just days before he was to leave the RFK estate at Hickory Hill, David was found passed out alongside a girlfriend in an upstairs room of the family home. It took long minutes for family friends to rouse the pair; they worried that the two had overdosed. The room was a mess, the window broken out, and the floor was wet with blood, littered with vials and syringes.

David Kennedy worried that his family would lobotomize him as they had his aunt Rosemary.

David claimed he had surprised a burglar who had smashed his way through the window (not likely, considering the room was on the third floor of the home). He also said he and his girlfriend struggled with the culprit before he fled. Family and friends knew better. It was just David being David.

By the time David finally arrived at Uncle Ted's home in McLean, it was obvious that the senior senator was not in any condition to assist his wayward charge.

"My uncle's as bad as I am," David said as he fled two days later. "He can't do anything for me."

Two years later, after a brief stint at Harvard where he seemed to subsist on a diet of cigarettes and Colt 45 Malt Liquor—David was back in New York. The family had plenty of room for him—Rose's apartment, Aunt Jean's condo, Aunt Jackie's townhouse—but David had burned too many bridges. He ended up in a rented Manhattan penthouse. He dabbled in writing, but mostly he was frequenting clubs and living the life of a disco-era playboy, even partaking in the family tradition of dating starlets, in his case, the beautiful actress Rachel Ward.

For the ambitious ingénue, it was a career boost to play house with a Kennedy, but David recognized the folly of the idea.

"I knew I was too fucked up," he said. "I was back on smack. She had no idea what I was up to."

But this sudden surge of self-awareness didn't mean David was approaching sobriety.

In September 1979, police from the NYPD's 28th Precinct were called to the Shelton Plaza, a run-down hotel in Harlem that was a well-known shooting gallery for heroin users. There they found David Kennedy in the lobby, badly bruised and in a daze. He was carrying 25 packets of heroin.

Again, David offered an implausible story: he had been driving through the desolate neighborhood when two black strangers on the curb flagged him down. After stopping to see what they wanted, he got out of his BMW and followed them into the Shelton where they beat him and robbed him of $30.

Soon the true story came to light—David had been trying to buy heroin. Not only had he not been lured into the fleabag, he was well-known there. His fellow junkies knew him by two nicknames: "Sweetwater" and "White James" (after James Caan's character in *The Gambler*). According to New York police sources, David had admitted to them, "I'm a stoned-out junkie."

(Despite the fact that it was determined that Kennedy had lied to the police and was driving a vehicle with expired tags, somehow no charges were filed against him. The Kennedy name had come in handy for David.)

David's self-diagnosis of himself as a "stoned-out junkie" was blunt, but accurate. He had already been diagnosed twice with bacterial endocarditis, a heart malady most often associated with intravenous drug use. His first bout had occurred in 1976, after a 40-day heroin shooting binge while enrolled at Harvard College.

"He is physically sick," Bobby Jr. told the New York tabloids. "He is receiving medical care."

Desperate to resolve the David problem one way or the other, the family next appointed Steve Smith, his aunt Jean's husband, as his legal guardian.

Smith decided to stage an intervention in the offices of the family trust fund on Park Avenue. He arranged for Ethel, Ted, Aunt Jean and David's brothers Joe and Bobby to be there. But David didn't respond well to their entreaties.

"We love you," Bobby Jr. told him. "You're killing yourself, and it's killing us to see you doing this to yourself."

"You oughta know!" David snapped back at Bobby Jr., who was like himself a junkie.

For the rest of his short life, David bounced back and forth between various rehabilitation facilities, five in all before his death, including the inevitable stop at McLean Hospital in Belmont, Massachusetts, as well as a two-month stay in Sussex, England. He dipped into his trust fund for $100,000 to join a twelve-month program in Sacramento. Perhaps it was fear that led him there. He well understood the fate of black sheep in the Kennedy family.

"My Uncle Ted told me to get my act together," he confided to a friend, "or I'll wind up in an institution for the rest of my life like Rosemary."

He became obsessed with the fate of his aunt Rosemary. He told others that his family would like to handle him the way they'd handled the problem child of an earlier generation—with a lobotomy.

Despite the year-long program, and his therapist's belief that David's problems were behind him, after departing the Sacramento rehab facility he was almost immediately arrested for drunk driving, his second offense. He pleaded guilty.

In 1984, *Playboy* magazine published an excerpt from a forthcoming, highly anticipated book on the family titled *The Kennedys: An American Drama*. The family knew that this would not be yet another Sorensen- or Schlesinger-like hagiography, nor would it be an easily dismissed *National Enquirer*–style hit piece. It had been written by Peter Collier and David Horowitz, two former liberals who had made a hard-right turn toward conservatism.

They had spent four years researching their topic, and dedicated countless hours to interviewing members of the family and hundreds of friends and acquaintances. The Kennedys did not fully cooperate; the authors were denied access to the letters of the clan's patriarch, Joseph P. Kennedy. But some of the Kennedys, including Chris Lawford and David and Bobby Kennedy, did speak with the authors.

"There was no pretense that there was any kind of friendship relationship here," Collier said later. "It was a kind of therapy for them. They wanted an authentic version of their family history. This is a family of vast silences."

An authentic version is what Collier and Horowitz got, on tape. Their book pulled no punches, nor did their on-the-record family sources. And what David had to say was particularly damaging. He spoke of visiting Southern California to see his cousin Chris and being met at the door by Peter Lawford.

"The first thing he did after saying hello," David said, "was offer me a pipe full of hash."

David admitted to shooting heroin in 1973 while at Middlesex. And he spoke of the isolation he felt inside his own family.

The family's reaction to David's role in the excerpted portion of *The Kennedys* was immediate. In the afterword to the book, Collier and Horowitz reported that "David was bitterly criticized for breaching the family faith. The word used in condemning him was *treason*."

David was devastated by the excerpt and his family's reaction to it. Once again, he turned to drugs and soon entered a month-long program at St. Mary's Rehabilitation Center in Minneapolis under the alias "David Kilroy." And one last time, he would end his detox with a monumental bender.

Upon leaving St. Mary's, David flew to Florida to be with his family during their "traditional" Easter weekend, as Ted Kennedy would describe it seven years later. Because of his drug addiction, he'd long since been barred from La Querida, the family's sprawling Palm Beach mansion. So he checked into the Brazilian Court Hotel a couple of miles south.

He would spend the next five days, his final five days, on what the British call a bat, with the hotel staff recalling that he was in the bar by 8 a.m. One night he picked up a woman at the bar, as well as some cocaine. His final night, he needed the assistance of another friend to get back to his room. Once there, he took his phone off the hook.

David didn't make his scheduled flight back to Boston on April 26, despite having told his newest girlfriend that he was coming home. His family was concerned enough to ask the hotel to check on his well-being. A room clerk found David fully clothed on the floor of his room, dead. He was 28 years old. There were no signs of violence or crime. An autopsy revealed that he had overdosed on a combination of cocaine, Demerol and Mellaril (a tranquilizer for which he had a prescription).

David's cousins Caroline Kennedy and Sydney Lawford drove down from the family compound to identify the body.

Authorities would later find a packet of coke in David's wallet and traces of it, as well as Demerol, in his room's toilet bowl and tank, an indication that someone might have tried to flush evidence of the overdose. The obvious suspects were Caroline and her cousin. They would later provide sworn statements to the Palm Beach County state attorney denying that they had ever set foot in David's room, despite the contradictory testimony of a hotel employee that he had seen Caroline in her cousin's room.

Two bellhops at the hotel—one from Rhode Island and another from Cape Cod—were arrested and charged with providing David with cocaine. It was later determined that the Cape Cod bellhop had previously worked briefly for the Kennedy family as a landscaper. He pleaded guilty and was placed on probation.

The Kennedys didn't just go into spin mode in the face of David's death. Their public-relations machine went on the attack, setting its sights on Peter Collier and David Horowitz. In the days after the funeral, the *Washington Post* reported that "some close to the Kennedys are saying that the magazine excerpt could have contributed to David Kennedy's death."

One of Ted Kennedy's aides told the paper that the *Playboy* story "sent David into a tremendous depression." Another "source close to the family" accused the authors of seeking out "the vulnerable members of the family. It was extraordinarily unfair to the kids—to take them at their most vulnerable."

"David thought these guys were his friends," the source added. "But in fact they took his life and spread it out for the public to see. They used him."

The authors immediately responded, saying that it was "absolutely absurd" to blame them for David's death.

"The Kennedys were guilty of epic child abuse," they said in a statement. "For them to hold two strangers responsible for what happened to David is disgusting."

The unnamed finger-pointers, described by Collier and Horowitz as "the political hacks around Ted Kennedy," surely knew that David himself squarely placed the blame for his downfall on his own family.

"I am what I am because I come from a whole line of alcoholics," he had said on tape. "Just look at how many of us are fucked up."

In fact, the book may have played a role in saving the life of one Kennedy—Chris Lawford, the cousin to whom David felt closest. After all, they had started using heroin together, and Chris eventually contracted hepatitis C. Lawford had briefly attended, then dropped out of Fordham Law School, eventually wedding a fellow drug addict. He too appeared headed for an early grave, but David's premature death scared him straight.

"It's really hard when you lose someone you care about," Lawford said years later. "I never expected to make it to 30. I shouldn't have."

After David's death, Lawford checked himself into another rehab program, in Cambridge, and has since maintained his sobriety.

Instead of mourning David, the Kennedys seemed to have decided to try to use his death as a way of undermining the unflattering portrait of themselves in the book. Such a strategy had totally backfired when they tried it with William Manchester and his *Death of a President* in

Block Island October 1993: Chris Lawford, right, recovering heroin addict, with his cousin, rapist Michael Kennedy.

1967, and it worked no better this time either. The new book would become a runaway bestseller. Every knock a boost, as the Kennedys' old rival James Michael Curley used to say.

As tough as the book was on David, it was even more unsparing of Bobby Jr., who was perhaps even sicker than his younger, now deceased brother.

From a young age, Bobby Jr. was, like many in the family, a not-so-merry prankster. At age 14, a week after his father's funeral, he spiked milk with laxatives at a birthday party for David at Hickory Hill. At a later memorial service for his father, he tricked a family friend into disturbing the solemnity of the Mass by ringing bells at the wrong time.

Like David, Bobby Jr.'s drug use began early. At 16, RFK Jr. and his cousin Bobby Shriver were arrested on Cape Cod after a taxi-driving informant told police that he had driven the pair to buy marijuana. Judge Henry Murphy told the Kennedys that the charges would be dropped if they could stay out of trouble for a year.

In the first of many such statements, Ethel told the press, "I was distressed to learn last night that my son had been charged with having been in possession of marijuana . . . but Bobby is a fine boy. We have always been proud of him and I will stand by him."

But staying out of trouble for 12 whole months was an impossibly high bar for Bobby Kennedy Jr. Less than a year later, he was arrested near the Kennedy compound after a police officer saw him, ice cream cone in hand, standing by an idling car with a woman inside. The door of the car was open, blocking traffic. As the cop approached, he noticed Kennedy's bloodshot eyes and asked the 17-year-old if he had been drinking. Kennedy said he had not, then took a bite out of his ice cream cone and spit it in the cop's face.

Kennedy's next appearance in court would be a departure from the usual family modus operandi. There was no smart gray suit and tie, no neatly combed hair. RFK Jr. appeared in a blue work shirt and patched jeans. His hair was shoulder length and he wore sandals into Judge Murphy's courtroom. And rather than offering contrition, Kennedy snapped to the judge that the arrest was "all a bunch of made-up lies."

Like Collier and Horowitz, another investigative journalist who examined the third generation of Kennedys pinpointed Ethel as the source of the lost boys' troubles. Contrasting RFK Jr. with his cousin JFK Jr., author Jerry Oppenheimer wrote that, "John, after his father's death, was brought up by a controlling and domineering mother, but one who obsessively looked out for his care and well-being. Bobby, after his father's death, was essentially given up by his angry, widowed mother."

It was left to Lem Billings, JFK's closest friend, to step in as a surrogate parent for RFK Jr. From the time he was 14, Bobby seemed to adore the 52-year-old closeted gay man. Some who were close to the family were surprised at the intimacy between the pair, and speculation abounded that Billings was infatuated with young Bobby, an unabashed heterosexual who would cut a wide swath among the Radcliffe girls when he entered Harvard.

"It was clear to us that Billings was in love with Bobby," one source told Oppenheimer.

Given Bobby Sr.'s lifelong homophobia, it seems doubtful that he would have approved of Billings's relationship with his second son, although after the assassination of JFK, Bobby had become somewhat more accepting of Billings. After all, they shared one thing in common— an unquestioning love of JFK.

Jackie, on the other hand, never warmed to Billings. As handsome as her son was, Jackie fretted about his sexuality. The fact that they lived in Manhattan only increased her apprehension. The reason she forbade him from going into acting was because of what she perceived to be the homosexual influences in show business, especially the New York theater.

Lem had attempted to ingratiate himself with "the Hunk" and his mother, but was banned once and for all after Jackie came upon a photographic scrapbook Lem had surreptitiously put together about JFK's only male heir.

Despite the 38-year age difference, Bobby appeared in complete control of his relationship with the older man.

Lem, who seemed unnaturally eager to please this next-generation Kennedy, allowed Bobby Jr. to introduce him to marijuana, LSD, angel dust, amphetamines, cocaine and finally heroin.

Eventually, the emotionally vulnerable Billings was accompanying RFK Jr. uptown to score their drugs. On one occasion, Bobby and Billings were chased through the streets of Harlem by black drug dealers.

Instead of trying to help his young charge overcome his demons, Billings enabled him, and he came to regret it. One drunken night near the end of his life, Billings was in tears as he told an associate, "I made a terrible mistake. I took drugs with [Bobby]. I made a terrible mistake. I let him down."

But Bobby Jr.'s addictions couldn't be blamed on the older man. The other Kennedys were well aware of his problems. As David sadly explained, "My brother Bobby's a junkie, but I take all the blame."

Lem Billings died at age 65 in 1981, a broken man, depressed and conflicted about his lifelong association with the Kennedy family. Just a few years before his death, he had morosely told a friend, "After I go, there'll be no more Kennedys."

Yet even at the end, despite his drunken threats, Billings never removed the Kennedy family photos from the walls of his townhouse. In his will, he left his Manhattan home to Bobby Jr.

And that was where Bobby would move a year later, after marrying his first wife Emily Black, whom he had met at the University of Virginia law school, alma mater of Uncle Ted.

The bride came from modest circumstances in Indiana, so the Kennedys offered to pick up the tab for the rehearsal dinner in Bloomington, Indiana, champagne, toasts and all. The bill came to $8,939.80—a huge amount for a small Indiana restaurant in 1982.

Ethel had no intention of paying until months later, when the restaurant filed a lawsuit, and its owner threatened to go on national TV and expose the Kennedys as deadbeats. Apparently, Hoosiers weren't as accommodating, or intimidated, as the shopkeepers and restaurateurs and merchants on the Cape and in Palm Beach.

Back in New York in the townhouse Lem had willed him, Bobby Jr. planned to go to work as a prosecutor in the office of Manhattan District

Attorney Robert Morgenthau. It was Morgenthau who had been lunching with Bobby at Hickory Hill on November 22, 1963, when J. Edgar Hoover phoned with the news from Dallas.

Working as a prosecutor was how Uncle Teddy had started in politics. And it was the same career path his cousin JFK Jr. planned to take a few years later, and it would be derailed in the same way—by JFK Jr.'s failure to pass the New York bar exam. Bobby Jr. would fail it only once, rather than twice, like his more famous cousin.

On the other hand, Bobby would accomplish a rather dubious feat JFK Jr. never came close to. Shortly after finally passing the bar exam, Bobby Jr. would be disbarred.

In *People* magazine's gushing story of his "story book" wedding to Emily Black in 1982, the reporter had asked Bobby Jr. if he had any faults.

"I have a tendency," Bobby admitted with false modesty, "to stay out too late and drink too much beer."

And to shoot too much heroin.

Bobby didn't mention that, of course, but by now he knew how bad his problem was. And so, in 1983, he had taken a commercial flight to South Dakota to visit a former priest who was attempting to help him overcome his addiction.

During the flight to Rapid City, passengers heard a ruckus from the restroom at the back of the plane. Inside Bobby was sitting on the toilet, semi-conscious, "white as a sheet, cold as an ice cube. There was a loss of muscle control."

He was trying to go cold turkey, always a bad idea for someone like the stone junkie Bobby had become. He was in the throes of withdrawal, and his condition prompted the flight's pilots to radio ahead for an ambulance. When the plane landed, however, RFK Jr. declined medical attention, despite needing assistance to make his way down the stairs. A police officer asked him his name.

"Bobby Francis," he answered.

The police decided to get a search warrant for Mr. Francis's luggage, and two days later they discovered heroin. He was charged with possession of the drug, a felony carrying a two-year sentence.

The family retained a South Dakota attorney with Boston roots. He was John Fitzgerald—the same name as Bobby's great-grandfather, Honey Fitz. This John Fitzgerald had moved west after surviving a spectacular car bombing in Everett in 1968 that had cost him part of his right leg. The bombing had been an attempt by the local Mafia to intimidate Fitzgerald's longtime client, Mob hitman Joe "the Animal" Barboza.

Bobby eventually pleaded guilty to the possession charges and was sentenced to two years' probation, periodic drug testing, treatment through Narcotics Anonymous and 1,500 hours of community service. He admitted himself to Fair Oaks treatment center.

"With the best medical help I can find," he said in yet another of those statements that the Kennedys were becoming known for, "I am determined to beat this problem. I deeply regret the pain which this situation will bring to my family and to so many Americans who admire my parents and the Kennedys."

There would be more pain, much more pain, in the years ahead.

CHAPTER FIFTEEN

A KENNEDY FAMILY PHOTO ALBUM

JFK, before he stopped wearing hats, meets his father, 1940.

JFK on the campaign trail, 1960.

JFK always had a wandering eye.

October 1963 Hyannis Port: JFK says good-bye to his father for the last time.

Primary night, 1962.

July 1967: Teddy and Joan leave St. Elizabeth's Hospital in Brighton with their infant son Patrick.

Sen. Kennedy gets the phone number of a constituent.

A rare photo: Teddy with nuns.

Joe Kennedy, paralyzed, with Richard Cardinal Cushing of Boston.

*Teddy was not popular with Boston parents
whose children's education was destroyed by
court-ordered busing.*

*Hyannis, November 1983: On the 20th anniversary of JFK's assassination, the family gath-
ered: Eunice, Pat, Ted and Jean.*

After Au Bar, Teddy needed a wife. Meet Victoria Reggie.

Newport, Rhode Island, August 1995: Ted Jr., Teddy, Bobby Jr. and Patrick Kennedy.

CHAPTER SIXTEEN

THE EIGHTIES

O NCE HIS 1980 CAMPAIGN for president was over and he'd taken penicillin shots for all the venereal diseases he'd picked up on the campaign trail, Teddy no longer even tried to keep up any semblance of sobriety. He and Joan quickly announced that they were finally getting a divorce, formalizing the end of their relationship.

In 1982, while Teddy was spending the weekend in Palm Beach, his nephew Tony Shriver arrived with the beautiful young drug addict Tatum O'Neal, who'd won an Academy Award as Best Actress in 1973 for *Paper Moon* at the age of 9.

Tipped off, the paparazzi rented a boat and lurked in the shallow waters off La Querida, hoping for a picture of the next generation of both Hollywood and the New Frontier. And the next morning, they did grab a revealing photo of a Kennedy, but it was Ted, by himself—walking along the beach naked, unabashed, unconcerned by either his gigantic beer gut or his "Fitzgerald breasts." The photo ran in tabloids around the world, and for years afterward, Teddy got invitations to address nudist groups.

A few years later, Teddy was in Monaco, cavorting with a 22-year-old graduate of the same college Joan graduated from—Marymount. Yet another Kennedy family tradition, serially seeking out women from the same school. For JFK, it had been Miss Porter's School. For Teddy, Marymount.

Again, he was photographed nude, only this time, he was on a yacht, and he was on top of a woman 33 years his junior. When that photo

Caroline's wedding to Edward Schlossberg, July 1986.

appeared in the supermarket tabloids, Sen. Howell Heflin of Alabama quipped, "It's good to see that the senator has changed his position on off-shore drilling."

That was Ted Kennedy—a national joke. The calamitous effects of his legislation—open borders, an out-of-control welfare state and the subsequent breakdown of the black family, a totally dysfunctional public education system dominated by greedy teachers' unions, tens of millions of abortions, a refugee program that would welcome thousands more terrorists like his brother's Arab murderer Sirhan Sirhan to the nation—the multiple disasters that Teddy had inflicted upon the nation were only now starting to become apparent.

Teddy seemed a buffoon, stumbling around the playgrounds of the western world, looking like "the husk he has so patently become," as the *New Republic* described him.

Despite his debauchery, Kennedy was still trying to further his goals, and in 1983, he decided to offer a plan to the Kremlin to overthrow the Republican president whose policies were driving the Soviet dictatorship to the brink, and Teddy to drink, or, more precisely, drink even more.

As his courier, Teddy settled on his old drinking buddy John Tunney, out of the Senate after a single term since 1976. In 1991, after the fall of the Evil Empire, a British reporter discovered in KGB archives a memo written by Victor Chebrikov, the director of the espionage service, to Yuri Andropov, the Soviet leader, laying out Teddy's offer to the Kremlin.

Andropov was himself an old KGB hand, who had been deeply involved in the overthrow of both the Hungarian revolution in 1956 and the Prague spring 12 years later. Kennedy wanted to introduce the dictator to the American people, in order to defeat Reagan. Through Tunney, Kennedy said he could accomplish this by assuring the Communists unlimited time on commercial television in the United States.

Teddy welcomes Mikhail Gorbachev to the JFK Library after the failure of their attempt to defeat Ronald Reagan in 1984.

"Kennedy and his friends," the Russian espionage service reported, "will bring about suitable steps to have representatives of the largest television companies in the USA contact Y.V. Andropov for an invitation to Moscow for the interviews . . . The senator underlined the importance that this initiative should be seen as coming from the American side."

In other words, networks like ABC, which would soon spike serious investigative work on the Hollywood scandals of Teddy's brothers, would agree to assist the Kremlin masters and Ted Kennedy in an attempt to rig the 1984 elections.

Teddy offered to go to Moscow to "arm Soviet officials with explanations regarding problems of nuclear disarmament so they may be better prepared and more convincing during appearances in the USA."

Of course, Teddy had his own vested interest in propping up the tottering Communist dictatorship.

Caroline Kennedy with her cousin, rapist Michael Kennedy, at Harvard graduation ceremonies, June 1980.

"The senator wants to run for president in 1988 (but) Kennedy does not discount that during the 1984 campaign, the Democratic Party may officially turn to him to lead the fight against the Republicans and elect their candidate president."

As a columnist for *Forbes* magazine noted after the discovery of the KGB memos, while Reagan risked his presidency to confront the Soviet slave state, Kennedy "chose to offer aid and comfort . . . On the Cold War, the greatest issue of his lifetime, Kennedy got it wrong."

In 1986, Teddy was again pushing "immigration reform"—open borders, in other words. This time he wanted an amnesty, for no more 1.3 million illegal aliens.

"We will secure the borders henceforth," he assured the president he had just failed to oust, even with the assistance of the Soviets. "We will never again bring forward another amnesty bill like this."

Hyannis Port, July 1983: Rose Kennedy, age 95, with her daughter Jean at the annual clambake for the Boston press.

By now, Teddy had found a new best friend in the Senate—Sen. Chris Dodd of Connecticut. Oddly, Dodd's father had detested the Kennedys when he served in the Senate from 1959 to 1971.

During the funeral services for JFK on Monday, November 25, 1963, Tom Dodd had sat in his Capitol office, drinking heavily, muttering and cursing the fact that his favorite game shows had been preempted.

Before his election to Congress, Tom Dodd had been an FBI agent. J. Edgar Hoover had always kept Dodd on a short leash, but tolerated him nonetheless until Dodd was picked up on an FBI wiretap drunkenly bragging that his pal LBJ was planning to appoint him as the next director of the FBI.

In 1967, Tom Dodd had been censured by the Senate for various corrupt acts on a vote of 92–5. It was the Senate's first censure vote since Joe McCarthy in 1954, and this time neither Kennedy ducked the vote. Both Bobby and Teddy voted to censure him. Tom Dodd was subsequently defeated for reelection, and died soon after at the age of 64.

Chris Dodd's political career was all about redeeming the family name—at least until he actually reached the Senate, after which he became crapulous Teddy's equally besotted sidekick, Falstaff to Ted's Falstaff.

In 1985, drunk as usual at the French restaurant La Colline in Washington, Dodd and Kennedy tore their framed portraits off the restaurant wall and stomped on them. The destroyed photo was replaced with a new one of the senior senator, this one inscribed *Laissez les bons temps roulette* ("Let the good times roll").

A new haute-cuisine French restaurant in the District quickly became another of their favorite watering holes. What Kennedy and Dodd liked about La Brassiere were the private dining rooms that were equipped with service bars—*de rigueur* for two drunkards who shared a thirst so great it would cast a shadow, as was once said of the poet Dylan Thomas.

In 1985, the two senators created what become known as their "waitress sandwich" in a private dining room on the first floor. They'd brought two young blondes as dates and gotten them drunk—their customary modus operandi. According to a story in *Gentleman's*

Quarterly (GQ), Ted had three or four mixed drinks in the first half hour after arriving, then switched to wine. When the women were in the restroom, a waitress entered. She was 5'3" and weighed 103 pounds.

Teddy, 6'3" and close to 300 pounds, grabbed the waitress, *GQ* reported, "and throws her on the table. She lands on her back, scattering crystal, plates, cutlery and the lit candles . . . Kennedy then picks her up and throws her on Dodd, who is sprawled in a chair . . . With (the waitress) on Dodd's lap, Kennedy jumps on top and begins rubbing his genital area against hers, supports his weight on the arms of the chair."

At that moment, another waitress entered, and both women began screaming. Teddy jumped off the waitress and Dodd said, "It's not my fault."

Kennedy dusted himself off and added, jokingly, according to *GQ,* "Makes you wonder about the leaders of this country."

In her memoir *Shockaholic,* the late actress Carrie Fisher recalled how shortly after her first stint in drug rehabilitation in 1985, she drove from Baltimore to Washington for a date with Sen. Dodd, of whom she knew next to nothing. Teddy tagged along, and after a long, liquid meal, he put the question directly to the woman who had portrayed Princess Leia in *Star Wars.*

"So," Teddy said, as a flushed Dodd looked on silently, "do you think you'll be having sex with Chris at the end of your date?"

"Funnily enough," she said, "I won't be having sex tonight."

"Would you have sex with Chris in a hot tub?" Teddy persisted.

"I'm no good in water," Fisher replied.

On July 1, 1987, President Reagan nominated Robert Bork for the Supreme Court seat being vacated by the retiring Nixon appointee, Lewis Powell. Bork was a distinguished legal scholar, a Yale Law School professor, who had served briefly as acting attorney general for Richard Nixon after the firing of Elliot Richardson in 1973.

At the time of his nomination, Bork was a federal appellate court judge. On constitutional grounds, he opposed *Roe v. Wade,* the court's 1973 decision legalizing abortion. On the bench, Bork had also failed to detect any references in the Constitution to any special rights for homosexuals. That was enough for Teddy.

He vowed to destroy Bork.

That afternoon, drunk as usual, Teddy stumbled onto the floor of the Senate and began an unhinged denunciation of the Marine Corps veteran:

"Robert Bork's America is a land in which women would be forced into back-alley abortions, blacks would sit at segregated lunch counters, rogue police could break down citizens' doors in midnight raids, schoolchildren could not be taught about evolution, writers and artists could be censored at the whim of the government . . ."

Kennedy then implored his sober colleagues not to allow Reagan, after carrying 49 states, "to impose his reactionary vision of the Constitution on the Supreme Court on the next generation of Americans."

Judge Bork had been "borked"—a verb that was quickly coined to describe what had happened. In October Bork's nomination was defeated, 58–42, and in his place President Reagan nominated Anthony Kennedy (no relation).

Kennedy is usually described as a "swing" vote on the Court although he has voted to impose both Obamacare and gay marriage on an unwilling population. (His own home state of California was one of 23 to vote in referenda to reject gay marriage.) Yet as soon as the Supreme Court approved it, gay marriage was declared "settled law" by homosexual advocates.

Again, despite Teddy's buffoonery and drunkenness, he had gotten his way, at the expense of the majority of the American people, in ways some of which would not even be recognized until after his death. As Shakespeare wrote, "The good a man does is oft interred with his bones/ While the evil lives on."

Six weeks after his "borking" speech, Ted Kennedy was out on his boat, the *Mya*, off Cape Cod, with a crew of one other man and five young women. On Sunday evening, Kennedy radioed that he had run aground and needed help. He was found eight miles from the location he had given the Coast Guard. A spokesman told reporters the rescue party had found "hundreds" of beer cans on the deck.

In September 1987, Teddy was in one of La Brasserie's private second-floor dining rooms with another young blonde, a Congressional lobbyist. They had consumed at least two bottles of Chardonnay. A waitress entered the room and saw Teddy "on the floor with his pants down on top of the woman, and he saw her and she just kind of backed away and closed the door."

In her final sentient years, even Rose was cognizant of her youngest son's behavior. At one point in Hyannis Port, slightly disoriented, she inquired where Ted was.

"In Virginia," one of her aides said.

"Virginia?" she said. "I hadn't heard of that one."

His behavior was so out of control that even his nephew Joe, the new congressman from Brighton, had to make sport of Teddy at the first St. Patrick's Day breakfast that he attended in South Boston, in 1987.

Senate President Billy Bulger asked Joe, "Where's your Uncle Teddy this morning."

"I don't follow Uncle Teddy in the morning," Joe answered. "After the decisions he's made the night before, I kind of leave him on his own in the morning."

The next year, Kennedy was among the Massachusetts delegation that went to the Vietnam Memorial to lay a wreath. A female reporter struck up a conversation, saying she'd like to interview him for a piece about his Uncle Ted.

"Does he know about the story?" Joe inquired.

Yes, the female reporter assured him. "I've been with him," she told Joe.

"Oh, you too?" said Joe.

In 1988, Teddy was running for his fifth six-year term. The sacrificial lamb was Joe Malone, a Harvard grad from Waltham, Italian despite his last name, who had worked for Ray Shamie when he ran against Teddy in 1982.

Malone was being groomed by the state GOP for higher office, and indeed, he would be elected treasurer in the state Republican landslide in 1990. Teddy of course gave Malone a wide berth. He even took off 40 pounds for the campaign, but mostly he just went through the usual minimal motions that were required of a Kennedy seeking reelection in Massachusetts.

Teddy's aides, as usual, called in "sound" to local radio stations—brief bits of audio recorded by the senator on the issues of the day. One Friday afternoon in May, Teddy was spotted at a pay phone at the Washington National Airport, trying to read a statement his staff had dictated to him, about the ratification of some treaty. He had to record a denunciation of "a band of renegade senators."

But Teddy, drunk, couldn't pronounce "renegade."

First he would say "renege." He'd take a breath and start again, flawless until he reached . . . "regnado." He'd start again—"regenada." "Regee . . . Renedgeo . . ." Finally, on the sixth take, Teddy nailed it.

By now the ticket agents from what was then Eastern Airlines were eyeing him nervously. When he glanced over at them, they rushed to assure him that he could take as long as he wanted—the plane wouldn't take off without him.

After a while, he returned to the pay phone, reached into his pocket for some change and called what was apparently his office for instructions on what he should tell any reporters who met his flight at Logan Airport in Boston.

He listened for a few seconds, then cut in.

"Well," he yelled at the hapless staffer, "what do you want me to say?"

In the fall, tradition required him to submit to interviews by the editorial boards of the state's newspapers. In Boston, he did the easy one first, at the *Globe*, where he knew that seldom, if ever, would be heard a discouraging word. Then he headed north to Rupert Murdoch's *Herald*, which he had recently tried to shut down.

He was told that his opponent, Malone, had recently admitted to using illegal drugs. Malone had gone to Harvard in the seventies—what else was he going to say? Would Ted like to follow suit and get it out of the way?

The question was asked by the same reporter who during the 1980 presidential campaign had interviewed Ilana Campbell, "the Countess." In a front-page story, she had said that "Ted and I used to take LSD and make beautiful love together."

Have you ever used drugs, Senator?

He put his head down and mumbled, "No, never."

Later, the same reporter asked Teddy a two-part question. Teddy looked up.

"That's a two-fer," he said.

"It's happy hour," the reporter replied.

Ted glanced up at the clock on the wall. It was 4:50.

"Not quite," he said.

Reluctantly, Ted agreed to a televised debate, but only one. Unlike his former boss Ray Shamie in 1982, Malone didn't even have to donate $10,000 to a charity to get a one-on-one with Teddy. But Ted insisted that it be held on the Saturday night before Halloween, on a single TV station, for just 30 minutes.

But even a half hour was too long, as it turned out. Ted's troubles began early, when he attempted to put the cap back on his pen as Malone answered the first question. His hands were shaking so violently that he couldn't even come close to getting the cap back on. When the moderator turned to Kennedy, he began talking about, of all things, "three-martini lunches."

Throughout the debate, Teddy kept mixing up words—not just in the usual way he bollixed words, turning "cop-killer bullets" into "crop-killer bullets."

Increasingly, he seemed unable to construct sentences with the words in their proper order, as in "Those are very two extremely important steps." Or he couldn't get the subjects and verbs to agree: "Those countries don't have a death penalty and they will not extradite them to a country that do."

His position on not executing illegal aliens, Teddy said, was based on his concern about "the protection of American kind of lives."

The Reagan administration naturally came in for criticism for having "underminded" peace proposals in Central America.

"More attention is going to have to be played to Mexico."

Nonetheless, Kennedy was reelected in November 1988, and two months later he found himself in yet another barroom affray, this time on the Upper East Side of Manhattan in a bar called American Trash.

Teddy reeled in about 2 a.m. and immediately began hitting on the young women, using his traditional line: "Are you from, er, um, uh, Massachusetts?"

At some point, he found himself into a conversation of sorts when a bouncer named Dennis McKenna (not to be confused with an alcoholic Irish-born Massachusetts state senator from Somerville of the same name.) McKenna came up to Ted and began yelling, "Why don't you politicians do something about drugs?"

"Get out of my face," Teddy responded.

"You're nothing like your two brothers," McKenna sneered.

Teddy threw a drink in his face.

CHAPTER SEVENTEEN

THE POSTER BOYS

N 1997, THE TATTERED façade of one-for-all-and-all-for-one Kennedy family unity finally crumbled into finger-pointing and scandal—this time in full public view.

The Palm Beach rape trial had been devastating to what little remained of the Kennedys' national image. But at least they had maintained a semblance of one-for-all-and-all-for-one family unity.

Now, however, there would be not only more rape allegations, but also denunciations by the late president's son and namesake of two of his cousins, one of whom would be almost simultaneously called out by his ex-wife as both an abusive husband and a bad Catholic.

And in yet another twist of fate, within months of the public feud erupting among the three Kennedy cousins, two of them would be dead, in their 30s, in the kind of horrific accidents that had haunted the family for so long.

What remained of old Joe's meticulously maintained media myth about his clan quickly unraveled after the death of the family's two matriarchs in an eight-month period that began with the passing of Jackie Onassis in May 1994.

She died in her apartment on the East Side of Manhattan of lymphatic cancer—which her son JFK Jr. privately blamed on all those long-ago injections from Dr. Feelgood. After her death, he went out onto Fifth Avenue to read a prepared statement to the gathered paparazzi, asking them to respect the family's privacy.

Cambridge, May 1993: Jackie attends her final Profiles in Courage award ceremony. She would be dead less than a year later.

In January 1995, Rose Fitzgerald Kennedy died at the age of 103 in the family compound in Hyannis Port. She had been virtually comatose for more than a decade, and had not spoken a word for two years.

Through various trusts, the two women had controlled the vast majority of the family's remaining wealth. As always the Kennedys tried as best they could to minimize their tax burdens, asking not what they could do for their country, but what their country could do for them.

Jackie's married boyfriend, Maurice Tempelsman, had proven a wise steward of Ari Onassis's money. Joe Kennedy would no doubt have been appalled by his favorite daughter-in-law's open, scandalous liaison with a European-born, Yiddish-speaking Hasidic diamond merchant, but he would have appreciated Tempelsman's investment acumen. But the most valuable part of her estate turned out to be the 327-acre oceanside resort on Martha's Vineyard that she had bought from the Hornblower family in 1978 for $1.5 million.

JFK Jr. and Caroline planned an auction at Sotheby's of their mother's personal belongings, but balked at the 55 percent death tax. Quietly, they lobbied to have the take from the auction—estimated to be at least $40 million—taxed as simple income, thus reducing the tax bite to a more manageable 39.6 percent.

The trial balloon went nowhere, and so, after the $43 million auction, in December 1996 the *New York Times* obligingly ran a story headlined, "Mrs. Onassis's Estate Worth Less Than Estimated," thus conveniently "leaving very little for charity."

As for Rose, at the time of her death, she had not set foot in Florida in at least 12 years. Yet the Massachusetts Department of Revenue, an agency renowned for its relentless pursuit of runaway residents, allowed her will to be filed in West Palm Beach, saving her heirs at least an eight-figure tax bite from the Commonwealth.

The closest facsimile to a Kennedy matriarch now would have to be Teddy's new bride, the former Victoria Reggie. After Au Bar, he had realized that even the *Globe* would no longer be able to carry him across the electoral finish line every sixth year with their traditional "Teddy-turning-his-life-around" puff pieces.

The marriage to Vikki helped Ted to fend off perhaps his most serious Republican challenger ever, Mitt Romney, an investment banker and son of former Michigan Gov. George Romney.

Romney was an attractive candidate—well-spoken, wealthy, happily married with five sons, two Harvard degrees. The electorate seemed increasingly weary of the Kennedys, and the ruinous social policies they had long championed. Romney and his surrogates spoke often of "Kennedy Country"—the urban areas devastated by 30 years of the Great Society's War on Poverty and Third World immigration.

As always, Ted tapped one of his younger relatives as the official campaign manager. That year the mantle fell to Michael LeMoyne Kennedy (his middle name came from JFK's best friend, Lem Billings). Kennedy was now running his brother Joe's Citizens Energy nonprofit. After assuming control, he had immediately given himself a six-figure raise.

Michael and Ted Kennedy, 1991, at the Sheraton Boston.

Romney had survived a bruising GOP primary challenge by an opponent who in one televised debate called him "Mr. Mormon." Early polls showed Romney, in his first campaign, running neck and neck with the 32-year veteran Teddy, who had appeared more disheveled, overweight and incoherent than ever in his initial TV appearances.

Alarmed by the campaign's ominous drift, the Kennedys unleashed what even their supporters considered a below-the-belt attack on Romney, lashing out at his Mormon faith.

The heavy lifting was left to Cong. Joe Kennedy, who accused the Church of Latter Day Saints of treating blacks and women as "second-class citizens."

"You ought to take a look at those issues," he advised voters.

The *Globe* ran headline after headline, always noting the inaccuracy of the charges against Romney, but only deep in the body of the stories. As the Kennedys well knew, it was only the headlines that most voters saw.

Teddy refused to disavow Joe's intemperate blasts. Finally, with his 87-year-old father at his side, Mitt brought up the obvious, that Teddy was engaging in the same tactics JFK had had to overcome in his presidential campaign 34 years earlier.

"I'm sad to say," Mitt Romney said, "that Ted Kennedy is trying to take away his brother's victory."

Finally, Joe issued a statement saying that he "deeply regretted" attacking Romney's religion. But by then the damage had been done. On election day, Kennedy cruised to a 17-point victory.

A few weeks later, Rose Fitzgerald Kennedy was dead. Michael Kennedy was supposed to be one of her pallbearers, but the day she died his cousin Michael Skakel had driven him to Maryland to check into an alcohol-rehabilitation center.

Michael Kennedy and his children, Kyle and Michael Jr., at Quincy Bay Marina, 1987.

In New York, at age 34 JFK Jr. was finally free from Jackie's controlling ways. He could now do what he wanted, and what he wanted to do, among other things, was learn to fly airplanes. Even as a child, he had loved traveling with his father on Air Force One. His first drawings were of jets, and in November 1963 when he was told his father was in heaven, JFK Jr. inquired whether he would still be able to fly on the big jet. His third birthday was November 25, three days after the assassination, and as his main gift Jackie had already selected a large toy jet.

His older sister Caroline was likewise interested in flight, and during her high school years at Concord Academy in Concord, Massachusetts, she had begun taking flying lessons at nearby Hanscom Field. But in January 1973, Jackie's stepson had died in yet another plane crash, this one at the airport in Athens. Jackie had immediately called the school and told them that there would no more flight lessons for Caroline. The same edict applied for JFK Jr., at least until Jackie's death in 1994.

But the bigger news for John F. Kennedy Jr. in 1995 was when he decided to do something almost no one in his extended family had done for two generations: he began actually trying to earn a living for himself in the private sector.

Along with his partner, businessman Michael Berman, he launched *George* magazine, a glossy monthly that sought to establish itself as a sort of *Rolling Stone* of political publications. JFK Jr.'s enduring popularity brought the publication a tremendous amount of initial publicity, and, like his father before him, his connections to Hollywood royalty would factor heavily in his plans.

Cindy Crawford graced the first cover, dressed as George Washington, wearing a facsimile of the general's uniform (except for the sexy midriff top under her blue coat).

JFK Jr. was able to attract a uniquely broad band of contributors. In an effort to broaden the magazine's base beyond the liberal left, he published Ann Coulter and Rush Limbaugh alongside more traditionally Kennedy-friendly talking heads like post–*Saturday Night Live* but pre-Senate Al Franken, George Clooney, and Clinton mouthpiece Paul Begala.

For a moment, the start-up *George* was the envy of all political magazines. This was significant in the days before the Internet all but rendered print journalism—especially monthlies—obsolete. For a few months, *George* enjoyed the largest circulation of any magazine of its kind.

But soon *George* was being criticized for its bland content. Its original premise, "Not Just Politics as Usual," didn't work. David Carr of the *New York Times* would later point out that JFK Jr.'s commitment to avoiding gossip in his monthly was a large part of its ultimate undoing. *George*'s transitory popularity was a function of the fact that its publisher bestrode the worlds of gossip and celebrity like a colossus, as had his father before him.

He hadn't been able to raise $9 million in seed money to start another *New Republic*, or even worse, a *New Republic* without attitude.

That's not to say John Jr. was staying out of the tabloids. It was big news when, in 1990, he failed the New York State bar exam—for the second time. The famous *New York Post* headline was "The Hunk Flunks." The paparazzi often photographed him skateboarding bare-chested on the East Side, or in Central Park.

Moreover, repeating the family tradition, before finally settling down in the final years of his life, the Hollywood-handsome JFK Jr. hooked up with a string of starlets including Crawford, Sarah Jessica Parker, Brooke Shields and Marilyn Monroe–obsessed Madonna.

But it was his relationship with Darryl Hannah that put him in the headlines most often. The two were photographed having very public arguments in New York City during their five-plus year relationship, which began after her tumultuous breakup with rock star Jackson Browne. Though tame by the standards of his contemporaries, JFK Jr.'s open spats were disconcerting to a public that still remembered the photo of the little boy on his third birthday in November 1963 saluting as the wagon containing his father's flag-draped coffin rolled by, pulled by a prancing white horse.

As a dutiful Irish son, JFK Jr. had waited until after his mother's passing to seriously consider matrimony. His bride was the beautiful Carolyn Bessette, five years his junior, who had worked in the fashion industry since her graduation from Boston University. In high school, her classmates had voted her "Ultimate Beautiful Person," and now she had proven them correct.

As his mother would have wanted, JFK Jr. tried to remain above the fray of the cutthroat world of publishing. But as circulation dropped and advertising revenue dried up, he did what all magazine publishers have always done.

An old-line magazine publisher once told his editor, "I don't want sex on the cover, I want wet sex on the cover!" And so did JFK Jr.

His former assistant, Rose Marie Terenzio would later report that JFK Jr. wrote to Madonna asking her to pose on the cover of his magazine as his mother Jackie, despite Terenzio's warning that it would create "a media shitstorm."

The concept was simple if not tasteless. "We'll have her in a pillbox hat, sitting on a stack of books," JFK Jr. said. Even the Material Girl, never a shrinking violet, realized this was a bad idea. Demurring in a faxed response she addressed to "Johnny Boy," Madonna told him she "could never do [her] justice." Instead, she proposed, "If you want me to portray Eva Braun or Pamela Harriman, I might say yes!"

(Perhaps Madonna did not realize that the irony of mentioning Pamela Harriman—a rape victim of JFK Jr.'s grandfather during a visit to Palm Beach in the 1940s. Maybe even JFK Jr. himself didn't know the extent of his family's sordid history.)

Grasping at one straw after another to save his magazine, JFK Jr. next invited actress Drew Barrymore—offspring of another notoriously scandalous clan—to pose on the cover of his magazine not in the style of an American patriot, but instead as Marilyn Monroe. And this wasn't just any depiction of the doomed ingénue.

Instead, Barrymore wore the fluffed hair and near-transparent gown that Monroe wore when she famously and breathlessly shocked the high-rolling audience at Madison Square Garden celebrating his father's 45th birthday in 1962. Her cheesecake shot dominated the cover and appeared above the words "Happy Birthday, Mr. President" in large type. There could be no mistaking the intent.

Jackie, who had refused to attend that 1962 birthday party for obvious reasons, would have been disgusted. Even worse, the shocking cover didn't reverse the magazine's failing circulation.

In Boston, however, JFK Jr.'s cousins Joe and Michael could still sell newspapers, if only because they were on the cover of both dailies, day after day, involved in one scandal after another.

JFK Jr., watched, fascinated and appalled, as the two brothers took the family down yet another notch, and then another, and another . . .

After a decade in Congress, Joe Kennedy had grown restless. The Republicans now controlled both branches of Congress. Neither of Massachusetts's seats in the U.S. Senate were going to open up anytime soon. Joe privately complained to friendly reporters that he wasn't as rich as everybody assumed, especially after divorcing his first wife Sheila Brewster Rauch, three years earlier. It likewise hadn't escaped Joe's attention that

Michael had now succeeded Joe as president of Citizens Energy—and was now paying himself more than twice as much as Joe had when he ran Citizens Energy.

But then Joe found out—by reading about it in the papers—that Sheila had written a tell-all book called *Shattered Faith: A Woman's Struggle to Stop the Catholic Church From Annulling Her Marriage*. In it, she recounted how she learned that her marriage to the congressman had been annulled, unbeknownst to her, by the Catholic Church three years earlier, so that Joe could immediately marry his former staffer Beth Kelly—a woman eight years her junior.

Joe Kennedy and his first wife Sheila.

Rauch, from a Main Line Philadelphia family, was flabbergasted—and angry. Her twelve-year marriage to Joe had produced twin sons in 1980, 11 years before their divorce. Now she was learning that the marriage, in the eyes of the Catholic Church, had never existed.

Rauch recalled that she vomited when she was first informed that Joe was seeking an annulment. Though she wasn't Catholic

Joe Kennedy and his second wife Beth.

(Joe's marriage to an Episcopalian was another departure from family tradition), Rauch refused to sign off on a pro forma acknowledgment that her marriage was invalid. But Joe was adamant.

As Sheila dug in her heels, he stormed, "How can you be opposed? What right do you have to be opposed? How can you prevent me from going on with my life?"

Devastated, Sheila replied, "I wish you well, but an annulment is something very different from a divorce. An annulment says that there was never a true marriage in the eyes of God. I don't know about you, but I took our marriage very seriously."

"Of course I think we had a true marriage," Joe said. "But that doesn't matter now. I don't believe the stuff. Nobody actually believes it. It's just Catholic gobbledygook, Sheila. But you just have to say it this way because, well, because that's how the Church is."

Worse yet, it appeared that the Church had broken its own rules, granting the annulment without going through its own review process. Now, with the spotlight cast upon it by Sheila Rauch, the Holy See had to reconsider the matter. In the end, nearly a decade later, the Church overturned the annulment.

By then it didn't matter. The congressman had already married Kelly in a civil ceremony—a mortal sin in the eyes of the Church. Theoretically, he would no longer be allowed to partake in holy sacraments, such as Communion. Theoretically. Canonical law meant as much to the Kennedys as criminal law.

But Sheila wasn't through with her ex. In her book, she described her former husband as a "person not endowed with patience or a willingness to listen." She implied that he was a bully, writing, "I know in retrospect there were other times when I should have faced up to Joe . . . I had never faced the truth that by the end of our marriage I had simply become afraid of him."

The timing of the stories couldn't have been worse. Popular Republican Governor William Weld had resigned his office in 1997 to focus on his nomination by President Bill Clinton to be ambassador to Mexico (which was ultimately thwarted by conservative GOP Sen. Jesse Helms of North Carolina). Weld was succeeded by his lieutenant governor, Paul Cellucci, a career pol with a six-figure credit-card debt and a rumored gambling problem. A State House lifer, Cellucci was well-liked on Beacon Hill but certainly no match for even a junior varsity Kennedy like Joe.

The Corner Office seemed there for Joe Kennedy II's taking. He was the odds-on favorite to win the governorship in 1998. But suddenly, his favorability ratings were plummeting as quickly as *George* magazine's ad revenue and circulation. His problems didn't end with Sheila's book. "The Wizard of Uhs," as one *Boston Herald* columnist took to calling the tongue-tied congressman, made a series of missteps that didn't play well with voters, many of whom no longer remembered the days when Kennedys traveled the seas in PT boats rather than Oldsmobiles.

Soon, Joe II found himself trailing in the polls behind not only Cellucci, but also his fellow Democrat, Attorney General, L. Scott Harshbarger. As his political fortunes plunged, Joe descended further into rhetorical incoherence.

There was the time he spoke on the House floor live on C-SPAN and, trying unsuccessfully to summon the ghost of his late uncle Jack, said "A rising tide *lefts* all boats."

Trying to position himself as a champion of the nation's veterans, he said "I stand back in the back seat to no one."

During a televised House Banking Committee hearing with the chairman of the Federal Reserve, Alan Greenspan, Joe tried his best to express his understanding of the plight of the lower middle classes.

"The American worker," Joe said, "finds himself in a hamster-like stance in a box."

To make matters worse, Sheila Rauch was back in the news, this time reporting that the couple's son Matthew, now 16 years old, had been taken to the emergency room at Cape Cod Hospital for treatment for burns he received from a "sparks-emitting device" he had used with his father on the beach in Hyannis Port. The device in question was, in fact, a large, two-fuse firecracker. Joe lit one of its fuses and idiotically handed it to his son, the results being third-degree burns and a trip to the hospital.

No charges of child abuse were filed; none of the "mandated reporters" at the hospital reported anything to the authorities.

Joe stumbled on in his campaign for governor. He showed up at an "empowerment zone" conference to address some "folks" from "the community." Kennedy preposterously described himself as a "poor Irishman," then surveyed the crowd and said, "Then I look out at all you, and I see that the blacks have taken over."

The Sunday morning that story appeared in the paper—buried as the last item in the *Globe*'s political-notes column, Joe K was back at it. Appearing on *Meet the Press* alongside Jack Kemp, he worked himself into a faux frenzy over how Republicans had given Big Tobacco a big tax break "in the dead of night." Only Joe II said "in the heat of the night."

By then, however, Joe had bigger problems to worry about than his inability to utter a coherent thought. His younger brother Michael was in a photo finish with a state grand jury.

Michael Kennedy was the middle child of RFK and Ethel's 11 progeny, and like some of his siblings, he inherited many of his father's familiar facial characteristics. But, unlike Joe, who was described in *Vanity Fair* as "[r]uggedly handsome . . . big grin . . . taller than his father was . . . hipper . . . ice-blue eyes," Michael's regressive features gave him the appearance of a caricature of RFK, his teeth a little too big, his brow a bit too heavy.

But like so many of his kinsmen, Michael had a way with the opposite sex. One of his many conquests was his family's voluptuous blonde babysitter Marissa Verrochi. The problem was, she was 14 years old.

Perhaps Michael had grown tired of his wife of 16 years, Victoria Denise Gifford, the daughter of football legend and broadcaster Frank Gifford. During their high school years, Ethel Kennedy had acted as matchmaker, when Michael was at St. Paul's School and Vicki was spending the summer at Hickory Hill.

By 1997, their marriage was on the rocks. But Giff had little time to console his daughter, after having become embroiled in his own tabloid sex scandal that same year. Despite what seemed to be a picture-perfect marriage to his third wife, television star and born-again Christian Kathie Lee Gifford, Frank was caught in an extramarital affair with an ex–flight attendant he had known casually for four years.

Meanwhile, in Massachusetts, Victoria caught her husband in bed with the babysitter who had worked for the family since the age of 12. Falling back on a tried and true excuse, Michael blamed his serial philandering on alcoholism. He enrolled in yet another treatment program, but continued to have contact with the girl, sometimes telling her that he planned to marry her once she turned 16.

Friends and neighbors of the girl would later tell the media that the affair had begun when she was 14. Whispers around Cohasset intensified as the indiscreet lovers were seen meeting in various locations around the town. Concerned friends of the girl's wealthy parents, Paul and June Verrochi, approached the couple about their suspicions. When the Verrochis confronted their daughter, she confessed to the affair.

The family was stunned, given their close ties to the Kennedys. Verrochi was a major Democratic fundraiser, and he sat on the board of the Kennedys' Citizens Energy Corp.

Many of the sordid details became public years later when Kennedy cousin Michael Skakel tried to sell yet another Kennedy tell-all, this one entitled *Dead Man Talking: A Kennedy Cousin Comes Clean.*

The subtitle was: *The First Account by an Insider of the Avarice, Perversion, and Gangsterism of America's First Family.*

It was yet another family tradition: a cousin spilling the beans on his more famous kinsmen for fun and profit. Like Paul Gargan, who had served as a source of the ultimate Chappaquiddick book, *Senatorial Privilege,* Skakel seemed to suffer from an inferiority complex. He was related to the Kennedys, but he wasn't really one of them. Like Gargan, he

Michael Skakel, Kennedy cousin and convicted murderer.

needed money. He was still at that point the prime suspect in the 1975 murder of his neighbor in Greenwich, 15-year-old Martha Moxley.

Skakel had been hired as his cousin's driver. Like everyone else in the family, Michael Kennedy was a menace behind the wheel. His convertible was well-known on the South Shore. Drunk or sober, he drove recklessly. Skakel's assignment was to keep his first cousin out of trouble, as best he could. Hanging around Cohasset, Michael Skakel saw everything. Michael and the babysitter carried on as if he wasn't even there.

"Michael asked for a back rub and lay on the sofa while she straddled him," Skakel wrote in his book pitch. "She used to brag all the time about sleeping with the Kennedy guy. But nobody believed her until the stories came out."

Skakel claimed he tried to warn Joe and Bobby Kennedy about their younger brother's behavior, but that they weren't concerned. The old admonitions about "jailbait" and the warning, "Fifteen'll get you twenty!"—those might be concerns for others, but certainly not for America's First Family.

"Michael has a pee-pee problem!" Skakel quoted Joe as saying dismissively. "What happened? Did he get caught fucking that babysitter? My brother can fuck anyone he wants."

Bobby told Skakel, "I don't see how that's any of your business."

But Skakel also said that as the facts came out, Bobby was shocked at his brother's behavior.

"Oh my God," Skakel quoted him as saying of Michael, "he's just like Willie (Smith)."

When Skakel asked him what he meant by that, Bobby told him that Willie "was guilty of rape, that his acquittal was the result of Kennedy power."

Meanwhile, Michael Kennedy's behavior was growing ever more unhinged. He broke into a garage where the babysitter kept her car. He was videotaped by a security camera leaving behind on the front windshield of her car what was later described as an "artificial penis."

Soon, Michael was packed off to another rehab center, this one for sex addiction, in Arizona. Following one of the rules of the facility, he had to compile a list of the names of all his sexual conquests. When his wife Vicki saw the list, she was shocked. Some of the women were her friends.

According to some sources, one of the women was the babysitter's mother, June Verrochi. Vicki and the children soon moved out of the family's Cohasset home.

As the babysitter Marissa turned 18, she and her parents entered therapy. Michael Skakel became one of Marissa's confidants—an especially strange turn of events, befriending one beautiful blonde teenage girl 15 years after allegedly murdering a different one.

But now Skakel had transferred his allegiance from his kinsmen to the Verrochis. As Marissa would testify a few years later at his murder trial in Connecticut, Skakel "took her under his wing" during "particularly distressful circumstances."

In 2002 she would testify at her friend's murder trial that "he protected me from the situation as best he possibly could."

One cold rainy Saturday night in November 1996, Skakel was with the Verrochis at their posh six-story townhouse in the Back Bay when June Verrochi cracked. Barefoot, in a white nightgown, she climbed to the roof of her building and threatened to throw herself off. In the rain-soaked alley below, Marissa begged her mother not to kill herself. Finally, Boston firefighters on a ladder truck were able to pull Mrs. Verrochi off the roof. In their report, the firefighters said she had a "faraway look" in her eyes.

A spokesman for the family told the *Boston Herald*: "She had received some unfortunate news that night, and she was under a doctor's care."

Asked if the news involved her daughter's affair with Kennedy, the spokesman said, "No comment."

Once they were both safely on the sidewalk, neither Verrochi woman would speak to the other. It was left to Michael Skakel to join June in the ambulance for the short ride to Massachusetts General Hospital, where she told staff about her daughter's rape by Michael Kennedy.

Soon thereafter, the district attorney of Norfolk County opened what he described as a "statutory rape investigation."

In yet another bizarre turn of events, a South Shore body shop owner working on Michael's Saab convertible contacted the police when he found the backseat of the car loaded with pornographic videotapes and magazines.

The Kennedys quickly came up with a cover story for this odd find. They explained that the car had been vandalized four weeks earlier, and apparently—incredibly—the vandal left porn in the car. When asked why Michael would leave someone else's pornography in his car for a month, the Kennedys' attorney replied, "I have no idea."

Ultimately, the Verrochis' high-powered attorney, R. Robert Popeo, announced that the babysitter would not testify against Michael Kennedy. If called before the grand jury, Popeo said, his client would take the Fifth Amendment. Without her cooperation, it would be impossible to win a conviction. Another Kennedy had skated.

Once the district attorney announced his decision, Michael Kennedy faxed a statement of contrition to the press—misspelling the babysitter's name. Another family tradition.

As always, the family's supporters rallied around the Kennedys. One caller to a Boston radio talk show scoffed at the alleged crime.

"Rape?" the caller said. "Come off it—everybody knew they were dating. These 14-year-olds today, they're like 25-year-olds used to be."

Hoping to put the scandal behind him, Cong. Joe Kennedy II continued his campaign for governor, bumbling his way through relentless questioning about his brother.

A local television reporter asked him if he had ever seen Michael and the babysitter at the family compound. When Joe replied "No," the reporter pushed.

"You never saw the girl with Michael?"

"Well, I mean I, I, not in the sense of being together in the way that I think you intended it."

Translation: He never saw them having sex.

"Did I ever, uh, in the last few years . . . no in, uh, not in uh, any incident that sticks out in my mind," he continued. "But I mean I'm certain at some point I might have seen them, you know?"

It was Joe's own brand of "gobbledygook" that was now on full display, as he futilely tried to defend his brother without seeming callous about the 14-year-old rape victim. Whatever he said just reminded everyone of his own record with young women, namely Pam Kelley, paralyzed on Nantucket when Joe recklessly overturned a Jeep on a narrow island road.

Asked for his comment on this latest scandal involving his nephews, Sen. Kennedy was equally adrift.

Stand
by
Vicki asks
DA to end
Mike K's
nightmare

your
man

By MAGGIE MULVIHILL and GAYLE FEE

Victoria Gifford Kennedy defended her scandal-plagued husband yesterday, making a secret statement to Norfolk County District Attorney Jeffrey Locke that she said should end his statutory rape probe of Michael Kennedy.

"This has been a very sad and difficult time for me (and) for my family . . ." Kennedy said in a statement issued by her lawyer.

"Now that I have been interviewed by the district

Turn to Page 22

'He preyed on her'

MICHAEL KENNEDY
Under investigation

Former
Kennedy
sitter
huddles
with DA

DA puts
Mike K
cousin
on the
hot seat

Alleged affair witness
linked to '75 murder

Mike K cousin told DA about underage sex affair

Source: Babysitter was only 14

By GAYLE FEE and MAGGIE MULVIHILL

A key witness in the Michael Kennedy case has accused Kennedy of having sex with his babysitter several times when she was underage, the Herald has learned.

The blockbuster revelation was told to investigators a day before the fami-

ly of the Cohasset babysitter called on District Attorney Jeffrey Locke to end his statutory rape probe.

A source close to Michael Skakel said Skakel told the DA Thursday that the babysitter confided in him late last summer or early fall that she and Ken-

Turn to Page 8

Ex-wife: Joe K bullied, scared me

By ANDREW MIGA

WASHINGTON — A new book by the former wife of U.S. Rep. Joseph P. Kennedy II describes how the congressman resorted to verbal bullying as he pushed for a church annulment he labeled

"Catholic gobbledygook."

"I was, after all, a Protestant in one of the nation's largest Catholic prohibitions," she wrote. "My former husband was powerful and popular. I was, as he so often reminded me, a nobody, and nobody in his town would be

on my side."

Sheila Rauch Kennedy, raised in a prominent Philadelphia Main Line family, said her decision to fight the annulment was a sharp departure from the passive way she handled most pressures during their 12-year marriage.

"I know in retrospect there were other times when I should have faced up to Joe. I had never faced the truth that by the end of our marriage I had simply become afraid of him," she wrote.

Turn to Page 23

BACK OFF: U.S. Rep. John Conyers (D-Mich.) lashes out at reporters yesterday after the journalists peppered U.S. Rep. Joseph P. Kennedy II, left, with questions about his knowledge of his brother's affair with a teenage babysitter. Kennedy cut short the press conference regarding TV liquor ads and stormed out of the room. More on the congressman, Pages 4, 23 and 28. *Photo courtesy of WCVB-TV*

DA seeks love letters allegedly written by Michael K

By GAYLE FEE and MAGGIE MULVIHILL

Investigators in the Michael Kennedy sex probe are seeking love letters Kennedy allegedly wrote to his babysitter paramour in which he reportedly declares his love for the Cohasset teen and promises to leave his wife for her.

Sources say the girl saved her packet of notes but investigators have not been able to obtain the potentially explosive evidence.

Bob Popeo, the attorney for the babysitter and her family, has told investigators he doesn't have the letters, sources say.

A source close to the investiga-

Turn to Page 22

KENNEDY

Source: Mike K and sitter at wild rafting party

By JOE BATTENFELD and MAGGIE MULVIHILL

Michael Kennedy and his teenage babysitter were carrying on their affair during at least one wild Kennedy family rafting trip that featured nude swimming and a vodka-laced sauna, sources said.

The annual family rafting trips, held between 1994 and 1996 in Maine, were dominated by a "late night party atmosphere," according to one source.

Sources said Kennedy family members were drinking heavily with the teenage babysitter, who was also seen swimming in the

nude at the time of one trip in 1994.

The girl was believed to be 16 years old at the time, well under the legal drinking age. It was not clear who provided her with the liquor.

Other family members present included

Turn to Page 9

Even by Kennedy standards, 1997 was a very bad year.

"I have nothing to, uh, add from the very beginning," he told reporters, "not gonna make any comment on it, just not gonna make any co-comment, since from the very beginning, not, not gonna say anything more about it, still under the, uh, district attorney's—I'm not gonna say anything more."

Joe made one final attempt to salvage his campaign for governor. In June 1997 he went to the state Democratic convention and tried to clear the air once and for all.

"I'm sorry," he told thousands of milling delegates. "So very, very sorry."

It wasn't nearly enough. Soon he withdrew from the race and announced he would not seek reelection to the House. After a contentious GOP primary against the popular state treasurer Joe Malone (who a decade earlier had run unsuccessfully against Teddy), Acting Gov. Cellucci would easily win the office that had once seemed Joe Kennedy's birthright.

It was after Joe's withdrawal from the race that JFK Jr. decided to publicly castigate his cousins, in his magazine's annual "Women's Issue."

In another attempt to goose newsstand sales, JFK Jr. posed nude, going all Garden of Eden, his private parts covered by an apple. In an accompanying "editor's note," he wrote cryptically, "I've learned a lot about temptation lately."

Without identifying his cousins by name, he left no doubt who he was referring to.

"Two members of my family chased an idealized alternative to their life," JFK Jr. wrote. "One left behind an embittered wife, and another, in what looked to be a hedge against mortality, fell in love with youth and surrendered his judgment in the process. Both became poster boys for bad behavior. Perhaps they deserved it. Perhaps they should have known better. To whom much is given, much is expected, right?"

It was such a complete departure from family tradition that few even bothered to note all the other "poster boys for bad behavior" in his family that JFK Jr. had neglected to mention.

Joe was particularly bitter about what he saw as the betrayal, although he tried to joke to reporters that he was ready for JFK Jr. to show up at the family's next touch football game.

"Ask not what you can do for your cousin," he said, "but what you can do for his magazine."

But the awful year of 1997 wasn't over quite yet. Another family tradition was to fly to Aspen for the Christmas holidays. A few years earlier, Chris Lawford had been arrested there, trying to pass a phony prescription for Valium.

That Christmas of 1997, the disgraced Michael joined the rest of his family on their annual ski trip, and as usual, they decided to play a foolhardy, dangerous version of touch football on the steep slopes, despite the repeated warnings of the local ski patrol.

As *Time* magazine later reported, "Members of the patrol had been warning the Kennedys off the game all week; [on the evening of December 30] a senior official of the Aspen Skiing Co., which runs the mountain, contacted Michael's mother Ethel to try to halt this family tradition . . . They wanted it stopped."

As usual Kennedy hubris would rule the day. Michael was described as an "expert skier" and "the ringleader" by social diarist R. Couri Hay, who was there and witnessed what came next.

"[Michael] skis off, he turns around to get a pass, he slams into a tree head first, he falls down unconscious."

Rescue efforts were futile. Michael was administered last rites of the Roman Catholic Church and pronounced dead, the cause listed as "massive head and neck trauma." His wife, the former Victoria Gifford, was not in Aspen. Instead, she had been in Vail with her own disgraced father. She quickly arrived in Aspen to retrieve her grieving children.

Actor Kevin Costner loaned the Kennedys his plane and Michael's body was returned to Hyannis Port. He was buried in Brookline next to his grandparents and his brother David.

JFK Jr. was shocked by his cousin's gruesome end. For three months, he quit the flying lessons he had begun after his mother's death. But as his magazine continued to flounder, so did his new marriage to Carolyn Bessette. By 1998, they had entered marriage counseling, and he had resumed his flying lessons. He bought a small plane.

January 1998: Siblings respond to the death of rapist Michael Kennedy: Joe, Kathleen, Max, Robert Jr. and Chris.

With *George* on its last legs, JFK Jr. began plotting his next move. Sen. Daniel Patrick Moynihan would be retiring in 2000, but Uncle Teddy thought the 2002 New York governor's race would provide a better opportunity for his nephew. Hillary Clinton already had her eye on the Senate seat, and in 2002, JFK Jr. would be going up against GOP Gov. George Pataki, who would be seeking a third term.

In July 1999, Rory Kennedy, the youngest of Bobby and Ethel's 11 children, born six months after her father's murder, was getting married on Martha's Vineyard. JFK Jr., despondent over his life, decided to fly to the Vineyard, where he could stay at his late mother's spectacular Red Gate Farm. His sister Caroline was worried about his mental state, but the day before he was to fly to Massachusetts, JFK Jr. assured her that he planned to live to a "ripe old age."

He took off that Friday evening from the Essex County Airport in Fairfield, New Jersey, in his Piper Saratoga PA32 II HP. With him were his wife and her sister. It was a dark, hazy night—treacherous weather for a novice pilot. He checked in with the control tower on Martha's Vineyard, but then disappeared off the radar screen.

Three hours later the word went out: JFK Jr. was missing. The nation was transfixed as CNN provided round-the-clock television coverage. The wreckage was found three days later. The three had died instantly upon impact. Their bodies were cremated on the Cape, their ashes scattered at sea. A few days later there would be a funeral Mass at the Church of St. Thomas More on the Upper East Side, where JFK Jr.'s aunt Pat had been wed to Peter Lawford 45 years earlier. Among the mourners: President Bill Clinton.

The National Transportation Safety Board, which investigated the accident, listed the official cause as pilot error due to Kennedy's "failure to maintain control of the airplane during a descent over water at night, which was a result of spatial disorientation."

JFK Jr. listed 14 beneficiaries in his will. Surprisingly, he left $250,000 to his cousin Bobby Jr., one of the two poster boys.

George magazine was quickly sold, and it went out of business in early 2001.

The latest Kennedy rape scandal would claim one more victim. In August 2001, June Verrochi died at the age of 51 "after a long illness," as the obituary put it. She was described as a "philanthropist." Her listed survivors did not include her ex-husband Paul Verrochi.

In 2010, Paul Verrochi, the former Kennedy confidant and Democrat party bundler, donated $5,000 to the Massachusetts Republican State Committee.

(TO BE CONTINUED)

COMING SOON
Kennedy Babylon, Volume Two

Including these chapters:

Joe and the "Pants Pressers"
Au Bar
JFK: The Final Days
RFK: The Final Days
Brother-in-Lawford
The Kennedy Women
You Don't Know Who You're Messing With!

And much, much more

Caroline & Max Kennedy under arrest Barnstable MA 8-20-2017
"I'm drunk... I know that!"
www.howiecarrshow.com

WORKS CITED

Andersen, Christopher P. *Jackie after Jack: Portrait of the Lady*. New York, William Morrow, 1998.

Blair, Joan, and Clay Blair. *The Search for JFK*. New York, Berkley Pub. Corp., 1976.

Bryant, Traphes, and Frances Spatz Leighton. *Dog Days at the White House: The Outrageous Memoirs of the Presidential Kennel Keeper*. New York, Macmillan, 1975.

Burke, Richard E. *The Senator: My Ten Years with Ted Kennedy*. New York, St. Martin's Press, 1992.

Capote, Truman. *Answered Prayers: The Unfinished Novel*. New York, Random House, 1987.

Clifford, Clark M., and Richard C. Holbrooke. *Counsel to the President: A Memoir*. New York, Random House, 1991.

Collier, Peter, and David Horowitz. *The Kennedys: An American Drama*. New York, Summit Books, 1984.

Dallas, Rita, and Jeanira Ratcliffe. *The Kennedy Case*. New York, Putnam, 1973.

Damore, Leo. *Senatorial Privilege: The Chappaquiddick Cover-Up*. Washington, D.C., Regnery Gateway, 1988.

David, Lester. *Good Ted, Bad Ted: The Two Faces of Edward M. Kennedy*. Secaucus, NJ, Carol Pub. Group, 1993.

Dinneen, Joseph F. *The Kennedy Family*. Boston, Little, Brown, 1959.

Exner, Judith, and Ovid Demaris. *Judith Exner: My Story*. New York, Grove, 1977.

Gibson, Barbara, and Ted Schwarz. *The Kennedys: The Third Generation*. New York, NY, Thunder's Mouth Press, 1993.

Hersh, Seymour M. *The Dark Side of Camelot*. Boston, Little, Brown, 1997.

Kaplan, James. *Sinatra: The Chairman*. New York, Doubleday, 2015.

Kennedy, Joseph P., and Amanda Smith. *Hostage to Fortune: The Letters of Joseph P. Kennedy*. New York, Viking, 2001.

Kessler, Ronald. *The Sins of the Father: Joseph P. Kennedy and the Dynasty He Founded.* New York, Warner Books, 1996.

Lasky, Victor. *J.F.K.: The Man and the Myth.* New York, Macmillan, 1963.

Lasky, Victor. *Robert F. Kennedy: The Myth and the Man.* New York, Trident Press, 1968.

Lawford, Patricia Seaton, and Ted Schwarz. *The Peter Lawford Story: Life with the Kennedys, Monroe, and the Rat Pack.* New York, Carroll & Graf Publishers, 1988.

Leary, Timothy. *Flashbacks: An Autobiography.* Los Angeles, J.P. Tarcher, 1983.

Lertzman, Richard A., and William J. Birnes. *Dr. Feelgood: The Shocking Story of the Doctor Who May Have Changed History by Treating and Drugging JFK, Marilyn, Elvis, and Other Prominent Figures.* New York, NY, Skyhorse Publishing, 2014.

O'Donnell, Kenneth P., and David F. Powers. *Johnny, We Hardly Knew Ye; Memories of John Fitzgerald Kennedy.* Boston, Little, Brown, 1972.

Parmet, Herbert S. *Jack: The Struggles of John F. Kennedy.* New York, Dial Press, 1980.

Piereson, James. *Camelot and the Cultural Revolution: How the Assassination of John F. Kennedy Shattered American Liberalism.* New York, Encounter Books, 2007.

Pitts, David. *Jack & Lem: John F. Kennedy and Lem Billings: The Untold Story of an Extraordinary Friendship.* New York, Carroll &Graf, 2007.

Pope, Paul David. *The Deeds of My Fathers: How My Grandfather and Father Built New York and Created the Tabloid World of Today: Generoso Pope, Sr., Power Broker of New York, and Gene Pope, Jr., Publisher of the National Enquirer.* Lanham, MD, Rowman & Littlefield Publishers, 2010.

Schwarz, Ted. *Joseph P. Kennedy: The Mogul, the Mob, the Statesman, and the Making of an American Myth.* Hoboken, NJ, John Wiley & Sons, 2003.

Shaw, Mark. *The Poison Patriarch: How the Betrayals of Joseph P. Kennedy Caused the Assassination of JFK.* New York, NY, Skyhorse Publishing, 2013.

Shearer, Stephen Michael. *Gloria Swanson: The Ultimate Star.* New York, Thomas Dunne Books/St. Martin's Press, 2013.

Spada, James. *Peter Lawford: The Man Who Kept the Secrets.* New York, Bantam Books, 1991.

Spindel, Bernard B. *The Ominous Ear.* New York, Award House, 1968.

Stack, Robert, and Mark Evans. *Straight Shooting.* New York, Macmillan, 1980.

Summers, Anthony. *Goddess: The Secret Lives of Marilyn Monroe.* New York, NY, 1985.

White, Theodore H. *The Making of the President, 1960.* New York, Atheneum Publishers, 1961.

Wolfe, Donald H. *The Last Days of Marilyn Monroe.* New York, Morrow, 1998.

Index